KU-053-674

Good Practice in Child Protection

A Manual for Professionals

Edited by Hilary Owen and Jacki Pritchard

Jessica Kingsley Publishers
London and Bristol, Pennsylvania

Acknowledgements

Finkelhor, D. (1986) *A Source Book on Child Sexual Abuse*. London: Sage. Reprinted by permission of Sage Publications Inc.

'The Standards of Child Neglect' is reprinted by permission of Hendrika B. Cantwell, M.D. a Clinical Professor of Pediatrics, University of Colorado, Consultant on child abuse and neglect at the C. Henry Kempe Centre and the Colorado State Department of Social Services.

All rights reserved. No paragraph of this publication may be reproduced, copied or transmitted save with written permission or in accordance with the provisions of the Copyright Act 1956 (as amended), or under the terms of any licence permitting limited copying issued by the Copyright Licensing Agency, 33-34 Alfred Place, London WC1E 7DP.

Any person who does any unauthorised act in relation to this publication may be liable to criminal prosecution and civil claims for damages.

The right of the contributors to be identified as author of this work has been asserted by them in accordance with the Copyright, Designs and Patents Act 1988.

First published in the United Kingdom in 1993 by
Jessica Kingsley Publishers Ltd
116 Pentonville Road
London N1 9JB

Copyright © 1993 the contributors and the publisher

British Library Cataloguing in Publication Data
Good Practice in Child Protection
I. Owen, Hilary II. Pritchard, Jacki
152.4

ISBN 1 85302 205 5

Printed and Bound in Great Britain by
Cromwell Press, Melksham, Wiltshire

L.H.M.C.	
Class	WA 320 Goo
Circ Type	
Donation	LIBS 4/95
	£ 16.95
Binding	
New Rebind Check	

LHMC BOOK

54008000196582

WITHDRAWN
FROM STOCK
QMUL LIBRARY

Good Practice in Child Protection

A Manual for Professionals

THE LONDON HOSPITAL
MEDICAL COLLEGE LIBRARY
TURNER STREET, LONDON E1 2AD

Books are to be returned on or before the last date below,
otherwise fines may be charged. Overdue books cannot be renewed.

Display 15/5/95

-5. MAR. 1998

-4 DEC 2001

19. JUN. 1995

30 AUG 2001

18. JUL. 1996

21. MAY 1998

25 OCT 2001

-8 NOV 2001

13 DEC 1999

-4 DEC 2002

11. JUN. 1997

26. AUG. 1997

4 JAN 2000

27. FEB. 1998

15 JUN 2000

of related interest

Child Abuse and Child Abusers
Protection and Prevention
Edited by Lorraine Waterhouse
Foreword by Professor Olive Stevenson
ISBN 1 85302 133 4

Play Therapy with Abused Children
Ann Cattanach
ISBN 1 85302 120 2 hb
ISBN 1 85302 193 8 pb

Grief in Children
A Handbook for Adults
Atle Dyregrov
ISBN 1 85302 113 X

Good Grief
Exploring Feelings, Loss and Death with
   Over Elevens and Adults
Barbara Ward and Associates
ISBN 1 85302 162 8

Good Grief
Exploring Feelings, Loss and Death with
   Under Elevens
Barbara Ward and Associates
ISBN 1 85302 161 X

The Abuse of Elderly People
A Handbook for Professionals
Jacki Pritchard
Foreword by Professor Eric Sainsbury
ISBN 1 85302 122 9

Handbook of Theory for Practice Teachers
   in Social Work
Edited by Joyce Lishman
ISBN 1 85302 098 2

DEDICATION

This book is dedicated to those children throughout the world whose human rights are denied them and who have no protection from harm.

ACKNOWLEDGEMENTS

We should like to thank everyone who has worked so hard to contribute to this book. We are also indebted to the children we have worked with and from whom we have learned so much.

CONTENTS

INTRODUCTION

Hilary Owen and Jacki Pritchard

Over the last five years the government has issued an unprecedented amount of guidance to all statutory agencies with a responsibility for protecting children, much of it attached to its legislative showpiece, the Children Act 1989. We use the word 'showpiece' deliberately, as there is a strong possibility that many of the good ideas it introduces may never be implemented properly because of the reduction in public spending which has taken place at the same time. There will be many opportunities for our clients to take our employers to judicial review in the coming years, and money saved by cutting services may well later be spent on claims for civil compensation awarded against our employers when our agencies fail to deliver the services to which families are entitled under the Act. There has been publicity recently about local authorities failing to provide aftercare to youngsters leaving their accommodation. More worrying is the fact that it is not unusual for social services departments to fail to provide social workers for children whose names are on Child Protection Registers, or who are subjects of care orders, because of pressure of work and lack of experienced social workers.

This book is written in the knowledge that, for many agencies, legislation and government guidance provide a model of good practice which they can only aspire to, never achieve. Despite the failure of government to provide many of us with enough resources to do our jobs properly, we are well aware that, when it comes to child abuse, we need to ensure that we have done everything we can to follow our child protection procedures, and have recorded our work meticulously.

Being acutely aware of the complexities of child protection work, and of the difficulty of the decisions which often have to be made, we have tried to ensure that this book is based very firmly indeed on the practice and experience of the agencies which deal with the various aspects of the work on a daily basis, from recognition of abuse, through investigation, communicating with children, effective communication with other agencies, contributing at child protection conferences, formulating child protection plans, assisting children to give evidence in court, and supervision of staff directly involved. Throughout, reflecting our own priorities, we have emphasised how the contributions of all agencies can best be used and co-ordinated to help the child and his or her family.

Despite scarce resources and unallocated cases, agencies are clearly at-tempting to achieve a high standard of practice in the work they are able to undertake. In order to achieve good practice, it is necessary to train workers to develop skills so that they ultimately function with a high level of compe-tence. But what does training mean?

> 'The process of bringing a person to an agreed standard of proficiency by practice and instruction'

> 'To guide or teach (to do something), as by subjecting to various exercises or experiences'

> 'To control or guide towards a specific goal'

> 'To do exercises and prepare for a specific purpose'

> (various dictionary definitions)

And do training sections provide this? Many probably do not. In a time of economic recession, training sections are often the first targets for budget/staffing cuts. There has been money around for training in order to implement the Children Act, but has it been used wisely? Have training sections researched in to what is really required, that is, what are the needs of the workers?

Some departments have excellent training sections who provide tailor made courses for workers, but there are still many professionals who feel that they lack knowledge and experience and believe that the training they are offered is inadequate. There are usually limits (because of financial con-straints) on attendance at courses outside of departments; consequently, workers have to be dependent on in-house training.

The purpose of writing this book is to fill some of the gaps which exist. Line managers should be able to identify the needs of their workers and make these needs known to their training section. But training does not just take place on courses; it can happen while 'working on the job', in supervision, in team meetings and in special sessions organised on worksites. Trainers, managers and workers need to remember that people learn from each other. Where managers and workers feel that training is inadequate, they need to be imaginative and to create opportunities themselves in order to learn. We hope that using this book will be one such opportunity.

A wide range of professionals have contributed to this book and it is hoped that this will help professionals to learn more about each other's roles and functions. There are contributions from a police officer, a probation officer, a paediatrician, a hospital nurse manager, a teacher, a lawyer, social work academics and trainers, senior representatives of prominent children's chari-ties, a child protection administrator, and ourselves as social work managers. To bring to the attention of professionals some of the newer concerns of child protection work, we are pleased to be able to include a chapter on protecting children with disabilities and special needs, and a chapter on female genital mutilation and how child protection procedures can be used to assist those children who are already victims, and those at risk from it.

We have attempted to achieve a balance between informative text, which anyone who works with children will find useful to read; and ideas for those involved in training, either within single agencies or on a multidisciplinary basis. The book can be used in any setting to facilitate learning about theory, practice and the multidisciplinary approach. Exercises are included in most chapters together with case studies, but it is recognised that users may prefer to use their own materials.

It is important to remember that all adults learn in different ways and whereas one worker may benefit from a course, a colleague may gain nothing from it. It is crucial that workers say how they prefer to learn/be taught. The exercises included in this book, however, do vary in content and every worker should be able to find something useful in order to develop their good practice further.

CHAPTER 1

MANAGING YOUR OWN LEARNING IN CHILD PROTECTION

ANNE HOLLOWS

INTRODUCTION

Other chapters of this book contain valuable information for personal study as well as suggestions for further activities to develop practice in particular areas of work. This chapter is designed to help the reader to identify how to make the best use of the material contained in the book. It looks at the process of learning and how it can be applied to attitudes and values, skills and knowledge. It considers issues around learning on your own or in co-operative groups. It also identifies issues that are unique to learning for better practice in the field of child protection. The chapter is based on current theories about how adults learn, applied to the practice of child protection.

Readers may find within the chapter a number of clues about their own learning, whether for work in child protection, or for any of the varied topics offered by evening classes or correspondence courses. For those currently working, or planning to work, in child protection the chapter should help the assessment of learning needs and indicate the options for meeting them. The information about adult learning theory is intended to empower the learning process by offering an insight into the different ways in which learning approaches work. There are some case studies, based on individual and group learners and some suggested activities to guide your planning.

It is desirable, in materials about child protection, that an author should present her own theoretical perspectives and constructs at the outset. In the same way, I want to identify my own commitment to learning. It could in general be summed up in the phrase 'life is a learning experience'. Learning, for me, can take place watching the news; in a post-course de-briefing; by observing a colleague undertaking a piece of work; by reading, talking, listening; and often by the casual observation of children. It can also take place in a structured environment organised by oneself or others. This is not an exhaustive list. The objective is to point out that we can learn from a huge range of experiences but we will optimise our learning if we have a framework for processing what we see or hear. Learning can, of course, be formal and less formal. It can be externally managed or self-managed. It may be validated or we may be dependent on our own assessment of how well we have learned.

Becoming aware of how we learn and of the different components of learning is one of the ways in which we begin to take control over our learning and thus of our potential to develop our practice. As with most things, adherence to a framework for learning, at least in the early stages, offers us the chance to develop and validate a personal system of learning.

Whether readers are planning independent learning, team learning or badgering a training officer for a different kind of service, the information below should assist the process of converting the chapters of this book into a positive professional and personal development plan. The case studies show how people in various settings in social work struggled with, and ultimately managed their personal development constructively. These are intended to offer encouragement and to act as an incentive to lateral thinking, rather than as prescriptions. On the assumption that those who are continuing to read this chapter are seriously seeking guidance about learning, the style from here onwards is deliberately more personal.

IDENTIFYING YOUR TRAINING NEEDS

We start with the obvious. What are you learning for? Learning can be described as meeting one of the following needs:

1. To remedy a deficit in performance – this means that you are aware that your work in an area has room for improvement, for example court room skills.
2. To maintain performance – you want to keep on top of the knowledge and skills in your job, for example recent research findings or the impact of new legislation.
3. To improve performance – when your work is satisfactory but you want to develop or extend certain skills within it, for example running a group to undertake therapeutic work with children who have been abused.
4. To meet anticipated changes in your job – this may mean moving to a new job or anticipating major changes brought about in your own job through legislative change or organisational re-structuring.

It will be essential to be honest about your motives from the outset, and to recognise that these may change as you learn more about the area of study and recognise your own performance strengths and weaknesses. Your work may be better than you think. You may discover that you are not really suited to the area of work you were planning to move into. You will find it helpful to keep a clear focus on your goals as you plan the sort of learning you undertake and look at how you are going to achieve it. Clear initial goals will help you to look critically at how effective you have been – your evaluation.

When you know why you are doing the learning you can begin to identify your aims, objectives and outcomes. These words and their precise meanings can be the subject of much debate among educationalists. It is important to recognise, too, that the borders between them are often indistinct. I choose to use them in the following way and will do so from here on.

First of all, aims. Aims are fairly broad. They are the point on the often distant horizon which you are aiming for and are not usually very detailed. Learners in child protection could have one or more of the following aims:

- to be a better child protection worker
- to improve skills in direct work with children
- to understand more about special needs and child protection
- to develop my knowledge so that I can apply for a job in child protection.

Objectives are more specific and tangible. It is often found that a single aim will generate several objectives. The reader wanting more understanding about special needs and child protection might, for example, want to know the incidence of abuse upon children with special needs. She might want to know about recognition of symptoms, about communication skills, about therapeutic interventions or about self protection issues – and much more besides.

Outcomes demand still more detailed thought. They consist of what you want to be able to do at the end of your period of learning. They may look rather like practice competencies. To identify your outcomes you should complete sentences which start with

'At the end of my learning I would like to be able to...'

and you should try to do this for each of your aims. You should be clear that objectives will not necessarily derive precisely from your aims.

Working out your aims, objectives and outcomes is a really important first step. At the Child Abuse Training Unit when we see trainers struggling to develop a new course, or when we see training materials which are not all they might be, we often find that the problem is a lack of clear aims and objectives. It happens to us too. How much more important, then, if you are trying to take some personal control over your learning and to invest time, energy, resources and even credibility into the bargain. We will see throughout this chapter how the careful planning of learning may avoid at least some of the pitfalls in learning about child protection.

At this point let us meet the characters within the four case studies and begin to trace them as they embark on managing their learning.

> Anna P. had three young children and returned to work part time. Although her training had been in children and families work she opted, partly through choice and partly through available part time work, to move to work in a hospital setting. But she never gave up her long term goal of working with children and families. The problem was, her authority never nominated her for training with children and families because she wasn't working in that area. Fortunately, she lived in a city with access to a number of extra-mural courses run by the local university. In fact, the choice was almost limitless but she approached it in a disciplined way. Her aim was to be in a position to undertake specialist work with children and families by the time the children were all in secondary school – some seven years hence. Her objectives were

to keep up with research, to maintain her knowledge of the legal system, and to develop good skills in assessment of children and families. Her desired outcomes were to be able to apply her social work skills, in the light of research and legal change, to front line work with children and families.

Joseph D. had been involved in a difficult court case. Although he had not been criticised, he was anxious to ensure that he, and others like him, were as well prepared as they could be in presenting cases in court. His aim was to improve his court craft. He decided that his key objectives would be to learn more about the presentation of evidence and to understand how to respond to cross examination. His learning outcomes were to be able to be a reliable and effective witness in civil and criminal proceedings around child protection.

Gwen T. was asked to do assessments on a number of children who had been the victims of a single abuser. At the end of the assessments she decided that she should set up a group where the children could be supported. Her aim was to prepare herself for the task and she set the specific objectives of learning about group work techniques to de-brief children about their abusive experiences, to help them understand why the events had taken place, to deliver an appropriate sex education programme and to learn how to develop a support network for the children. Her learning outcomes were to be able to develop and run a programme of group activities for children who had been sexually abused; to record the process and to evaluate its effectiveness.

Bridie O. is a child minder, her sister-in-law Emilia is a foster carer, and Emilia's neighbour Maya is a school nurse. Over coffee one evening they decided that they were all coming across child abuse cases all the time and they didn't really know much about the topic. Their aim was to develop their very basic knowledge about the subject area and to understand how it impacted upon their work. Their objectives were uncertain – how can we know what we want to do with the knowledge until we know where the knowledge might lead us, they said. But they were clear about the outcomes. They all wanted to be sure that they were treating children appropriately and that they would recognise and respond appropriately to signs and symptoms of abuse. From that they were able to work back to objectives including skills in recognition, knowledge of local procedures, understanding the different roles of all the agencies involved.

ACTION POINTS

1. Write a brief statement about why you want to do some structured learning.
2. Identify your learning aims, objectives and outcomes.

How Do We Learn?

It is worth spending time to take a brief look at the field of adult learning. Not only does it provide a framework for understanding our own learning process, it may also offer some insights into our professional work with adults. A word of caution is, however, essential. Much of the research upon which adult learning is based was undertaken among middle class, white Americans, so the theories, while valuable, cannot be claimed to have a necessarily universal application. They do, however, have aspects in common with theories of anti-oppressive practice and are firmly rooted in the notion of the empowerment of the learner.

Learning combines work on attitudes and values, knowledge and skills. For adults it is a process whereby increasing independence from the educator is offered to the learner which is based on enabling the learner to plan and take responsibility for their own learning. It involves offering insight into the learning process. Using one's own and others' experiences as a resource for learning is essential for adults. It requires, fundamentally, a continual review of knowledge and skills in the light of experience.

Institutional teaching frameworks alone cannot support good adult learning. Ideally, learners and educators are able to engage in a continual, interactive process which involves both thought and action. Learners need to be able to reflect on experience, to consider new information and review the skills which they can apply to a situation. It follows that some of the better learning experiences involve problem solving work around case studies or tasks which resemble those of day to day work experience. By the same token, some of the less successful learning will involve the lecture from a visiting expert. In many cases the expert will offer a single model for practice, often limiting the opportunity for questioning. There may be little opportunity for participants to share and build upon their own experience of work in this area. To apply expert knowledge, you will require opportunities to reflect on the extent to which the knowledge is based upon a particular theoretical framework. Do your personal values and attitudes resemble those of the expert or is there a clash which threatens the value of the material? Are the skills described by the expert those you feel comfortable in using or developing?

We also have different learning styles. Some of us prefer to read material. When we listen to speakers some of us write copious notes while others make a few brief jottings. Some of us are badly distracted by the trainer or lecturer who moves around the room in an energetic presentation while others are horrified by the speaker who remains fixed to the spot. Some of us adapt well to role play or sculpts while others loathe such activities. These are not just aspects of our personality. They are real clues to how we learn best and, if we use them, we can try to find styles of learning which will be most effective for us. While it is rare to find a course or follow a learning programme which avoids all our dislikes, at least recognising what they are will help you to reflect upon your reactions to learning offered in a particular style.

If you are managing your own learning it is essential to have a clear understanding of what works for you in learning. Only then can you go out and get your learning. This bit of knowledge is, quite simply, the empowerment of the learner. But before you become too set on a particular style of learning it may be useful to think about other learning you have done. It may be that your own education, in school, college or university, has left you feeling you are not good at something. You might still try it out to see whether you have changed – or whether your present environment makes a particular approach easier to apply.

Anna P. liked to read and to listen. She had an essentially academic style. She discovered that audio tapes were available on some of the areas which interested her and started to listen to them when she was in her car. She also opted for an academic programme run by the university extra-mural department.

Joseph D. did not consider himself a reader. He just wanted to keep practising his skills under cross examination but he could not find any way of doing this. A friend suggested he read some court room dramas to get his head round some of the dialogue. He enjoyed the stories and discovered he could concentrate on the written word!

Gwen T. was struggling with a mountain of reading too, but she felt she could not just plunge into her work. Her last training course had, she felt, been too theoretical. She badly needed to see a group working. She heard of some groups being run by a colleague and arranged to attend as an observer.

Bridie, Emilia and Maya thought about going on a course at the local college but they were really quite frightened of what might be expected of them. Bridie and Emilia had been out of school for fifteen years and had never passed any exams. They didn't really know where to start. Then a colleague lent Maya a video tape of an episode from the Cagney and Lacey series about a child abuse case. They sat and watched it one night and started to talk. They concluded that they needed to be together if they were going to achieve anything.

ACTION POINTS

1. Think about something new you learned to do in the last five years. It could include learning to speak a new language, mending a car, woodwork or craft, for example. Jot down how you learned to do it, such as reading a book, talking to someone who could do it, going to a class.

    ◦ Did you succeed?

    ◦ Did you enjoy the learning experience?

    ◦ Could you have learned more effectively and how?

2. Think about some professional learning in the last five years which was disappointing.
   ◦ What were the problems?
   ◦ How could it have been done better?
   ◦ Did you get any benefits from it?
   ◦ Did you do anything to draw your disappointment to the attention of the trainers or your managers?

Where Do We Learn?

There are basically three settings for learning:

- individual learning or private study
- group, or class room work
- on the job, or workplace learning.

Individual study can take place at home, in a library, in an office. In a sense it is the most flexible form of learning because it requires just one individual and some learning materials – audio tapes, books, work packs or blank sheets of paper. It lacks an opportunity for shared reflection, discussion, interactive exercises, feedback or observation.

Group work can range from conferences and lectures through to small, informal groups. It is probably the most versatile in its potential for learning styles, although the size of the group may have implications for organisation and cost. Group learning does not necessarily require a formal facilitator. The one area for caution with group learning is in skills development. Skills learning may be practised and rehearsed in groups but it will not be refined and tested until you are back on the job.

Workplace learning generally implies observation of others, live supervision or close mentoring of your own performance. There are now some workplace tools under development (e.g. Morrison, T.A. Workbook on Supervision (in press)) which may assist the development of better supervision in the workplace.

The settings for learning are important in two key ways. The first is knowing what you prefer as a setting and in being aware of its strengths and weaknesses. The second is relating the setting in which you are learning to what you are learning. There are some areas of child protection practice which dictate a particular learning setting. Skills development, as we have already noted, can be started in a group and refined in the workplace. Inter-agency working skills can be initiated by watching videos alone, or by observation placements in a different agency. But there will be a need to find opportunities to meet with other professionals and undertake some exercises to establish a common value base for shared work.

Exploring your personal responses to abuse requires the presence of an experienced facilitator. Some of the graphic material contained in case studies can have quite unforeseen consequences and it is essential to do some work under guidance.

In an earlier publication (Hollows, A., Armstrong, H. and Stainton Rogers, W. *Good Enough Training,* 1989) I identified six key areas of learning for work in child protection:

- providing support
- exploring feelings – or attitudes and values
- acquiring knowledge
- developing skills
- working together
- developing critical abilities.

This list provides key headings under which to group your learning needs. Mapping the six headings against the three settings for learning provides an indication of the advantages which different settings offer for different functions of learning.

> Anna P. was unsure about her opportunities for group learning: she had been excluded from training in the workplace and as a part-time staff member there were few points of the working week where she had much contact with colleagues. In the first instance her needs were essentially knowledge based. She started to read on her own, but found it unsatisfactory because she lacked an environment where she could talk through the reading and relate it to her experience. She then signed up for and joined a child observation course which ran in the evenings, undertaking observation exercises in her spare time. This led to two things: first, she found a study group to whom she could relate, and among whom she built lasting relationships; second, she came across programmes for a wide range of training courses. As her children grew older she opted to take courses in counselling, arranging her practical work in settings where she could work with children and families. As the time approached when she felt she could make her move into the new area of work, she had a set back when she realised that her lack of knowledge on the Children Act would limit her ability to perform well in interviews. She contacted a friend who trained for another authority and arranged to borrow the Open University Pack on the Act.
>
> Joseph D. was struggling. He could not persuade his training officer to run a course in court skills. He went to court and sat through criminal trials but only grew less confident in his ability to cope in the area. He went to a conference on the issue and got some useful ideas but still had difficulty in applying them in his own work. How could he tell whether he was improving or not? Cases with court involvement began to become a real anxiety for him.
>
> Gwen T. observed some group sessions and then found a course on group work skills in her agency. She enjoyed it and was delighted when some of the course members agreed to her suggestion for a monthly meeting to follow up their work. She was doing some fieldwork teach-

ing for a local Diploma in Social Work course and she mentioned her interest and current work to one of the tutors. They invited her to attend a conference and she also contributed to a teaching session on child sexual abuse. She also talked to one of the researchers about the evaluation part of her work.

Bridie, Emilia and Maya were not sure where to start. They were unfamiliar enough with the idea of formal study, without trying to manage it all themselves. They each talked to contacts in their agency. All were offered helpful suggestions, involving buying material for distance learning. But most of it was expensive and they were not sure they would finish it. Eventually, Bridie went on a course for child minders and she made an opportunity to talk with the trainer. It turned out that there were some copies of one of the training packs they had thought would be useful in the local training department. Not only that, but the training officer knew of two more people who wanted to do the same thing. The training officer's time was limited but she offered to spend a couple of hours with the group to start them off.

ACTION POINTS

1. What settings for learning are available to you? Write a list of all the possibilities and note which are the most likely to be achieved.
2. Now look at what you want to learn. Try to match it with the settings you have identified. What are the advantages and disadvantages of the setting for the learning. How can you overcome this?
3. Note that you may be able to affect the settings available to you when you have considered the next section on supports for your learning.

IDENTIFYING SUPPORTS FOR YOUR LEARNING

In much of the above material there has been an implicit assumption that someone, somewhere would be supporting your learning. It should by now be clear that for most aspects of adult learning some kind of learning support is required. Getting learning started may be dependent on somebody else: to press for your admission to a training course; to offer suggestions; to direct you to sources of material. Checking out attitudes and values with an individual or group is part of the process of reflection which is itself learning. Getting feedback on our progress both in general and in the particular area of skills development is essential. Some areas of learning will be slow and others may be challenging. When you are tempted to give up, you need access to an individual or group who can help to maintain your morale. Learning in the field of child protection creates additional needs for support of which the following two are critical: the duty of care which we owe to the children and families with whom we work and the duty of care which we owe to ourselves. We need to have some confidence in the quality of our developing knowledge and skills. For some aspects of learning we cannot make much progress without some support. But how can you identify and secure support for the process?

You will need to make a judgement about whether your private learning is something you want to share with your supervisor or line manager. You may have very sound reasons for keeping your learning process private, but in such cases there will be a need to ensure that it does not have an impact on your daily work. On the other hand, if you are hoping to engage in some kind of workplace learning you will require the agreement, and probably the active support, of your line manager. If you discuss your plans with your line manager and gain their co-operation you may find that they will back your application for training courses. Nonetheless, you may find it helpful to do some of the groundwork suggested in this chapter before going to your manager.

Ideally, line managers should take pride in staff who want to improve their own practice and who use their own initiative to do so. In workplaces where regular appraisal of staff is combined with training needs analysis there should be better opportunities for accessing training programmes. In any workplace where people come together to provide services for children and families there should be a supervision structure where staff development needs are a regular part of the agenda. You may be able to use this to meet your longer term training needs. Supervision is also likely to be the most appropriate vehicle for supporting your learning.

Many learners appear to follow courses of study quite independently. Looking behind the scenes, however, may reveal that their study is not as isolated as it might appear. Open University courses, for example, are based on a lot of private study but also offer tutorial groups and summer schools. Most of those who undertake examination preparation by correspondence course are actually working in the subject area on a day to day basis. There is an extent to which all learning requires some opportunity for reflection with others – the practice which we have already discussed – if it is to be effective. Forming a study support group could meet this need. This may not necessarily be a group of people with whom you regularly work or with whom you regularly study but it could mean that other people who are studying in the same area would benefit from the opportunity to meet on a monthly basis to talk through some of the work they have been doing. Where a whole team is doing some thinking and studying, some of this process can take place in team meetings or team supervision sessions, but few of you will be lucky enough to work in teams where there is such an integral learning culture. A further possibility is to find a **mentor**. A system of mentoring is being developed by the Central Council for Education and Training in Social Work (CCETSW) around their post-qualifying study and there will be growing numbers of people in social services departments who will have the skills to undertake this sort of process. It may be worth approaching staff within child protection specialism or within the training team to see if they would be prepared to allocate a regular time commitment, for example one hour per month, to talk through the work you undertake in your own time. If you cannot achieve this you may find someone in a local voluntary organisation or from a local social work training course. Some professionals are enthusiastic about providing this sort of support and guidance but they all have heavy demands on their time and a refusal should not be seen as lack of interest, or as a set back. You may need to exercise some persistence and commitment to find a mentor or support system for your learning. Nonetheless you will find it worth its weight in gold as it will substantially increase the development you can undertake.

Anna P. did not feel able to discuss her learning with her colleagues or manager. For some time she ploughed on alone until she joined the child observation course. Gradually, she developed a network of others who were following independent learning in the field. She also got to know, as a personal friend, a consultant trainer who was able to provide support and guidance in some of the areas of study.

Joseph D.'s situation came to a head as his stress levels around court appearances became more obvious. He was so pre-occupied by his anxiety that he was really unable to take any initiative in meeting his learning needs for himself. After a difficult start, he began to confide in his line manager who developed with Joseph a programme of activities to respond to his needs. As well as arranging for him to attend a four day course, she agreed to spend some time with him in preparation for his court appearances over the next two months. He also got to know a local solicitor and began to find out more about the legal system.

Gwen T. had a line manager who had little experience in the field she was working in. He recognised her need for support, however, and arranged for her to have a monthly meeting with a local child psychiatrist. She also obtained some informal support from the staff of the Social Work Department at the local university where she was a field-work teacher.

For Bridie, Emilia and Maya there was a clear understanding that the learning they wanted would fall outwith their professional task. They could, in principle, have survived as a study group on their own, but they were close friends and were keen to expand their group so that it would be definably different from their social meetings. They were introduced to two residential workers, keen to follow a similar course of study, and Maya found a health visitor to join them too. The trainer whom Bridie had met agreed to give them two sessions, each of an hour, to start them off and offered some telephone support if they got stuck.

ACTION POINTS

1. Note down the sources of support you need to get you started. (You may be able to start your learning without support).
2. By now you should have a broad idea of what you are going to learn, and how. What are the support implications of this?
3. Brainstorm all the possible sources of support who are (a) available to you and (b) available in your locality. How can you make links with them?
4. Think carefully about how your line manager may be able to support your learning. Approach a discussion with a clear statement about what you want to learn, how you propose to do it and what she or he can do to help.
5. Whether or not you discuss this piece of learning with your line manager, you do need to ensure that your training and development needs are a regular feature of you supervision sessions.

MAKING THE SPACE FOR YOUR LEARNING

The opportunity to develop knowledge and skills and to explore attitudes offers a chance to develop ourselves in a way which should enable us to value ourselves more. This should have benefits both personally and professionally.

If you plan to do some learning in a structured way there are a number of small steps which should help to define the space which you give to your learning but also make it a valued activity. The idea of a private place for study is often attractive because it carries a symbolism of space which is rarely available for social workers or others who work with children and families. Achieving the reality is often quite difficult.

It is important to work out how much time you can commit in advance. Your estimates will probably be on the short side and you should bear this in mind as you plan your learning. If you need to do some preparatory reading for a group discussion, the time should be built into your schedule. If you cut corners, you will be the main loser but you may also have obligations to a learning group to keep to your time commitments for study. It is often helpful to fix a regular time each week for your study – a regular evening or portion of the weekend. It is probably not a good idea to commit yourself to more than you are likely to achieve. Once you start borrowing from your private study time you will find it very hard to repay the borrowed time and you will fall behind with your schedule. One of the key aims that we discussed earlier was maintaining your own morale as a learner and that means setting yourself tasks which are achievable.

Physical space for learning may ease the time constraints. If you can afford it, creating a defined space for your study in physical terms – a table and chair, a bookshelf, an attractive picture, a small vase of flowers will all help to give you a feeling of valuing your own efforts and that will also be critical when your study competes with other demands for your time. If your learning requires the completion of written tasks, this may provide you with the opportunity to obtain a computer and to learn to use it.

> Our learners all found different ways to make time and space for their learning. Anna P. had a big house with room for a study. She planned her learning over seven years and she knew she would be able to increase her time commitment as her children grew older. They, in turn, became used to respecting their mother's study time and space. Joseph's early efforts to train himself had not benefitted from clear planning. He identified the need for space, particularly in his day to day work. When he knew a court case was coming up, he acknow-ledged the need for considerable preparation and systematically ob-tained feedback on the process. The space he needed was in his working time. Gwen's progress was somewhat erratic until she began to recog-nise the need to maintain her reading and knowledge base. She set aside an evening each week when she could read and make notes from all the references she was accumulating. The study group turned their learning into a social event. They committed themselves to a three hour session each fortnight. They drew up a rota of homes to visit and always had coffee and cake in the middle of the session. For their private study, they committed two hours in the alternate week. They agreed to set a group task to negotiate time and space with their families and sup-ported each other to accomplish this.

ACTION POINTS

1. Work out, with absolute honesty, how much time you can allocate to study.
2. Look at where you are going to study. You may find it helpful to think about what sort of equipment you will need.
3. If you do not live alone, you may need to negotiate both time and space for your study. You may even be able to negotiate support and encouragement for your efforts.

GETTING THE CHANCE TO PUT YOUR LEARNING INTO PRACTICE

Putting your learning into practice will depend to the extent on which your current work permits it and your line manager is aware of what you are trying to do. Some courses of study will require clinical work. Getting opportunities to undertake child observations will require negotiations with family doctors, health visitors, schools, family centres or youth centres. You may already have contacts with whom you can arrange clinical work outside of your profes-sional commitments. If, like Anna P., you are working full time in a different situation then the time will come when you have to consider opportunities to move into another area of work. Your personnel department should be able to offer you some advice and guidance on this, as well as professionals in your agency. If you have been spending your private study time in trying to acquire new skills you must remember that your learning will not be complete until you have undertaken some practice. If it proves absolutely impossible to get opportunities for practice within your organisation then you could consider approaching voluntary organisations in your area. *Obtaining supervision for this work is critical*. Some family centres who integrate community activities with quite complex areas of therapy make extensive use of volunteers and supervise them very well. One NCH family centre provides, within any two week period, a group meeting of volunteers plus an individual supervision session. Any organisation which is seriously undertaking therapeutic work will have a high commitment to quality supervision of clinical practice. If you are working in any new area, but particularly in the development of your therapeutic skills, you should insist on this. Otherwise you will expose yourself and those with whom you work to great risks.

Keeping a documentary record of your practice learning is very important. You may find it useful to do occasional process recordings. This used to be a regular feature of student placements on social work training courses, although it is rarely used now. Nevertheless, it is a helpful technique when you are stuck with a case and want to look closely at the communications and interactions both within a family, and between yourself and a family or its individual members.

To make a process recording you should identify your intentions in advance and be sure to remember as much as possible of the process of the interview. You should be prepared with pencil and paper or tape recording machine, so that immediately you leave the interview you can sit in your car or go somewhere close by and make your recording. Writing the notes by hand will be time consuming but it will be very helpful to put down all your thoughts about the interview, not just what happened and what was said, but what you thought was being meant and why you may have decided to ask questions or make responses in the way that you did. These sorts of documents provide endless sources of further analysis in particular cases and are a good way of reflecting on your own input and level of skill.

Building a portfolio of recordings or case studies or child observations will help you to reflect on your learning and the change in your practice. It will help you to identify your on-going learning needs. It will also be of value when you come to apply for a different position which gives you the chance to put your learning directly into practice.

> Our learners have all made some progress. Anna P. has now obtained a job in an assessment team in a children and families unit. At last she has an opportunity to bring together the various strands of learning and practice. Joseph D. is now much more confident about his court skills. He is discussing with his supervisor whether he might harness his learning experience and undertake some fieldwork teaching. He says he will be able to teach all his students how to cope with court work. Gwen has completed her group work and is now applying to do

a Master's degree in child protection studies at the local university. The group is still meeting. Emilia helped to run a half day event for foster carers and now a similar group is starting in another part of the town. Maya has done some further training at her school. Bridie is looking at the possibility of doing a nursery nurse course.

ACTION POINTS

1. What are the practice outcomes for your learning?
2. For each practice outcome, identify at least two ways in which you will be able to get some opportunity to use your learning.
3. For each method, try to find a viable form of supervision. Then choose which you prefer.
4. It may be helpful to draw up a clear contract for your practice work, with your supervisor.
5. Develop a method of recording and reviewing your case work and keep a portfolio of your activities.

SELF EVALUATION AND NEXT STEPS

It is difficult to approach the task of evaluation if you have not previously been very clear about your aims, objectives and outcomes. These are the standards against which you can measure your progress. Different aims will require different styles of evaluations. You can test yourself up to a point; but it will be much better to engage your mentor, learning group, or supervisor in the process of exploring your progress. However enthusiastic you are about your own learning, you will find it of immeasurable benefit to have your learning validated in some way within the workplace and this requires a certain amount of openness about what you are trying to achieve. Every evaluation does, to some extent, identify new targets for action. The circular diagram overleaf illustrates how this happens.

Once you discover that you can manage some aspects of your own learning, you may become increasingly enthusiastic about the process. You may decide next time to try a different approach. It may be that you have worked alone so far and you now seek a group with whom to learn – or perhaps the reverse may be true. Every time an individual in the social work profession decides to develop their own learning in some small way it is one small step to building a learning culture in an organisation. At present, one of the most significant difficulties in social work is that people are not always encouraged to learn and to see their career as a learning activity. Taking some control for your own learning will help you to do this. You begin to understand the priorities for your work and you will begin to become much more familiar with the potential sources for meeting your training needs. As you move through the organisation in different positions or into management, you will be able to make much more effective use of the organisation's training potential too.

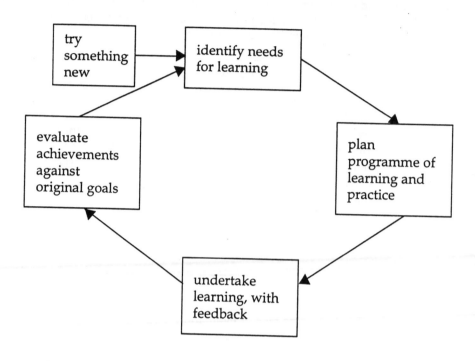

RESOURCES FOR FURTHER STUDY

Hollows, A., Armstrong, H. and Stainton Rogers, W. (1989) *Good Enough Training: Managing and Developing Training in Child Sexual Abuse*. National Children's Bureau.

This book provides some detailed guidance on a number of issues covered in the text. Although it was designed around child sexual abuse it has a wider application. CATU staff use it regularly as a basis for planning training activities.

Brookfield, S. (1986) *Understanding and facilitating adult learning*. Open University Press.

This book explores in detail the concept of adult learning as a facilitative process. Both the complexities and the values of adult learning are examined critically and thoroughly. If you want to know more about adult learning this is a good way in.

Armstrong, H. (1989) *What's in the Box (volume 1)* National Children's Bureau.

Armstrong, H. (1991) *What's in the Box (volume 2)* National Children's Bureau.
  A series of evaluations of published training materials. These are now maintained by CATU and available through our office at the National Children's Bureau.

Morrison, T. (in press) *A Workbook on Supervision.* Harlow, Essex: Longmans.

CHAPTER 2

THE CHILDREN ACT AND CHILD PROTECTION

PAT MONRO

Whenever social workers are investigating or taking court action in respect of a child, it must be remembered that the recording of the work carried out will be of major importance. It is not only a question of recording what has happened, but also why action has or has not been taken, what alternative action was considered, with whom the matter was discussed, and what advice was received and from whom. The records must show clearly who made them, and if they have been typed, when they were dictated and subsequently approved as being accurate. They should always be signed and dated.

It is a fundamental principle of this legislation that the state should not intervene in family life without good cause. The Act specifically prohibits the court from making any order unless it is satisfied that it will be better for the child than making no order at all. Clarity of thought and of presentation of evidence, both oral and by use of well written records has never been so important.

The Children Act 1989 contains a number of provisions which enable local authorities to take action in an emergency situation to protect a child. It has been made clear by the courts that a local authority wishing to protect a child should do so by using the public law provisions contained in the Act, i.e., by applying for an Emergency Protection Order followed by care proceedings under s31, rather than by applying for a prohibited steps order or specific issue order, which are available under s8 (Nottinghamshire County Council v P. CA *Times Law Report* April 8 1993).

INVESTIGATION BY THE LOCAL AUTHORITY

1. The specific duty imposed on a local authority to investigate where a child protection issue arises is to be found in s47 CA 1989.

   This requires that where a local authority are informed that a child who lives or is found in their area, is either:

   (a) the subject of an Emergency Protection Order (EPO) or in police protection or

(b) they have reasonable cause to suspect that a child who lives, or is found in their area is suffering, or is likely to suffer significant harm or

(c) they have obtained an EPO

then the authority shall make, or cause to be made, such enquiries as they consider necessary to enable them to decide what action if any they should take to safeguard or promote the child's welfare.

2. The local authority do not have a discretion to investigate. They must do so, either themselves, or through some other person or agency. The extent of the enquiries made will be a matter for their discretion, subject to certain requirements laid down by s47.

They must consider:

(a) whether to make an application to the court, or use any of the powers given them by the Act

(b) where an EPO has been made, but the child is not in local authority accommodation, should she be?

(c) if the child is in police protection, should the authority seek an EPO?

3. Steps must be taken to see the child, not just to obtain information (s47 [4]).

4. Where access to the child, or information as to her whereabouts is refused, either to the authority, or to someone acting on their behalf, the authority have a duty to apply for an EPO, Child Assessment Order, or a s31 order, unless they are satisfied that the welfare of the child can be safeguarded without doing this (s47 [6]).

5. If a decision is made not to apply for one of these orders, the authority must consider whether they should review the case at a later date, and if so, the date when that review will begin.

Co-operation between agencies

1. Where as a result of the enquiries made by the authority, it appears that there should be an investigation into matters concerned with the child's education, the authority must consult with the appropriate education authority.

2. Where an authority are conducting enquiries under s47, there is a duty imposed on certain agencies to assist with those enquiries if called on to do so, unless 'it would be unreasonable in all the circumstances to do so'.

   The agencies named are the education, housing, health authority, any NHS Trust, and any other local authority, as well as any person authorised by the Secretary of State (there are none to date).

3. Where it appears that the child concerned is usually resident in the area of another authority, the investigating authority must consult with that other authority, which may be requested to carry out the investigation. However the responsibility for the investigation remains with the authority in whose area the child was found.

Area Child Protection Committee

All investigations under s47 must be carried out in accordance with ACPC procedures. No distinction is to be made between the child who is at home with her parents, and the child who is being looked after by the local authority. The investigation must be planned, and the plan recorded. *Working Together* (1991) describes the prime tasks as being:

- to establish the facts about the circumstances giving rise to the concern
- to decide if there are grounds for concern
- to identify sources and levels of risk
- to decide protective or other action in relation to the child and any others.

In order to plan an efficient investigation, avoid duplication of work, and to identify the role of each agency, *Working Together* refers to the need for a Strategy Meeting to be called at an early stage, between the statutory agencies. An important consideration at this stage is to clarify to what extent the information gathered during the investigation will be exchanged. This is particularly relevant as far as the police are concerned. They may conduct interviews with a number of people, and a social worker will usually be present at the interview with the child. However, the police officers concerned will not usually have authority to release copies of the statements taken, nor a copy of the video interview with the child. The absence of this material may significantly affect the action which is open to the local authority at the conclusion of the investigation [for more detailed discussion on this point, see section on Evidence].

CHILD ASSESSMENT ORDER

This is not an order to be used in an emergency situation, but where further information is required in order for a decision to be taken about the need for further action. The order should be sought only where there has been a s47 investigation which cannot be successfully completed, possibly because it has been frustrated by the carers.

1. An application for a CAO may be made by a local authority or the NSPCC. The court must be satisfied that:

   (a) the applicant has reasonable cause to suspect that the child is suffering, or is likely to suffer, significant harm

   and

   (b) an assessment of the child's health or development, or of the way the child has been treated, is required to enable the applicant to determine whether or not the suspicion is correct

   and

   (c) it is unlikely that such an assessment will be made, or will be satisfactory, without an order.

2. Seven days notice that the application is to be made must be given to the following people:

- the child's parents (which included an unmarried father)
- anyone else who has parental responsibility
- any other person caring for the child (there is no definition of 'caring' in the section, but clearly this will include a child minder or a relative with whom the child is staying at the time the application is issued)
- any person who has a contact order allowing them to have contact with the child
- the child (whether this has been granted under s34 CA 1989 or under another provision)

An order may be granted even if notice has not been given, as long as the applicant is able to show that reasonably practicable steps have been taken to ensure service.

3. The court must appoint a guardian ad litem for the child as soon as possible after the proceedings are commenced, unless it is satisfied that it is not necessary to do so in order to safeguard the interests of the child (s41). The authority should urge such an appointment on the court, since a court may be reluctant to make an order without obtaining advice from a person independent of the authority.

4. The CAO must specify the date by which the assessment is to begin, and for how long it will have effect. This period cannot exceed seven days.

It is not entirely clear from the wording of the section (s43 [5]) whether it is possible to obtain an order which allows for the child being assessed over a period of time, for example for one day in each of seven consecutive weeks. Where the concern is for the weight gain of a young child, such an order may be more appropriate than one which requires assessment over one seven day period.

5. The only assessment which can be carried out is the one specified in the order.

It is obviously crucial that the authority has clear plans prepared for the assessment. The court cannot authorise a blanket assessment for an unlimited period. The following information should be obtained in advance of the hearing;

- what assessment is necessary? For example
  - paediatric
  - neurological
  - social work
  - educational
  - psychiatric
- who will make the assessment?
- how long will it take?

- when can it start?
- can it be carried out while the child is at home? if not, why not?
- who should be present?
- how will the assessment be recorded?
- if the assessment is to be recorded on video, whose property will that be, and when will copies be available?

6. If the child is of sufficient understanding to make an informed decision, she may refuse to submit to a medical or psychiatric examination or other assessment. (This will include assessments by e.g. social workers, an educational psychologist, and assessment by means of a video interview.)

    Social workers who discuss assessments with a child need to be particularly careful to record the discussion and what was said about the implications of the child agreeing to the assessment. The child must not be given the impression that there will be any confidentiality attached to what she may say, or what may be found during the assessment.

    Where possible, it may be advisable to leave this discussion to the guardian ad litem. She has the duty to advise the court as to the child's understanding where there is any doubt, and as a person independent of the local authority, her recommendation to the court about this may be less open to criticism than that of the authority, who will clearly be anxious to persuade the child that it will be in her interests to agree to the assessment.

7. The child may not be removed from home for the assessment unless the court directs this, being satisfied that it is necessary for the purpose of the assessment. The order must specify the period authorised, and must contain directions as to the child's contact with other people while she is away from home.

8. Where the court considers that there are grounds for making an Emergency Protection Order, and that it ought to make this order rather than a CAO, s43 [4] prohibits the making of a CAO. The court is empowered to make an EPO in these circumstances although there has been no application for such an order.

    It is essential that social workers planning an application for a CAO consider the implications for the authority should an EPO be granted at this stage. Duties in relation to placement of the child, contact, application to discharge the order, and others will arise. The social worker at court must be in a position to deal with these issues, and cannot assume that an adjournment would be granted for further information to be obtained.

    The court may consider making an order other than a CAO or EPO. It is arguable that a s8 order can be made by the court when considering an application under Part V of the Act. (See xi under section on EPO for further details).

9. The child's welfare will be the court's paramount consideration when making a decision on the application for a CAO. In addition, s1 [5] requires the court to be satisfied that making an order will be better for the child than making no order at all.

Since this is an application under Part V of the Act, the welfare checklist (s1 [3]) is not considered by the court, although the matters listed in that sub-section will no doubt be relevant when looking at the welfare of the child.

10. Once an application for a CAO has been made, there can be no further such application for six months, unless the court gives leave (s92 [15])

11. Any party may appeal against the making of an order by the magistrates court, whether this was described as a direction (such as for a medical examination) or an order (CAO). The appeal (under s94) is to the care centre, and must be lodged within 14 days.

POLICE PROTECTION

1. The police have power under the Police and Criminal Evidence Act 1984 s17 [1e] to enter premises without a warrant to save life and limb. This provision does not authorise removal of a child found on the premises. If police want to remove the child, they must then rely on powers given to them under the Children Act.

   Where a police officer has reasonable cause to believe that a child would otherwise be likely to suffer significant harm, he may either remove the child to suitable accommodation, or take steps to prevent the child being removed from a hospital or any other place where the child may be at that time. (s46 [1]) The maximum period of police protection under this section is 72 hours.

   This power is frequently, but mistakenly, referred to as 'a police protection order'. It is not an order, therefore there is no appeal against the exercise of the power. It could be challenged by a writ of habeus corpus or possibly by an application for judicial review; but this is unlikely, given the limited period during which a child can be kept in police protection.

2. As soon as reasonably practicable the police officer must

   (a) notify the local authority of the action taken, reason for the action, and where the child has been placed. The authority must then investigate the case (s47 [1]), and may request the police to make an application for an EPO (s47 [3c])

   (b) inform the child (where she appears capable of understanding), of what action has been taken, and why, and what further action may be taken,

   and must take reasonably practicable steps to give this information to

   ◦ the child's parents,

   ◦ any other person who has parental responsibility,

   ◦ any other person with whom the child was living at the time when she was removed

   (c) take such steps as are reasonably practicable to discover the wishes and feelings of the child

(d) ensure that the case is inquired into by an officer designated for this purpose by the chief officer of the police area concerned

(e) ensure that where the child has been removed into police protection, she is placed either in local authority accommodation

or in a refuge (which has been approved under s51 CA 1989)

3. A child cannot be kept in police protection for longer than 72 hours (s46 [6]).

As soon as the inquiry by the designated officer is complete, the child must be released, unless the officer in charge of the inquiry considers that there is still reasonable cause for believing that she would be likely to suffer significant harm if she is released.

Where this is the view of police, and where for whatever reason the local authority is not applying for an EPO, the police may apply for an order, on behalf of the authority, with or without its knowledge. In these circumstances, the authority has an obligation under s21 to provide accommodation for the child. The authority may not appeal the making of an EPO (since this order cannot be appealed [s45 [10]] However, a duty is imposed on the authority to return the child home, or allow her to be removed from where she is (e.g. hospital), where this appears to be safe.

It should be very unusual for police to apply for an EPO without the agreement of, or following a request by, a local authority.

4. The police do not have parental responsibility for a child who is in police protection. However the designated officer has a duty to do what is reasonable in all the circumstances of the case for the purpose of safeguarding or promoting the child's welfare, 'having regard in particular to the length of the period during which the child will be so protected' (s46 [9b]).

This duty to act is in the same terms as the power given by s3 to a person who does not have parental responsibility, but has the care of the child. However, in view of the limited period during which the police can act (i.e., the 72 hours), the duty should be exercised cautiously.

Where there appears to be an urgent need for the child to be medically examined and then treated, s46 would allow the police to arrange this, and to give necessary consents. They would, in those circumstances, have a good defence to any subsequent action for assault and trespass, and likewise the doctor would be protected. However, good practice will require that the consent of a person with parental responsibility will always be sought first, if this is practicable. Where there is any doubt as to the need for emergency action, caution would dictate that an application for an EPO should be made, and directions sought under s44 as to medical or other examinations.

5. The designated officer shall allow a range of people to have 'such contact (if any) with the child', as in his opinion is reasonable and in the interests of the child. They are:

- the child's parents
- any other person with parental responsibility
- any person with whom the child was living before she was removed
- anyone who has a s8 or s34 contact order allowing contact with the child
- anyone acting on behalf of any of those persons

The contact allowed under this section is expressed in terms of the right of the persons listed to have contact with the child, rather than the right of the child to have contact.

When a local authority is providing accommodation for the child their duty is to allow the child to have contact with various people (s34). However, when they provide accommodation during a period of police protection, the duty is the same as that imposed on police (s46 [11]). The reasoning behind this distinction is unclear. Another distinction is that there is no requirement on police to consider the wishes of the child when making a decision about contact; before the local authority make any decision concerning a child being looked after by them, they must consider her wishes and feelings (s22 [4]), and likewise a court making a decision relating to contact (see the welfare check-list in s1[3]).

Although the child's siblings are not specifically included in the list, clearly they fall within it; as long as they were living in the same household. If they live elsewhere, they have no right to contact, nor do other relatives or friends. They must then depend on the exercise of the discretion given to the police (s46 [9b]). If contact with the child is allowed while she is in police protection, the circumstances in which it takes place will be entirely at the discretion of the police officer, for instance it may be supervised. The police cease to have any responsibility for contact once the child is placed in local authority accommodation.

EMERGENCY PROTECTION ORDERS

1. Any person may apply for an EPO. The court must be satisfied that –

- there is reasonable cause to believe that the child is likely to suffer significant harm if
- the child is not removed to accommodation provided by or on behalf of the applicant
- or the child does not remain where she is (s44 [1])

It is clear that the court may grant an EPO on the application of any person. Although it is rare for applications to be made other than by a local authority or the NSPCC, it could be used by an individual concerned about a child where the local authority have declined to take action, or where there are concerns about a child in the care of the local authority. Where there are immediate concerns about a child, and there is no involvement by a local authority, it may be quicker to obtain an EPO on the child, then to make an application for a s8 order. If the EPO was granted, there would then be time to consider what other proceedings might be appropriate.

2. (a) If a local authority apply (s44), they must satisfy the court that:

   ○ they are making a s47 investigation in respect of the child

   ○ *and* the enquiries are being frustrated because access by the local authority to the child is being unreasonably refused

   ○ *and* the applicant has reasonable cause to believe that access to the child is required as a matter of urgency

   ○ *or* when either a local authority or NSPCC apply the applicant has reasonable cause to believe that a child is suffering, or is likely to suffer significant harm if

     * she is not removed to accommodation provided by or on behalf of the applicant

     * *or* she does not remain in the place in which she is then being accommodated.

   (b) No definition of the term 'likely to suffer significant harm' is given in s44. However, the definition of harm found in s31 [9] will apply. Therefore:

   ○ harm means ill treatment or the impairment of health or development

   ○ development means physical, intellectual, emotional, social or behavioural development

   ○ health means physical or mental health

   ○ ill treatment includes sexual abuse and forms of ill treatment which are not physical.

   In the Court of Appeal, in Newham London Borough v A. G. (1993) [1 FLR 281] the President of the Family Division considered the interpretation of the phrase 'likely to suffer'. Although this was in relation to care proceedings, and s31, the decision is clearly relevant for the court considering an application for an EPO. Sir Stephen Brown stated that when interpreting and giving effect to the phrase 'likely to suffer significant harm' in s31 of the Children Act 1989, it would be wrong to equate 'likely to suffer' with 'on the balance of probabilities'. He said that the court was not applying a test to events which had happened, and deciding on the evidence whether, on the balance of probabilities, an event actually had happened. In considering 'likely to suffer', the court was looking to the future, and had to assess the risk.

   The President also indicated the hope that courts would not be invited to perform a strict legalistic analysis of the statutory meaning of s31. He said that, although the words of the statute had to be considered, they were not intended to be unduly restrictive when the evidence clearly indicated that a certain course should be taken in order to protect the child.

3. Where the application is being made because access to an authorised person has been frustrated, the applicant must be able to satisfy the court that she had been able to produce evidence of her identity if called on to do so (s44 [3]).

4. An application for an EPO may be made ex parte (without notice to any other person) if the justices clerk gives leave. If an order is then made, the application must be served within 48 hours on the child and any person who has parental responsibility. Where the court refuses to make an order on an ex parte application, it may direct that the application be made inter partes, that is after notice has been given to the other parties. One clear day's notice must be given of an application for an EPO. The application must be served on the child and anyone with parental responsibility. A parent who does not have parental responsibility must be notified of the application. The rules do not require that this notice be in writing, but this would be good practice.

5. As soon as practicable after the application for an EPO is issued, the court must appoint a guardian ad litem for the child, unless the court considers that the appointment is not necessary to safeguard the interests of the child.

6. When the court is hearing an application for an EPO, it must consider the welfare of the child (s1 [1]), and whether it is better for the child to make an order than no order at all (s1 [5]). It will therefore consider the encouragement to the authority in Schedule 2 para 5, to provide accommodation, or money for accommodation, to the alleged perpetrator, to enable that person to move from the home, instead of the child being removed. The authority must be able to justify a decision to remove the child, and demonstrate what consideration has been given to an alternative course of action.

The authority must also satisfy the court as to their plans for the child if an order is granted, in the light of the requirements of s23. Unless it is not reasonably practicable or consistent with the child's welfare, the authority must make arrangements for the child to live with:

- a parent/person with parental responsibility or
- a relative, friend or other person connected with her.

In addition, and again subject to this being reasonably practicable and consistent with the child's welfare, she must be placed near to her home, and with siblings, if they are also accommodated by the authority.

Where a child with disabilities is provided with accommodation, s23 [8]requires that the authority ensure, as far as reasonably practicable, that the accommodation is not unsuitable for the needs of the child. Note that the section is not drafted as an obligation to find suitable accommodation as such.

Scope of an EPO (s44 [4])

1. It has the effect of a direction to any person who can produce the child, to do so if requested by the applicant. The child concerned must be named in the order if this is reasonably practicable; if not, the order must describe the child as clearly as possible (s44 [14]).

2. It authorises the removal of the child to accommodation provided by or on behalf of the applicant; or the prevention of the child's removal from the place where she was immediately before the order was made.

3. The court may direct that the applicant, when exercising the powers under the EPO, can have the option of being accompanied by a doctor, nurse or health visitor (s45 [12]).

4. The applicant has parental responsibility for the duration of the order, together with those other persons who already have it. However, the extent to which those other persons will be able to exercise their parental responsibility will be limited, given the automatic consequences of an EPO, the power of the court to make directions, and the discretion given to the applicant in relation to contact.

5. Where the court making the EPO considers that a person other than the applicant has information as to the child's whereabouts, a provision may be included in the order requiring that information to be disclosed upon request by the applicant. A person who has such information may not refuse to give it on the ground that by complying they or their spouse would be incriminated in an offence; but anything said by that person or their spouse in giving the information cannot be used against them in any proceedings other than for perjury.

6. An EPO will not automatically authorise the applicant to enter premises to search for a child. Specific authority must be sought from the court at the time the application is made (s48 [3]).

7. Where the court is satisfied that there may be another child on the premises who ought to be made the subject of an EPO, the order may authorise a search for the other child at the premises concerned. If that other child is found as a result of the authorised search, and the applicant is satisfied that there are grounds for making an EPO in respect of that child, the order for a search then operates as if it were an EPO. The applicant must then notify the court of the effect of the order.

8. Where it appears to the court that a person attempting to exercise powers under an EPO has been prevented from doing so, because they have been refused entry to the premises, or access to the child, or they are likely to be obstructed in this way, the court may issue a warrant to the police authorising a constable to assist the person concerned, in exercising their powers, and the warrant authorises the use of reasonable force if necessary.

A warrant must be addressed to, and executed by a constable, and if the applicant for the warrant wishes to accompany the constable they may do so, unless the court directs otherwise. The court may direct that the constable executing the warrant have the option to be accompanied by a doctor, nurse, or health visitor.

9. Can the court make any order other than an EPO on an application for this order? In family proceedings, the court has the power to make any of the s8 orders (specific issue, prohibited steps, contact, or residence), or a family assistance order, whether or not there is an application for one of those orders. However, s8 defines family proceedings, and omits proceedings under Parts III and V from the definition. Therefore it has been assumed that when an application for an EPO is made, the court will either make the order, or not make it, but no other options are available. Some doubt has been thrown on this assumption by the case of JR v Oxfordshire County Council (1992) [2 FCR]. An application was made for a secure accommodation order, under s25 (a Part III application). Hearsay evidence was not allowed, since the proceedings were not family proceedings within the meaning of s8, and hearsay evidence was only allowed in such proceedings.

On an appeal against the decision of the family proceedings court, it was held that s8 had to be read in conjunction with s92 (2), which provided that proceedings under the Act should be treated as family proceedings in relation to magistrates courts. The consequence of this decision in the particular case was that hearsay evidence was admissible on an application for a secure accommodation order.

The decision has a far reaching effect on proceedings brought by a local authority. It means that before making any application for a Children Act order, the local authority must consider the possibility that a s8 order, or Family Assistance Order will be made, rather than the order sought. It also means that the guardian ad litem will have a broader remit than was envisaged when the Act was implemented.

Limitations of the order

1. The applicant must only use the power to remove the child, or prevent her being removed, to the extent necessary to safeguard the welfare of the child (s44 [5]).

2. The parental responsibility acquired with the order must only be exercised as far as it is reasonably required to safeguard or promote the welfare of the child (having regard to the duration of the order) (s44 [5]).

3. The court may give directions as to contact between the child and any named person (s44 [6]).

4. The court may give directions as to the medical or psychiatric examination or other assessment of the child. Conditions may be attached to the order, which may include a direction that there is to be no such examination or assessment, or none without the prior direction of the court. (s44 [8]).

The child may refuse to submit to the examination/assessment, if she is of sufficient understanding to make an informed decision. Similar considerations apply as those on the making of a Child Assessment Order.

5. A direction as to contact or examination/assessment may be given:

    - at the time the E.P.O. is made

    - at any time while it is in force

    It may be varied on application to the court on one day's notice being given to the other parties.

6. If no direction has been given by the court, any person with parental responsibility will be able to consent to an examination or assessment, subject always to the right of the child (in accordance with the Gillick principles) to object.

Return of child subject to an EPO

1. During the course of the order, the applicant may decide to allow the child to go home, or to be removed from the place where she was required to remain by the EPO (e.g. a hospital). In fact, if the applicant considers that the child would be safe, the child must be returned or allowed to be removed (s44 [10]).

2. Where the child is to be returned, she must be returned to the care of the person from whom she was removed, or, if that is not practicable; to a parent, or person with parental responsibility; or to such other person as the applicant considers appropriate. In this case the court must give agreement to the plan (s44 [11]).

Further removal of child

While the EPO. remains in force, the child may again be removed, or prevented from being removed, if the applicant considers that a change in circumstances makes this necessary (s44 [12]).

Contact during an EPO

Subject to any direction given by the court, the applicant must allow the child reasonable contact with:

- her parents

- anyone who is not a parent but has parental responsibility

- any person with whom the child was living immediately before the order e.g. brothers/sisters

- any person who has contact under the terms of a court order

- any person acting on behalf of those persons. It is unclear what is intended by this provision. It may include a lawyer acting for a parent who is an alleged abuser. A refusal to allow contact with a person who falls within this category should be carefully recorded, as indeed should any decision concerning contact during an EPO.

Offences relating to an EPO

Any person who deliberately obstructs the removal of a child, or prevention of removal of a child, under an EPO commits an offence (triable in the magistrates court) for which the penalty is a fine.

This also applies to any person who deliberately obstructs the entry to premises and search for a child under s48.

Time limits

1. An EPO may be made for any period not exceeding eight days. Where the eight days ends with a public holiday or a Sunday, the court may specify that the order is to come to an end at noon on the day following the holiday (s45).

2. If the application for an EPO is made by police, during a period of police protection, the eight days is calculated from the date when the child came into police protection (s45 [3]).

3. Any person who has parental responsibility following the making of an EPO, and is entitled to apply for a care order on the child, may apply for an extension of the EPO. In practice the only persons in that position will be a local authority or the NSPCC, since no one else is authorised under the Act to apply for a care order.

4. The court may extend the EPO by a further period of up to seven days, *if* it is has reasonable cause to believe that the child concerned is likely to suffer significant harm if the order is not extended. One clear day's notice of such an application must be given (s45 [5]).

5. An EPO can only be extended once (s45 [6]). This may cause practical difficulties, where for example an EPO expires on a Monday. An application to extend the order starts on that day, but is not completed. If the court extends the order overnight to the following day, how can a further extension for the remaining six days be made at the conclusion of the hearing?

6. An application for the discharge of an EPO may be made by the following persons:
   - the child
   - a parent
   - any person with parental responsibility
   - any person with whom the child was living immediately before the order was made.

   The application to discharge the order cannot be heard within the first 72 hours after the order was made. One day's notice of the application must be given.

   No application to discharge an EPO can be made by any person who was given notice of the original application for the EPO and was present at the hearing.

   No application can be made to discharge an extension to an EPO.

7. There is no appeal from the making of an EPO, or from the refusal to make an EPO, or from any directions given by the court when making an order.

EVIDENCE

1. The Children (Admissibility of Hearsay Evidence) Order 1991 states that in civil proceedings before the High Court and county court, and in family proceedings in the magistrates court, evidence given in connection with the upbringing, maintenance, or welfare of a child will be admissible in spite of any rule which may otherwise make hearsay evidence inadmissible. Hearsay evidence is evidence of a statement made to a witness by a person who is not called to give evidence themselves when the purpose of giving that evidence is to establish the truth of what is in the statement. It is not hearsay evidence when the purpose of relating it to the court is to establish the fact that a statement has been made, rather than the truth of what has been said.

   The effect of the Order is that hearsay evidence is admissible in children's cases. The court will assess the weight to be attached to any evidence which is not first hand, and will want the best evidence possible. In R v B County Council ex parte P (1991) 2 All ER 65 Butler-Sloss LJ stated 'a court presented with hearsay evidence has to look at it anxiously and consider carefully the extent to which it can properly be relied on'.

2. The court may take account of any statement contained in the report of a guardian ad litem and the court may take account of any evidence given in respect of matters referred to in the report, insofar as the evidence is relevant to the question which the court is considering (s41 [11].

   Similar provisions apply to the court welfare officer under s7. [4].

3. A copy of a record of, or held by, a local authority, produced to the court by the guardian ad litem will be admitted as evidence of any matter referred to in the report of the guardian ad litem, or the oral evidence given by her. (s42).

4. A court hearing an application for an EPO may take account of:

   - any statement contained in any report made to the court in the course of, or in connection with the hearing or

   - any evidence given during the hearing, which is, in the opinion of the court relevant to the application

ABDUCTION OF CHILDREN FROM THE LOCAL AUTHORITY

Recovery order (s50)

1. The court may make a recovery order, where it appears to the court that there is reason to believe that a child in police protection, or who is the subject of an EPO

(a) has been unlawfully taken away or is being unlawfully kept away from the responsible person or

(b) has run away or is staying away from the responsible person or

(c) is missing

The responsible person is the person who has care of the child under the EPO or during the period of police protection.

2. The application for a recovery order must be made by any person who has parental responsibility under the EPO, or the designated officer where the child is in police protection.

3. The order will:

    (a) direct any person who is in a position to do so to produce the child on request to an authorised person

    (b) authorise the removal of the child by any authorised person

    (c) require any person who has information as to the child's whereabouts to disclose that information, if asked to do so, to a police officer or officer of the court.

4. If it appears to the court that there are reasonable grounds for believing the child to be on particular premises, the order may specify those premises, and authorise a police officer to enter and search for the child, using reasonable force if necessary.

5. s50 [7] defines an authorised person as:

    - any person specified by the court

    - any constable

    - any person authorised after the recovery order is made, by a person who has parental responsibility by virtue of the EPO, to exercise any power under the recovery order.

The authorisation must identify the recovery order, and the authorised person must, if asked to do so, produce an authenticated document showing that s/he is authorised.

Child Abduction Act 1984

1. It is an offence under s2 to remove or keep out of the lawful control of the person having lawful control, a child in police protection or subject to an EPO. The offence cannot be committed by a parent, guardian, or person who has a residence order.

2. s49 CA 1989 makes it an offence for any person knowingly and without lawful authority to take away a child who is in care, subject to an EPO or in police protection, from the responsible person. It is also an offence to keep such a child away from the responsible person, or to induce, assist or incite such a child to run away or stay away from the responsible person. The responsible person is any person who has care of the child under a care order, EPO or while she is in police protection.

Refuges

s51 CA 1989 makes provision for voluntary organisations and local authorities to set up refuges for children who appear to be at risk of harm. A refuge must be certified by the Secretary of State, under the provisions of The Refuges (Children's Homes and Foster Placements) Regulations 1991, and may be a voluntary home, a registered children's home, or a foster home.

The refuge must notify police within 24 hours of a child coming to them, and as and when the designated officer is aware of the identity of the responsible person, they must be notified that the child is being provided with a refuge, and given a contact telephone number for the person providing the refuge. The police must be informed when the child leaves the refuge.

Provided the refuge has been properly certified, they will be protected from the provisions of s49 Children Act and s2 Child Abduction Act in relation to the commission of offences.

Reg. 3 [para. 9] prohibits the provision of a refuge to a child for more than 14 consecutive days, or for more than 21 days in a period of 3 months. If a child remains in breach of the regulation, it does not create an offence, but the certification may be withdrawn.

INHERENT JURISDICTION OF THE HIGH COURT

The ability of a local authority to use the inherent jurisdiction of the High Court has been severely restricted by the Children Act. s100 prohibits the court from exercising its inherent jurisdiction so as to place a child in the care of a local authority, or to require that a child is accommodated. A local authority may apply for leave to invoke the inherent jurisdiction, but this will only be granted if the result sought cannot be achieved by the making of an order under the Children Act.

CHAPTER 3

RECOGNITION OF ABUSE

ALICE SWANN

INTRODUCTION

In the 1990s there are few people who do not accept that child abuse and neglect exists. However, as relatively recently as the early 1960s our counterparts would have had a different perspective.

In the 1960s there was an emphasis on the recognition that not all physical injuries to children were accidental. In the previous decade Kempe and his staff in Denver, Colorado were recognising child abuse in the children they were seeing at their centre. In 1961 Kempe, who was then chairman of the American Association of Paediatrics, chaired a Symposium at which the term 'Battered Child Syndrome' was first used. Kempe deliberately chose this label to gain the attention of the medical profession in particular and he was successful. Up to that time the medical profession had viewed child abuse as a social problem and for them confidentiality was a barrier to their becoming involved.

In 1962 the famous 'Battered Child Syndrome' paper was published (Kempe *et al.* 1962). In that paper Kempe highlighted the fact that there was an undiagnosed condition in which young children were receiving serious physical harm from a caregiver, usually a parent. From that point there was a rapid movement to studies that were concerned with the best way in which to deal with children and their families. As this developed, there was a growing recognition that children could also be injured emotionally and sexually as well as physically.

In the 1960s social workers were not centrally involved. This only happened in 1972 when monitoring systems were being set up by local statutory agencies. Social workers now have a primary role in protection, investigation, giving evidence in court, provision of services, treatment and rehabilitation.

Many events have alerted people within our society to this problem. Following the death of Maria Colwell, the public inquiry which was ordered by Sir Keith Joseph, then Secretary of State, received much publicity (D.H.S.S. 1974). This inquiry established that child abuse and neglect was a major social problem. Fundamental changes in policy and practice were introduced. At the same time, Sir Keith Joseph also published his department's analysis of social deprivation and the term 'cycle of deprivation' was introduced.

Social workers were then given the role of breaking this cycle and their input was accepted as essential by other professionals. A decade after the 'Battered Child Syndrome' paper, professionals were beginning to think in terms beyond that narrow syndrome.

Other inquiries have followed the Maria Colwell inquiry and it is disheartening to note that many of them have found the same evidence of professional misjudgment and failures of communication within and between the various agencies involved. Whilst there has been recognition of the statutory responsibilities for social services there has been an increased awareness of the importance of any professional who comes in contact with the child, especially those in need of protection.

For some professionals this responsibility may seem onerous, especially if they are reporting concerns about an injury, element of neglect, or suspicions of child sexual abuse. The key for such professionals is to remember that they are expressing a concern and not making a diagnosis.

PHYSICAL ABUSE

Definition

> Physical abuse of children is intentional, non accidental use of physical force... on the part of a parent or other care-taker in interaction with a child in his care, aiming at hurting, injuring or destroying that child.

Age range

Any child or young person is susceptible to physical abuse. Those most at risk are often under two years of age (McHenry *et al.* 1963).

Typical sites for accidental bruises

An acknowledgement should be made at this point that diagnosing non-accidental injury can be very difficult, even for well trained and experienced clinicians.

The non-medical professional involved is not expected to make the actual diagnosis but would certainly be expected to report an injury that is of concern. For such a professional it is beneficial to have a clear idea of the pattern of accidental bruises on children. These types of bruises are familiar to anyone who deals with children. A good rule of thumb is that accidental bruises are more common at places on the body where bone is fairly close to the skin. Accordingly, such a child may present with cuts, bruises and abrasions on places like forehead, nose, chin, elbows, knees and shins. Please note there is such an entity as 'an accident prone child'. These children will have bruises, albeit more numerous, in the above type of pattern.

Typical sites for non-accidental injury

A good rule of thumb for non-accidental types of bruises is to remember that
they are present frequently on soft tissues like soft parts of the cheek, buttocks,
lower back, and upper legs. There may also be marks on the neck, genitals
and mouth. Any mouth injury is of particular concern but one that should be
highlighted is that of a torn frenulum. The frenulum is a mid line tissue
containing a vein which is situated between the upper lip and upper gum.

Pattern for accidental bruises	Pattern for non-accidental bruise
Where bone is close to the skin	*Soft tissue*
forehead	cheeks
nose	mouth
chin	neck
points of elbows	tissue surrounding elbows and knees
points of knees	lower back
shins	buttocks
	upper leg
genitals (astride)	genitals

Injuries of concern	*Caused by*
Bruises	Hand
	Fist
	Foot
	Implement
Burns	Accident
	Neglect
	Deliberate action
Breaks	Direct blow
	Grabbing and twisting
Bites	Child
	Adult

Bruises

HAND

The most common bruises inflicted by the hand are grab or slap marks. Both these types of injuries have a distinctive pattern, particularly slap marks. These frequently occur on the buttocks and cheek. Often the outline of the fingers is obvious. Grab marks are also distinctive but for the clinician these are more difficult marks to diagnose. When present they are usually located around the joints, such as knees, hips and elbows. This is where a child has been forceably held. Babies may have such marks on their backs or faces. If a child is grabbed to the extent to which bruising is left there can be other serious complications such as fractured limbs, or potentially fatal consequences as found in the Shaken Infant Syndrome. For obvious reasons, one of the most worrying locations for grab marks is on the neck. As the neck is so well protected it is relatively rare for accidental marks to appear there.

For all of the above much force has been used by the assailant. If the reader has any doubts about this try this simple exercise. Grab your own arm tightly and sustain this for a minute. You will have inflicted some pain on yourself but almost certainly you will not have left any bruises. For the child who has had bruises inflicted by grabbing the force used is therefore much more than you have inflicted on yourself and there is no doubt it is excruciatingly painful.

FIST

Bruising that has been inflicted by hitting a child with the fist is not as defined as the slap and grab marks already considered. There are two exceptions to this however. If a child is punched in the ear or eye fairly distinctive bruising occurs.

It is very difficult for the clinician to distinguish between an accidental black eye and a non-accidental black eye. The eye is another very well protected part of the body. However, if the eye is hit by a fist there is some very distinctive bruising.

Unless you have witnessed a child acquiring an accidental black eye it is a good rule that you report any black eye noted on any child. It is of particular concern if the child has two black eyes.

Some children who are engaged in contact sports like rugby or boxing may acquire a bruised ear. However, this is not a common injury so any child with a bruised ear, particularly if there is bruising on the skull behind the ear, should be reported to the appropriate authorities. The force involved in inflicting a bruised ear is of such intensity that two possible complications could be a ruptured ear drum or fractured skull.

A torn frenulum is one of the most common and specific non- accidental injuries. A hand or a fist blow across the mouth or force feeding with, for example, a bottle or spoon may produce this particular injury. There may be bruising around the mouth as well as bleeding from the torn vein.

The frenulum heals very rapidly and so it needs a very speedy response in order to assist the clinician in the diagnosis. This is also a common accidental injury which can occur when a toddler or young child falls with something in his mouth. Unless the professional involved has witnessed such an injury, any injury of this kind to the mouth of a young child should be reported immediately.

FOOT

The child who is kicked usually acquires diffuse bruising. Occasionally there may be the mark of the footwear on the child which will assist in the diagnosis.

IMPLEMENTS

The most common implements used are straps, belts and sticks. For a child beaten in such a manner there are usually several lesions of a very similar if not identical pattern. Some distinguishing features might also be obvious, for example outline of the buckle or the end of the strap. The most frequent sites for these type of injuries are the buttocks, lower back and upper thighs and these are usually hidden by clothing. However, some may be partially exposed if the clothing has slipped.

Burns

- Accidental
- Neglectful
- Deliberate

It is my opinion that this is the most under- diagnosed form of non-accidental injury. Many children are burned and this may be a true accident, a result of neglect or deliberate. It is very difficult for the clinician to distinguish between accidental and non-accidental burns. In turn it is often unclear whether a burn is due to neglect or deliberate. The professional who is concerned must therefore report any burn, except the most superficial ones that have clearly happened accidentally. It is of particularly grave concern if a child is deliberately burned because of the sadistic element.

There are, broadly, two types of burns: contact burns and hot liquid burns.

CONTACT BURNS

A child may be burned by a hot object being placed against the skin or vice versa. The most common of these is a cigarette burn.

Any cigarette burn should be reported to the authorities, particularly if a child has more than one burn and the burn is in a location that cannot be explained by brushing against a cigarette, for example a cigarette burn on the palm of the hand. Indeed, children frequently acquire accidental cigarette burns but these are usually very superficial.

A child may be held against a hot object like a radiator or ring of a cooker. These burns leave distinctive marks on the skin characterised by their symmetry and depth.

HOT LIQUID BURNS

A child may be non-accidentally burned by having a hot liquid splashed on him or part of the child being immersed in a hot liquid. The experienced clinician will carefully consider the distribution of such a burn.

BREAKS (FRACTURES)

- Direct blow
- Grabbing and/or twisting

The reader of this chapter will rarely be the first to notice such fractures as children are usually brought to the attention of clinician whether the fracture is accidental or non-accidental. Non-accidental fractures like many of the other non-accidental injuries have a distinctive pattern.

They may be caused by a direct blow and this would include a fracture to the skull. Fractures may also be caused by someone grabbing a child with force and then twisting or tugging at a limb. The obvious signs of a fracture are swelling or deformity. However, this may not always be present and if a child is unwilling to use a limb medical attention is essential. A fractured skull may present clinically as a soft swelling on the head.

Bites

Children frequently get bitten by either animals or humans. Animal bites are usually obvious and distinctive. Children may bite other children and again distinctive marks are left on the skin. Adults who bite children inflict larger wounds and these always must be investigated. Adults usually bite children for two reasons: the first to teach a child not to bite another child and the second for sadistic reasons. Whilst one discourages an adult from the former, the latter is obviously of grave concern. It is of note and concern that in many of the child fatalities bite marks were noted. Bite marks are not themselves fatal but are frequently one of the elements in sadistic injuries to children. Accordingly, any bite mark must be taken seriously.

Whilst many of the above injuries may seem obvious, it is worth remembering that parents or carers will usually keep children within the home whilst such injuries are healing to avoid detection.

REPORT

This section lists injuries and circumstances that definitely should be reported to the appropriate authorities.

- black ear
- two black eyes
- black eye (for which you did not witness accidental injury)
- belt marks
- strap marks
- slap marks
- grab marks
- burns
- adult bite marks
- baby with any bite marks
- torn frenulum
- marks on neck

- knowledge of someone shaking a child
- a baby with bruising of any type
- child saying she is frightened of a particular person
- child reporting that she is being hit, kicked etc.

NEGLECT

Definition

> Neglect exists when chronic inattention is given to the child(ren) by their parents or caretakers in the areas of medical, educational, stimulative, environmental, nutritional, physical or emotional needs (Cantwell 1978).

Age range

All age groups, with the pre school children being the most vulnerable (Cantwell 1980).

Neglect is difficult to diagnose as, by definition, it has to be present for a period of time. The professionals involved in the day to day care of children have an important role in the recognition of neglect, in that they have a unique opportunity to observe the child and in many cases other members of the family in many different areas of the child's life. Clinicians who are assessing the level of neglect need to refer to such professionals in daily contact with the child.

Cantwell's definition is useful as a reminder that it is not necessarily only the very dirty hungry child who is neglected as other needs of that child may not be met.

Using this definition as a framework, the various needs of the children will be listed under separate headings. If the professional notes that over a period of time these needs are not being consistently met there could well be neglect and evaluation is essential. Please note that parents may not be able to meet adequately many of the needs that are listed below if they are under the influence of alcohol, drugs or have a psychiatric illness.

Medical needs

1. Routine visits to the doctor (for check ups and vaccinations).
2. Child with injury or illness.
3. Child with handicap or chronic health problem.

Educational needs

1. Regular attendance at school.
2. Consistent time keeping.
3. Child in a condition that is conducive to learning, for example to be fed, clean and warm with no major worries about what is happening at home.

Stimulative needs

1. Age appropriate allowing the child to accomplish their developmental appropriate tasks.
2. New experiences being offered to the child. The two most important elements to meet these needs for the child are play and language. Language is essential for a child not only to communicate with others but to rationalise, understand and consider all that is happening to him and eventually the rest of the world around him. This in turn can only happen if the child is stimulated, particularly through play and language. Play helps the child control their motor functions, practice skills useful in life and provide the means to express feelings (Pringle 1981).

Environmental needs

1. Safe housing.
2. Adequate supervision of child. It is of particular concern if a child is left to supervise other younger children.
3. Protection from dangerous substances. For example fire, hot liquids, medicines or corrosive materials.
4. Protection from violence within the home. The child should not be exposed to repeated violence within the home even if that violence is not directed towards the child himself.
5. Parental knowledge of whereabouts.

Nutritional needs

1. Adequate food.
2. Appropriate food.
3. Investigation of medical conditions that might affect growth.

There are still children in this modern age in Great Britain who suffer from inadequate nutrition. In some cases it may be that the food offered to the child is inappropriate. Professionals should be alerted to hungry children and it should be of particular concern if weight loss is noted. Medical conditions may be present that impair growth even with adequate nutritional care, for example coeliac disease or cystic fibrosis. These children have organic reasons for failure to thrive. However, non-organic failure-to-thrive is a serious manifestation of emotional deprivation and requires a full evaluation.

Physical needs

1. Adequate clothing and warmth.
2. Protection from harsh discipline and non-accidental injury.

Emotional needs

1. Love. This love should be unconditional and given without resentment. The child should have a sense of approval and acceptance by others. There should be no unreasonable criticism.
2. Security. The child should feel secure within the family. For this it is essential that there is a consistency and dependability within the home. In the provision of such security there needs to be an orderliness within the home.
3. Discipline. This should always be age appropriate and have a direct relationship to the misdemeanour. It can be particularly abusive if a child is shouted at frequently (Pringle 1981).

Evaluating emotional deprivation is extremely difficult for the experienced clinician and beyond the remit of this chapter. The following is a list of the more common manifestations of severe emotional deprivation and should always be of concern.

- severe behavioral problems
- inability to play
- excessive withdrawal or timidity
- excessive sadness
- indiscriminate attachment
- failure to thrive.

REPORT

1. Knowledge that parent/s is/are under the influence of drugs or alcohol.
2. Knowledge that parent/s has/have psychiatric illness.
3. Injury or illness of child not being treated.
4. Child who is not attending school.
5. Knowledge of marital violence.
6. Knowledge of child unsupervised.
7. Knowledge that child is being expected to take care of other children.
8. Persistently hungry child.
9. Persistently dirty, smelly child.
10. Unhappy child.
11. Child with inability to play.
12. Child who is obviously under-weight and small of stature.
13. Child who reports being threatened, criticised unreasonably or shouted at.

SEXUAL ABUSE

Definition

> The involvement of dependent, developmentally immature children or adolescents in sexual activities that they do not truly comprehend, to which they are unable to give informed consent or that violate the social taboos of family roles. In other words, it is the use of children by adults for sexual gratification (Schechter and Roberge 1976).

Age range

This is over the complete age range, with many studies showing two maximum age groups of reporting of child sexual abuse of 7 years and 14 years. Our centre is now reporting that at least one third of children who are sexually abused are boys (Swann and Kalston 1991).

There are three main ways in which concern of sexual abuse may arise.

1. Disclosure by child.
2. Behaviour of child.
3. Physical symptoms and signs.

Disclosure by child

For professionals involved with the day to day care of children this is very often the most common way in which sexual abuse becomes apparent. The child may make a very clear disclosure, for example 'Uncle Don hurts my pee pee' or 'My babysitter does rude things to me'. Other disclosures may be less specific in that the child may share with the professional that they wish to share a secret or make a non-specific comment about the person, for example 'I don't like it when Billy babysits for me'.

Behaviour of child

Finkelhor and Browne's model 'Traumogenic Dynamics in the Impact of child sexual abuse' (Finkelhor 1986) provides an excellent framework that not only lists behaviours of concern but places them in context. Part of this model is reproduced below.

Traumatic sexualization

Behavioural manifestations

- Sexual preoccupation and compulsive sexual behaviour
- Precocious sexual activity
- Aggressive sexual behaviours
- Promiscuity
- Sexual dysfunctions: flashbacks, difficult in arousal/orgasm
- Avoidance of or phobic reaction to sexual intimacy
- Inappropriate sexualization of parenting

Stigmatization

Behavioural manifestations

- Isolation
- Drug or alcohol abuse
- Criminal involvement
- Self mutilation
- Suicide or suicide attempts

Betrayal

Behavioural manifestations

- Clinging
- Vulnerability to subsequent abuse and exploitation
- Allowing own children to be victimized
- Isolation
- Discomfort in intimate relationships
- Marital problems
- Aggressive behaviour
- Delinquency

Powerlessness

Behavioural manifestations

- Nightmares
- Phobias
- Somatic complaints: eating and sleeping disorders
- Depression
- Running away. Unwilling to go home from school
- School problems, truancy
- Employment problems
- Vulnerability to subsequent victimization
- Aggressive behaviour, bullying
- Delinquency
- Becoming an abuser
- Fear of being alone with an adult
- Unwilling to undress for PE or games

Many of the behaviours that are outlined in this framework and many others are non-specific, for example clinging, aggressive behaviour and isolation. Some behaviours, however, are fairly specific and should alert the professional as to the possibility of sexual abuse. These include

1. SEXUAL PREOCCUPATION AND COMPULSIVE SEXUAL BEHAVIOURS.

To decide whether or not such a manifestation is inappropriate, one has to have knowledge of what is appropriate for the age of that particular child. It is normal for a child to be curious about sexual matters, particularly about body parts of the opposite gender. Doctor–Nurse games are familiar with most people who work with children and usually involve a game where genitals may well be looked at and even touched but it is usually in a 'hospital' setting. Any activity that goes beyond such normal activity should be reported, for example a boy trying to place his penis into a girl's vagina or persistent masturbation in public.

It is also a concern if a child wishes to masturbate another child. Whilst a child may draw genitals within their drawings it is of concern if the drawings consist of pubic hair, erect penis or if sexual activities are being depicted.

2. SUICIDE ATTEMPT

It is well known that children who are sexually abused frequently present with depression. The most serious manifestation of this could well be an attempt at suicide. Any such attempt should be reported to the appropriate authorities.

3. SELF MUTILATION

This is often a manifestation of the stigmatization a child feels. It is more common in teenage girls and should alert the professionals to the possibility of sexual abuse.

4. REFUSAL TO TAKE PART IN GAMES/SWIMMING ETC.

Whilst there may be other reasons for this if the child persistently refuses, this may well be an alerting feature.

5. RUNNING AWAY

Any child who runs away from home should be given the opportunity to discuss why he or she took such action. Those involved should bear in mind that sexual abuse within the home may be the reason.

Physical Symptoms and Signs

These can be considered under two broad groups

1. Those due to injury.
2. Those due to infection.

DUE TO INJURY

The child may present with bleeding from the vagina or anus. She may have difficulty and/or pain in passing urine or faeces.

DUE TO INFECTION

The child may acquire an infection secondary to sexual abuse which may or may not be a definitive sexually transmitted disease. Professionals should be alerted if a child has got a persistent vaginal discharge or has warts or some type of rash in the genital or anal area. It is acknowledged that professionals may not necessarily have reasons for seeing the genitals or anal area of a child. However, in some circumstances in a normal caretaking role they may be aware of some of the above.

REPORT

- Disclosure by child
- Explicit sexual play
- Sexual preoccupation
- Very depressed child
- Child who attempts or is speaking of suicide
- Child who is self mutilating
- Child who is running away
- Bleeding from vagina or anus
- Persistent difficulty or pain in passing urine or faeces

- Persistent discharge
- Evidence of warts in genital or anal area.

EXERCISE 3.1

This exercise is to provide the opportunity for the professionals to think about situations they are encountering in terms of their level of concern. A horizontal scale should be displayed from 0–10.

> 0 = no concerns whatsoever
> 10 = abuse/neglect

The group, under leadership, should consider the following case studies and, as the account unfolds at regular intervals consider at what level on the scale their concern could be placed. A marker should be placed at the point in time where they would consider it imperative to report their concerns to the appropriate professionals.

Case studies

CASE 1

Jamie is a three and a half-year-old who is attending nursery school. His mother, aged 19, is single and living in an apartment in very difficult social circumstances. She has very little support from her family or from the community. Jamie is a robust child who is known as accident prone and always 'covered in bruises'. Indeed some of these have been acquired at nursery school.

STAGE 2

On a particular Tuesday morning Jamie returned to nursery school having been absent on the previous Friday and the Monday of that week. He was rather quiet. He had two bruises on his forehead with a large one present just above his left eye. His mother informed the staff that he had fallen down the stairs; the child agrees with this.

STAGE 3

On Tuesday, the same day of Jamie's return, the health visitor calls into the nursery school. She has heard on the grapevine mother may well be involved with drugs. The following day Jamie has a black eye (left).

STAGE 4

On Friday afternoon the mother confides with a member of staff that she is having difficulty in managing Jamie. The following Monday morning she informs the same member of staff that she has had 'a terrible weekend'. The member of staff, when taking Jamie to the toilet, notices strap marks across his buttocks.

CASE 2

Mr and Mrs Brown are married and have two children. Tommy, their eight-year-old boy, has been in care for five years because of neglect and a minor non-accidental injury. Both parents were in their late teens when Tommy was born and this was an unplanned pregnancy. The parents are now in their mid twenties and their second child Emma is now aged two and a half. This was a planned pregnancy and the couple have been attending a family centre regularly for assessment of their relationship with Emma and also with a view to returning Tommy to the family home. Mr Brown has a job as a bus driver and both parents present as very caring parents.

STAGE 2

Mr Brown has lost his job because of abuse of alcohol whilst driving his bus. Although the family continue to attend the family centre the staff have noted that Mr Brown seems rather depressed. On one occasion Mrs Brown had a black eye. Emma, however, is cheerful and thriving.

STAGE 3

Mrs Brown was admitted to hospital overnight following an assault by her husband. The staff are now noting that Emma is much more withdrawn and unwilling to play within the family centre. She is not as clean as she usually would be and has head lice. On one of the visits to the family centre her mother informed staff that she had a minor burn over her chest. This happened when she had pulled a cup of tea over herself.

STAGE 4

Appointments at the family centre have not been kept for some time. Staff, because of their concern, called to the family home and found the child unattended within the house.

CASE 3

Mr and Mrs Green are married. Both are highly paid professionals and Mrs Green is labelled as a 'career woman'. They have an only child, Christopher, aged four, who attends a private playschool. Mrs Green has always made a very clear statement that he was 'unplanned' and viewed her pregnancy as an interruption of her career. Christopher is a small, thin child who settles extremely quickly into playschool.

STAGE 2

Staff at the playschool have notice that whenever strangers come in to the building he displays indiscriminate attachment. At lunch time he would frequently have three helpings of a meal and occasionally he will eat scraps from other children's plates. It is difficult to engage this child in play activities but he can be involved with encouragement.

STAGE 3

This child is becoming more withdrawn. He rarely smiles and will not play.

STAGE 4

After a holiday period when both parents were off work and had sole care of Christopher, staff noticed that this child had lost a significant amount of weight on return to the playschool.

CASE 4

For this case consider how high your concern would be concerning sexual abuse.

Mr and Mrs Black are married and live in poor housing in a local estate. They have three children: Sarah aged six, Anthea aged five and Mark aged three. Mr Black is a road sweeper and Mrs Black works in a local fish factory. Mr and Mrs Black have had a violent relationship for many years and, following an assault on Mrs Black and two of her children, she requests hostel accommodation.

STAGE 2

The staff at the hostel notice Sarah likes to play doctor/nurse games. These will consist of her laying another child on the bed and wishing to examine them, including looking at the other child's bottom. Staff notice that when the child is playing with her dolls she will put two in bed together. On one occasion she lay the 'daddy doll' on top of the 'mummy doll' and moved the father doll in explicit manner. She then put the 'daddy doll' on top of a 'little girl doll'. When a member of staff asked what was happening the little girl stated that 'the daddy was hurting the little girl's bottom'. On further questioning from the member of staff she stated that the little girl's mummy was working in the fish factory. This child was insisting that the doll did not depict herself.

EXERCISE 3.2

This exercise is to highlight, for the professionals, who will become involved in the child's life if the child discloses to that particular professional serious sexual abuse, for example incest.

This exercise will consist of a participant role playing as the child who will inform the professional about the incestuous relationship with her father. The professional will then decide and state who he or she would inform following this allegation. That person will then join the two participants in the middle of the room. This third person in turn will state who they will inform and choose someone to represent that professional. This will continue until invariably there will be several people surrounding the child who will know about this within a day or two of the disclosure. As the exercise proceeds this will involve not only social workers and their seniors but police officers, police surgeons, foster parents and so forth.

A marker should be put on the people whom this child already knew before the child made the disclosure. Invariably this will be a very small number of people and it should illustrate the number of new contacts that this child will be in touch with at a very traumatic time.

REFERENCES

Cantwell, H.B. (1978) Denver Department of Social Services. Personal Communication.

Cantwell, H.B. (1980) 'Child Neglect in the Battered Child' C. Henry Kempe, Kay E. Helfer (eds.) Chicago, Il: The University of Chicago Press.

D.H.S.S. (1974) Report of the Commission of Inquiry into the care and supervision of Maria Colwell. London: HMSO.

Finkelhor, D. (1986) *A Source book on Child Sexual Abuse*. London: Sage.

Kempe, C.H., Silverman, F.N., Steele, B.F., Deoegermueller, W. and Silver, H.K. (1962) The Battered Child Syndrome. *J Am. Med. Assoc.*, 181, 17–24.

Parton, N. (1987) *The Politics of Child Sexual Abuse.*

McHenry, T., Girdany, B.R. and Elmer, E. (1963) 'Unsuspected Trauma with Multiple Skeletal Injuries during Infancy and Childhood'. Paediatrics, 31: 903–8.

Pringle, M.K. (1981) *The needs of children 2nd ed.* London: Hutchinson.

Schecter, M.D., and Roberge, L. (1976) 'Sexual Exploitation' in Helfer, R.E. and Kempe, C.H. (eds.) *Child Abuse and Neglect: The Family and the Community.*

Swann, A. and Ralston, L. (1991) 'The Importance of the Child's Account in the Valuation of Child Sexual Abuse'. (Paper read at BAPSCAN First National Conference, Leicester, Sept 1991).

CHAPTER 4

AWARENESS AND RECOGNITION

JO CROW

To be able to recognize abuse, one has to be aware of the different ways abuse may present itself. The Department of Health defines four types of abuse.

Physical: This is suggested when there is bruising, burns or scalds, or a bony injury. Although these indicators often occur normally in a child's life, non-accidental injuries show in slightly different ways and are often accompanied by unconvincing explanations. Included in the definition of physical abuse is deliberate poisoning and Munchausen's Syndrome, sometimes related.

Neglect: This is when the carer fails to meet the basic needs of the child, including when a child is left on its own, unsupervised. It often manifests itself when a child fails to thrive.

Emotional: This is when there is a lack of affection and love.

Sexual: This is when an adult or older child uses a child for their own sexual gratification.

The following is intended to alert professionals working with children to indicators of abuse, and to offer some insight into why abuse takes place.

PHYSICAL ABUSE

Physical abuse which manifests itself as bruising, can be caused by any injury to soft tissue. It was originally known as 'The Battered Baby Syndrome', but it is usually now called 'Non-accidental Injury' (NAI).

Most children have bruising, some more than others, but usually over bony areas, such as the knees and elbows, rather than on the softer, more protected areas. A baby of only a few months is unable to bruise itself. There may be a story of hitting itself with a rattle, but a baby is unable to hold a rattle well enough for this to happen. Bruising caused by abuse may be evident as a small pair of bruises where the child has been pinched. They may also appear at both sides of the mouth, where a child has been force fed. A bruise made by a hand may show the outline of the hand, or fingertip marks or whatever else may have been used to hit the child. Some children may be found to have corresponding bruises on the arms or legs, and sometimes on the sides of the body; these have been caused when the child has been held down. The ones on the body of a small child may have been caused as a result of being held too hard, when, perhaps, the carer was angry 'Bruises caused by biting usually look oval, with a gap at each side'. The age of bruising may vary, and as the bruise becomes older, its colour will change to a yellowish hue. This can help determine whether all the bruises were caused at the same time.

There are a few exceptions to the rule. Children with cancer or leukaemia may develop bruises, especially around the eyes. There are also some children's illnesses which present with fine bruising. The mongolian blue spot, (a pigmentation found usually on the backs of babies with family histories originating from Asia, Africa, the Caribbean or China, and which fades in the first year of life) can be mistaken for bruising.

Burns and scalds often occur from the unguarded fire, or the carelessly left hot cup of tea, incidents of concern in themselves. However, it is the severe burn that may not have a history, or a history that does not correspond with the child's development that is most worrying. A child may pick up an iron that has been left to cool, and be burnt, but that would not explain an iron-shaped burn on the back. A child who runs into a cigarette that someone is holding will usually have a slight tail to the burn as the cigarette is snatched away, but a deep circular mark may be a purposeful burn. Some people make a child touch a fire, as the child will not listen and keep going too near the fire, so they try to prove to the child that it is hot.

The scald with a knocked over cup of tea will have splash marks, but the child who has its hands held in boiling water will have a definite line along the hands or arms. The Non-accidental injury is not always easily recognized; someone may have thrown, in anger, hot water over the child, and the injury would appear the same as that of a child pulling a cup of tea off a table, or a kettle from a work top. Blisters usually appear at the site of a scald, especially if not treated with cold water immediately, and will have a variability of the depth of the injury.

Sometimes the child will be sat on the electric element of a cooker, and this will present as a circular mark. Sometimes the abuser will heat something metal and hold it against the child and in this instance the burn will take on the shape of the object.

The other type of injury inflicted under this heading of 'physical' is the bony injury. Children often fall and hurt themselves, especially at the age when they are climbing or riding bikes, but the story may not be consistent with the injury.

A small child may be reluctant to use an arm, and there may not be any swelling: this may be due to a 'pulled elbow'. This injury may occur either when the child is being swung, as they often are when walking between adults, or if they try to pull away from an adult, when they are being naughty. This injury is not a fracture, and can be easily manipulated by a doctor and the child will move its arm soon afterwards. If there is swelling and a deformity as well as pain then there is a probability that there is a fracture. With a young child there may not be a complete break as the bone is soft and what is known as a 'greenstick' fracture occurs, when the bone is bent slightly.

A broken bone can be caused either from a hit, or under force while being held: this is especially seen when the ribs are involved.

A limb held in an unusual angle and force exerted against it will also present with a broken bone. If an arm is twisted with unusual force, the bone may break, but in a different way which is known as a spiral fracture. There are very few accidental injuries that will present with a spiral fracture, so if this is seen on an X-ray, the story must be assessed very carefully.

With a fracture caused by abuse, there is often multiple bruising as well. Obviously, when any bony injury is suspected an X-ray is needed for confirmation and if, when diagnosed, abuse is suspected, the doctor may order a skeletal survey. This is when X-rays are taken of all parts of the body to show if there are any other fractures. An old healing fracture will also be shown on an X-ray, and it may show healing fractures of different ages.

The child who has a head injury may be drowsy or be vomiting, and a small baby may have a 'boggy' area over a fracture. The story of how the injury occurred may be well above the developmental milestones of the child, or may be not of an injury that would involve such damage. The child who is shaken will not have a fracture but may have a subdural haematoma. This is bleeding under the protective layer around the brain, and therefore the baby may be irritable due to the pressure on the brain. A neurological examination will help to diagnose this type of abuse, as will a brain scan, where a special type of X-ray is used.

A child who presents with any frequent injuries should have the histories very carefully assessed.

Munchausen is a medical problem, where the patient manufactures symptoms of an illness. In children it is usually the mother who keeps bringing the child with a problem, and this is known as Munchausen by proxy. It is often a cry for help and may present in numerous ways. There may be blood in the nappy, and this may be where the mother has been inflicting injuries on herself to produce blood to put in the nappy. It may present as fits that are never witnessed by anyone else. In these types of cases there is no direct harm at first, but the child may be submitted to numerous investigative procedures, while nothing is diagnosed. They may also visit different doctors and hospitals and therefore no one place has a complete picture.

The more dangerous cases are when a mother gives a child either some medication that may have been dispensed for her, or some other substance. These may cause symptoms, for example drowsiness from tranquillisers, and if not diagnosed early may cause permanent damage to the child. There have been some cases where the child has died as too much as been administered.

NEGLECT AND EMOTIONAL ABUSE

Neglect and emotional abuse are often linked. They often occur when the parents have little or no parenting skills, and therefore do not give the child the care and attention it needs. They will not give them toys to play with (which they need to help them develop properly), and deprive them of the stimuli they need. This type of abuse is often recognized by the way the carer and child respond to each other. The carer may not take any notice of what the child is doing, and the small child especially is noted not to talk to them or, as small children often do, show them what they are playing with.

Neglect is sometimes manifested in the small child when she or he receives one or more injuries which have resulted from being left unattended, such as burns, broken bones or bruises from falling downstairs, or ingestion of poisonous household substances such as bleach, or even alcohol.

An older child may be regularly ridiculed and disparaged and therefore the child becomes withdrawn. The child may also be deprived of playing with toys even in its own room as the mother wants a spotless house, and the house may almost have a clinical appearance rather than be a caring environment. The child who is abused in this way may present as failing to thrive, falling below its percentiles (the expected rate of growth). This needs to be medically investigated, as sometimes it may be due to a metabolic cause rather than child abuse. Children may also be neglected if there is someone in the family who is chronically sick. This may be a sibling with cancer, or a parent, and the other parent is so busy caring for the invalid that the child is neglected.

The emotional or neglected child may have poor hygiene, to the extent, for example, that they lose most of their teeth and have learning difficulties at school. They also may be noticed to cling to anyone willing to show them any affection, or may find it difficult to make relationships, even with their peers. Sometimes these children are over-aggressive to others, while trying to get attention, or acting out what happens to them. The older child or teenager may have a self-abusing behaviour, trying glue-sniffing, drug abuse, or succumbing to anorexia nervosa, or even suicide.

SEXUAL ABUSE

Many people think that a sexually abused child will present with sore or bruised genitalia, but this is not always the case. In addition, whilst men and boys perpetrate the vase majority of child sex abuse, some cases have been found to involve women, or girls. One of the signs of a sexually abused child is that there may be behaviour changes due to the perpetrator threatening them, possibly with the fact that its mother or father will not come back if it tells anyone what has happened. The older child may become obsessive about cleanliness, as it knows that sexual abuse is wrong, and feels dirty. The older child, like the emotionally abused child, may self abuse.

Some children suffer from 'blurred' roles, especially if it is a girl being abused by a male. She may see herself taking over, or in a similar role to her mother, and this may show in her behaviour, especially to younger siblings.

The younger child will often have the 'frozen look', where it takes no interest in what is going on around it, and does not respond to anyone. The child who soils itself or is constipated may be an abused child. A child who has frequent urinary problems, identified by either incontinence or frequency may also be an abused child. The child at school may be reluctant to go to the toilet and therefore become incontinent, and then to add to their problems their peers start calling them names.

If the child has been forced to take part in oral sexual abuse, it may present with either mouth infections or petechial bruising (numerous small bruises) to the roof of its mouth. While eating certain foods, they may be reminded of a similar sensation while being forced to partake in oral sex, and therefore may suddenly start vomiting in the middle of eating for no apparent reason.

Obviously, the child that does complain of a sore vulva or anal region needs to be investigated, but there may be some innocent reason for it. Also, the child may be noticed playing with dolls in an inappropriate way, or may approach their peers in a promiscuous way. The abused child may have an unusual knowledge of other people's anatomy, or may have an unusual vocabulary, although in these days this is harder to use as a guideline, as there is more on the television for them to see and hear.

A child may unintentionally disclose abuse, as he or she may be overheard by a teacher talking to a friend at school, about what happens at home.

POTENTIAL ABUSERS

Now the different types of abuse that may be seen have been described it is important to give consideration to the abusers. Due to media coverage, the wrong impression of who abuses is often given.

If we start at the beginning of a child's life there is a possibility there is poor bonding at birth. This may be due to a difficult birth, premature birth, an unwanted pregnancy; or, due to a medical problem, the child is rushed to another hospital and the mother is unable to accompany it. Later, there may be post natal depression, which manifests itself in many ways, one being that the mother does not want her baby. Post natal depression may not be apparent at first but the mother may suffer from it a number of months later.

As the baby develops, it may cry constantly and, due to lack of sleep, it may be that one of the parents becomes irritable. In the past, when people did not move around as much as they do today, there was always the family network to help out. Today, though, people often have to move where their work takes them, and so young couples find themselves in strange surroundings with no friends or close family. When the child is taken to either the doctor's surgery or to the hospital casualty department, it is sometimes a cry for help.

If a baby is a difficult feeder, whether it is breast or bottle fed, it will take up more of the mother's time, and if she has other young children, she becomes tired and may hit the children, or the baby may not be fed properly and fail to thrive.

Often, there is often only a single parent, who may be trying to keep a job, and when not working they are trying to run a home, and therefore may never have a few hours to themselves. This is common in the poorer paid jobs, but it also occurs in the case of higher paid employment where there is sometimes stress in management jobs, or the worry of the loss of employment.

There may be a problem economically: the family living on benefit may find it difficult to manage and so the parents become irritable. There may be financial problems in situations where, before the baby, both partners had well paid jobs, but the one parent (it may be mother or father) gives up their job to look after the child: there will be only one salary to live on and pay the mortgage. This may also lead to jealousy, if this partner feels that they have given up employment that they enjoyed. Jealousy may also be present if one partner feels that the baby has taken their place in the affections of the other carer.

The parents themselves may not have had a good childhood, and therefore do not know what to expect of their child. They may expect too much by thinking that their child should be top of the class in all subjects, and put pressure on the child to achieve this. The parents may, on the other hand, take no notice of the child's achievements at school, and so the child becomes disillusioned and depressed.

While discussing the neglected child we have already mentioned the sibling of an ill, or maybe disabled, child whose care involves the carer spending more time with him or her than with the sibling, who is left to amuse themselves. Another potential abuser is the carer's cohabitee. There is no blood link, and the cohabitee may have no experience with children. The relationship, especially in the early stages, may not have a stable background and therefore there may be stress, and a young child may increase the stress, and be the one that is abused.

There is often reduced responsibility if one of the parents is a habitual drinker, who may become easily irritated while drunk, and this may happen in any household. There is an added problem if the drunken parent attacks the other parent, as the child may try to interfere, resulting in abuse.

The hyperactive child will put stress even on a loving family atmosphere, and may cause stress between the parents. The patience of a carer in an unstable relationship may already be reduced, and with a hyperactive child it may be reduced further. There is evidence that children of young parents are abused more often; this may be due to the fact that the parents are not fully mature themselves. The mother may treat the baby as a doll, but unfortunately the baby does not behave like one. Older parents sometimes do not have the patience that they may have had, and perhaps the incessant chatter and the questions of a small child become too much for them and they hit out. The older mother who may be suffering from the start of the menopause may have less patience.

The carers, if abused themselves, may grow up to become abusers, and this is one of the many reasons why it is so important that child abuse is stopped: however, if it has been present for many years, in one way or another, it will be a difficult task. Abusers may also become very adept at hiding the abuse.

It is evident that there is no one area in our society that is more prone to child abuse than any other, and it may be possible to highlight some other reasons when abuse may take place. Having perhaps identified a child who is being abused, there are some other factors that should be taken into consideration.

It may not be the actual carer who is the active abuser and, therefore, there is the possibility that they do not know abuse is taking place. They may, on the other hand, know that it is taking place, but feel they are unable to stop it. It is always difficult for people to understand that if a non-participant in child abuse has to choose between the child and the abuser, they often leave the child and go with the abuser.

It should also be recognised that the abuser may feel guilty, and will often become aggressive towards professionals and defensive about the injury that has occurred, before they have been accused of anything.

There are some 'broad spectrum' signs that might lead one to consider whether a child is being abused. A child who is at school may suddenly have a behaviour change, and may become disruptive in class. Their standard of work may degenerate, and they may also be found to be stealing things. Their attendance record may become poor. When they do attend there may be evidence of bruising. The younger child who was happy to come to nursery or playschool may start clinging to their mother, and be reluctant to be left. They may not eat as well as they did, and there may be toileting problems.

It is often not until the child goes to school and talks to their peers that they realize that what happens in their home is not normal; this is why sometimes the child's behaviour changes, although abuse may have been happening for a while. The child may also take on the guilt, either because they have been made to feel guilty, or they are trying to protect the abuser. A child who has been frightened by abuse, may be reluctant to make eye contact. This will be shown with small children who are usually trusting. In a strange environment they are often shy at first, but usually will make eye contact after a short time.

Over the years people's reactions to many things change. Only a few years ago it was an accepted practice for a child who was doing wrong to be smacked. This would not lead to a child having a bruise, but it was enough to stop the child doing whatever it was doing. Slowly, feelings about this have changed. Some pressure groups (EPOCH, for example) are now trying to stop smacking altogether, and are saying that it is an abuse. There are many different reactions to this, but if we are working with children in any way we must protect the child from danger. This is one cultural practice that we are trying to change. Other cultures in the UK may need to change also. For example, female genital mutilation is still practised in some cultures, which may not be noticed unless the baby's nappy is being changed, or some complications arise, for instance if there is some infection. Unfortunately, sometimes the children are sent back to their parents' country of origin to have this performed. Therefore, education is needed about the risks and longlasting effects of this procedure (see Chapter 6).

It is often a difficult task to identify child abuse, especially in small children, as they are prone to accidents. Here are a few pointing factors that might help recognition:

- When there is an injury which needs medical intervention, but the parents are reluctant to seek or delay in seeking medical advice.

- The parents may take the child to different doctors or hospitals, so no one has a complete picture of all the injuries that may have been inflicted.

- Sometimes, as already has been mentioned, the story given of how the injury occurred, is not consistent with the child's age and development.

- The story may change, or the parents seem to argue over the story, and are unable to agree.

There is one source of information that has not been mentioned very much: the child itself. Listen to what the child is saying. A small child may tell us directly, but it may be difficult as they may not have the vocabulary they need. Some children have vivid imaginations and may tell stories that only have some truth to them. Older children may tell us directly. This has to be dealt with carefully. If the child is made to feel that it has done something wrong, due to the questions asked, then it may deny what it has said later. The questions should be left to the specialists.

It is obvious that there are occasionally times when a child presents with only one of the signs that have been mentioned, but often there is a mixture of some or all. The physically abused child may have bruising, but due to deprivation of love there may also be signs of failure to thrive.

It must also be taken into account that some of the accidents that happen to children are due to neglect because the parents have not taken the right safety precautions within the child's environment. These parents need education about how they can create a safer environment for their child.

One other area is often linked with child abuse and that is Cot Death (SIDs – Sudden Infant Death). The parents of a baby who is found dead in its cot obviously go through the grieving processes, of which one is guilt. This often appears early after the death, and may be wrongly interpreted as guilt about what the parents may have done to cause the death.

This chapter has tried to show that children who are abused often show signs that may be easily attributed to some other reason. It is therefore easy to see how children slip through the network. On the other hand, not every child who has an unexplained bruise, or broken arm with an unusual history is an abused child.

REFERENCES

Carver, V. (ed) (1978) *Child Abuse, A Study Test.* Milton Keynes: The Open University Press.

Department of Health (1991) *Child Abuse A Study of Inquiry Reports 1980–1989.* London: HMSO.

Meadow, R. (ed) (1989) ABC of Child Abuse. London: *British Medical Journal.*

Moore, J. (1985) *The ABC of Child Abuse Work.* Aldershot: Gower Publishing.

Stainton Rodger, W., Hevey, D. and Ash, E. (ed) (1989) *Child Abuse and Neglect.* London: B.T. Batsford.

CHAPTER 5

RECOGNITION OF ABUSE BY WORKERS IN OTHER SPECIALISMS

JACKI PRITCHARD

INTRODUCTION

It is often assumed that specialist workers in social services departments do not need training on child protection issues because they are unlikely to come across child abuse cases. This is a very dangerous assumption to make. We have learnt during the course of the past ten to fifteen years that abuse can happen in all sorts of circumstances and environments; there are no social or class barriers.

I should define what I mean by specialist workers. These could include workers who specialise within a department which works on a generic basis, for example under eights worker, adoption and fostering officer, intermediate treatment officer, social worker for the blind, worker for the physically handicapped, community worker, approved social worker and so on. This chapter will also be of relevance to workers whose Departments have reorganised into specialisms.

It is imperative that all workers in social services departments receive some form of training in child protection work, because any worker may come across child abuse. A social work assistant working with the elderly, who is visiting a home where children are living with parents and grandparents, could witness bruising on a child. Would that worker know what procedures to follow?

The aim of this chapter is to suggest areas which need to be covered in such training programmes and to include some exercises which could be utilised in different work settings. I have found it particularly useful to train specialist workers within their own teams, but for them also to meet with workers who are working regularly with child abuse. I learnt that this was an effective way of working when I was a team leader of a generic social work team, which included generic social workers, under eights specialists, an adoption and fostering officer, an intermediate treatment officer, and a family support worker. As well as sharing experiences and information in the training sessions, workers formed useful links with each other which they were able to use in the future.

I hope that this chapter will be useful to the specialist workers I have mentioned above, but also to other specialised staff such as those who work with the physically and mentally disabled, residential workers, nursery staff and so on.

HOW TO TRAIN

Training can be either formal or informal. It is important to find out initially how the workers will best learn quickly and effectively, given that training on child protection is likely to be limited. Everybody responds differently to the methods used – for example people either love or hate role play. Therefore, it is important that trainers find out what form of adult learning will best help a particular group of workers.

Training can take place in all sorts of ways and in different settings. When we talk about training, people tend to think of attending organised courses. Most training sections are stretched for budgets, so that workers may find it impossible to obtain funding to attend courses organised outside their own department. I firmly believe that, if training resources are limited, it is the responsibility of managers to use their own resources either by organising training sessions for their workers and imparting their own knowledge and expertise or by asking others to help in the training process. By others I mean people within the department or professionals from other agencies who may offer to help if the training can be reciprocated. In this way there is no cost to anyone except of their time.

In a time of limited resources managers and workers have to be imaginative and make the best use of what is available to them. Supervision can be used effectively as a tool for training (for a full discussion see Chapter 16). Training can also be done on an informal basis, such as using team meetings as a focus for discussion and development of a particular issue which may worry some workers who are not working daily in the child protection field. For example – how do you present information effectively and concisely at a case conference? What are the boundaries of confidentiality when working with other professionals? What information is given to the parents of an abused child? Case discussions in groups (e.g. teams) can be helpful to workers in obtaining ideas but also for inexperienced workers to learn about procedures and practice.

WHAT WORKERS NEED TO KNOW

It is impossible to predict in what sort of circumstances a specialist worker may come across a case of child abuse; consequently, training should be aimed at a very basic level so that workers learn about basic policies, principles and practice. It must be stressed that in no circumstances whatsoever should a specialist worker be expected to carry out a child abuse investigation. However, they may become involved in some work related to the investigation and they need to know how to proceed.

Because workers (and this includes both those who are working with child abuse every day and others who are not) have a fear of finding themselves in a situation where they do not know what to do or they fear making a mistake, the trainer at the beginning of any training session should emphasise that it is all right to admit you do not know something and participants should be encouraged to keep asking questions. Workers sometimes feel that they cannot ask questions because they are considered to be 'experienced' and 'should know the answer'. This is a myth. Having experience does not mean that one cannot learn more or widen one's knowledge base; also, nobody can be expected to know everything or be a 'Jack of all trades, master of none'!

The key points in this type of training are that workers need to know the basic procedures and to identify key people to whom they can go if they are not sure about what to do. I have found that it is helpful to introduce the philosophy of child protection work and the procedures of the local area child protection committee by asking an 'expert' (e.g. the Department's Child Protection Co-ordinator) to explain and simplify the guidelines we have imposed upon us (i.e., *Working Together* document, Home Office *et al.* 1991). Every worker should have his or her own copy of the ACPC procedures or at least easy access to them on their worksite. In training sessions, workers should become familiar with the procedure manual, so that they know how to use it effectively. Whatever is outlined in training sessions should be followed up in supervision sessions and team meetings. It is difficult to assimilate massive amounts of information on a training course and often questions only arise once the theory is being put into practice. There should therefore be follow up training sessions to reinforce procedures and good practice.

Another aspect which should be included in training is the recognition of child abuse. Again, this can be kept at a very simple level. Workers need clear, straightforward explanations about injuries (perhaps with the use of slides, photographs) and signs/symptoms of abuse. Other chapters within this book address this issue (see Chapters 3 and 4).

Most workers turn to their team members, worksite colleagues and team leader for support and information. However, it is useful to widen these supports by establishing who are the key people to go to for information in child protection work. This can be achieved by using Exercises 5.1 and 5.2, either in formal training sessions or in group meetings, for example a team meeting.

EXERCISE 5.1: MAP OF SUPPORT

Objective

To identify key people in the organisation who can help by offering practical and emotional support/advice.

Participants

Task to be carried out by individuals.

Equipment

One flipchart sheet and pen for each participant.

Time

20 minutes to complete task, then the participant will feed back to line manager or group.

Task

Individuals are each given a sheet of flipchart paper and asked to draw themselves in the centre of the page. They are then asked to draw in colleagues, other professionals, agencies (by using boxes, lines, arrows) whom they would approach for advice or support about a child protection issue.

EXERCISE 5.2: MULTIDISCIPLINARY HOUSEBUILDING

Objective

To identify the key people who work in the child protection field

Participants

Small groups (maximum 6)

Equipment

Flipchart paper and pens

Time

25 minutes for task, then each group will display the house they have built.

Task

In their groups participants are asked to build/draw a house with rooms on the flipchart paper. The idea is to house different professionals who work with child abuse in the separate rooms. The ground floor should house the people who have most contact with child abuse cases; the attic should house people who are involved but are also quite detached from the grassroots level.

It has already been said above that specialist workers may find themselves dealing with a case of child abuse when they least expect it and probably in the normal course of their duties. It is impossible to prepare for every situation, but it is useful in training sessions to think about some possible scenarios. It is important for trainers to address the issue of 'what to say'. It is accepted that workers will have developed interviewing and counselling skills, but it is important for them to think about talking to children who have been abused and also how to engage with the parent(s) of that child. Workers have to be aware that they must not ask leading questions; they should not probe too much at the first disclosure but neither should they lose the opportunity of listening to the child (see Parts 3A and 3B Memorandum of Good Practice, Home Office and Dept. of Health 1992).

It is very important to go back to basics in this sort of training. Once a worker is qualified it is very rare that he or she will have the opportunity to have further training on basic interviewing skills. I have found that it is beneficial sometimes to think about what you actually say to someone and what actions you take in certain situations. Exercise 5.3 has been designed to encourage workers to think about the exact words/sentences they would use in a conversation. This is particularly important when confronted with child protection issues.

EXERCISE 5.3: WHAT DO I SAY?

Objective
To get participants to respond verbally to certain situations.

Participants
Task to be performed in a large group

Equipment
Flipchart and pens

Time
Will vary according to how many situations the trainer wishes to address. Not more than one hour.

Task
The trainer will present situations to the group and ask them to respond immediately.

Preparation

The trainer should have compiled a list of situations which can be used as headings on separate sheets of flipchart paper before the exercise begins. Some examples:

- how do you introduce yourself after knocking on the door
- how do you get invited over the doorstep
- how do you proceed in a difficult interview when you as a worker feel uncomfortable, you do not want to be there and you are dreading having to bring up certain issues
- how do you try to engage someone in a conversation when they are remaining silent
- how do you stop a client digressing, knowing that they are avoiding answering certain questions
- how do you terminate a difficult interview.

It was said above that most specialist workers will find themselves dealing with child abuse when they are engaging in a normal visit. They may be told something out of the blue (e.g. 'I saw my next door neighbour punch his little boy') or they may see something (e.g. a child who is severely bruised round the face) which necessitates an immediate response and follow-up action. Workers will already have specialist skills, but these need to be transferred to deal with child protection situations. Exercise 5.4 is designed to make workers think about their own responses, in other words what would they actually *do*.

EXERCISE 5.4: WHAT DO I DO?

Objective

To make workers think what they do when they are told something which could become a child protection issue.

Participants

Task to be carried out in pairs

Equipment

Cards/paper/pens

Time

Ten minutes in pairs (i.e. five minutes' work on each situation); then join with another pair to discuss responses for 20 minutes

Task

Each person will be given a card, which explains who they are and gives the statement they have to say to their partner when the exercise begins (*not before*). The pair will decide which card they will work on first. The cardholder will then say who they are and read out the statement; his/her partner will respond. The pair will discuss the response/conversation which ensues.

Preparation

The trainer needs to write on individual cards a role and a verbal statement. Some examples:

- $2\frac{1}{2}$-year-old boy: 'My Dad likes a draw'
- 14-year-old girl: 'My brother raped me last night'
- 5-year-old child: 'Mummy smacks me when she's had a drink'
- 4-year-old girl: 'Daddy plays with my tuppence when he bathes me'
- Foster child or child in a residential unit: 'You've got to get me out of here; I'm being abused'
- 3-year-old boy: 'Simon burnt me with a cigarette lighter'
- 9-year-old boy: 'My bottom hurts'
- 5-year-old girl: 'Me and my dad have got a secret'
- 12-year-old girl: 'I don't want to live here anymore. I'm frightened'

There is a lot to be said for the saying that 'practice makes perfect'. It is by doing that we learn and we also learn from our mistakes. We usually hate people watching us if we do make mistakes, but this can also be a very constructive way of learning. Hence, the need for role play. The following exercise develops role play in pairs, so that people can feel comfortable initially before moving on later to a simulation exercise.

EXERCISE 5.5: ROLE PLAY

Objective

To learn from role play situations

Participants

Role play is carried out in pairs

Equipment

Cards defining role and background situation

Time

10 minutes for each role play, then 10 minutes for discussion in pairs. Followed by general discussion in large group.

Task

To role play situations and then discuss in pairs. Participants need to consider what happened in the role play, and what action would follow. Experiences, difficulties, issues which have arisen will be fed back from pairs to the whole group

Preparation

Cards need to be prepared before the training session. Trainers will probably have their own case material but some examples follow:

ROLE PLAY 1

ROLE: Natalie, aged five years

You are out in the park with the family support worker, whom you trust and with whom you feel safe. You have just sat down to eat ice-creams. You start by saying that your mum's boyfriend, Uncle Peter, hurt you last night. The fact is that he has abused you sexually. This has only happened on one occasion. Your mum is at home feeding the baby.

ROLE: Family support worker

You have taken five-year-old, Natalie, out to the park while her mother feeds the new baby. Just as you have sat down to eat ice-creams, Natalie tells you that Uncle Peter, who is mum's boyfriend, hurt her last night. You have known Natalie and her mum for some time now.

ROLE PLAY 2

ROLE: Matthew, aged three years

You have been hit by your childminder, which has resulted in a cut by your left eye. When the under eights worker arrives you are screaming that the minder should not come near you. The worker takes you into the garden to talk.

ROLE: Under eights worker

You arrive at a childminder's house to do a routine visit. As you walk into the lounge, you find three-year-old Matthew starts screaming at the minder not to come near him. Matthew has a cut near his left eye. You take Matthew into the garden to talk to him.

ROLE PLAY 3

ROLE: Childminder

You are out with two children whom you childmind on a regular basis. You are very tired and the children have been extremely demanding. You reach the end of your tether. You start shouting at the children and then you slap one of them across the face. When you look up you see your Under eights worker across the road. She is now walking towards you.

ROLE: Under eights worker

You are walking along the street when you see one of your childminders on the other side of the road. She is shouting at the two children with her and then you see her slap one child across the face. Just as she has done this she looks up and sees you. What do you say when you go over to speak to her.

ROLE PLAY 4

ROLE: Three-year-old boy

You are talking to a woman (Under eights worker) who is visiting your playgroup. She sees you have got a black eye and a bruise on your chin. She asks you how you got these. You tell her that Sally, one of the playgroup leaders, hits you.

ROLE: Under eights worker

You are visiting a playgroup. A three-year-old boy comes to sit with you. He has a nasty black eye and bruise on his chin. You ask him how he got these injuries. He tells you Sally hits him. Sally is one of the playgroup leaders.

ROLE PLAY 5

ROLE: Michael, aged 14 years

You are currently taking part in a supervision group run by Intermediate Treatment officers from social services. One of them has come to meet you to take you somewhere. In the car you have been talking about your family. You have admitted that you hate your father, but have said that you are cannot say why. The truth is that your father has sexually abused you since you were seven years old.

ROLE: Intermediate Treatment Officer

You have gone to meet 14-year-old Michael in order to take him to a supervision group you are currently running. Whilst driving in your car, you have been talking about his family. He says he hates his father, but says he cannot tell you why.

ROLE PLAY 6

ROLE: Eleanor Harvey, aged ten years

Your mum and dad have applied to become foster parents. The social worker has come to talk to you today to see how you feel about having a foster brother or sister. You tell her you do not want a brother because boys do nasty things to girls, like Joe next door, who is 14 years old. This is because Joe has been sexually abusing you for some time now and threatens to hurt you if you tell your parents.

ROLE: Adoption and Fostering officer

You have been working with Mr and Mrs Harvey for several months now, because they have applied to become foster parents. Today you are interviewing their ten-year-old daughter, Eleanor, to see how she feels about having a foster brother or sister. She tells you that she does not want a foster brother because boys do nasty things to girls.

ROLE PLAY 7

ROLE: Barry, nine-year-old boy with learning difficulties

Yesterday you were hit across the face with a ruler by your teacher. Some red marks are evident on your cheeks. When you came home last night you told your mum but she did not believe you because you have not told the truth in the past. Your social worker has come to visit you at school today. You tell her about the incident.

ROLE: Social worker for children with learning disabilities

You have popped into school in order to see Barry, a nine-year-old boy with learning difficulties. You have known Barry for several years and know that he sometimes tells lies. Today he tells you that yesterday his teacher hit him across the face with a ruler. There are some red marks on his cheeks.

ROLE PLAY 8

ROLE: Samantha, four-year-old

You are sobbing in a corner of the room at nursery and refusing to move. You have not spoken to anyone since coming to nursery. One of the staff is sitting with you and trying to get you to talk to her. You need to tell her that the man next door hurt you while you were playing out in the garden this morning. He has sexually assaulted you.

ROLE: Any member of staff in a social services day nursery

Four-year-old Samantha is sobbing in a corner of the room and refusing to move. You are sitting with her and trying to encourage her to talk. She has not talked to anyone since coming into school.

ROLE PLAY 9

ROLE: Clive, eight years old

You know that your mum is 'sick', because she has been like this before. When she goes 'funny' she is not herself. She talks to invisible people. She sometimes hits you when she is like this. You know that your mum might have to go away again. You think it is because you are naughty. She has hit you across the face with a stick today; your face is all swollen and your nose keeps bleeding.

ROLE: Approved social worker

You have been asked to go out to section Mrs Rogers, mother of eight-year-old, Clive. When you arrive at the house, you see that Clive has a swollen face and his nose is bleeding. You have been told that Mrs Rogers can be violent. You need to ask Clive about what has been going on.

ROLE PLAY 10

ROLE: 12-year-old girl

You are attending youth club. You have just been to the toilet and as you come out through the cloakroom the youth worker has come up to you, kissed you on the cheek and touched your breasts. You ran away because you are frightened.

ROLE: Community worker

You are attending a tenants' association meeting in a centre where a youth club is also happening. On your way to the toilet you see one of the youth workers kiss a girl and fondle her breasts. The girl has run off. You go after her to speak to her.

It is important for any worker to know about the roles and functions of other professionals. Learning about other professionals can be facilitated by using a simulation exercise. As the exercise proceeds, participants will question their own and others' practice, but they will also realise what gaps they have in their knowledge, which will help learning in the future. Exercise 5.6 explains how to conduct a simulation exercise and two scenarios are described, together with the roles to be acted out.

EXERCISE 5.6: SIMULATIONS

Objective

To learn about policies, procedures and practice by acting out what could happen during the course of one working day.

Participants

Each person takes on a role.

Equipment

Large room

Plenty of chairs (Two pairs of chairs need to be placed in the middle of the room, back to back, to act as two telephone lines)

Information sheets about the case and roles

Clock

Posters indicating locations around the room

Time

Thirty minutes to prepare room and the participants. One hour to simulate the exercise. Thirty minutes for analysis and discussion.

Task

Each participant will be given information about the role they are to play. He or she will assimilate the information, act out the situation – by communicating with other participants as necessary. This can be done in various ways, for example by visiting, interviewing, telephoning people in the locations. If a person wishes to telephone someone they need to sit on one of the telephone chairs and shout out to whom they wish to speak. That person then comes to sit next to the caller and the conversation takes place. If both lines are busy the caller has to wait until a line becomes free. Each participant should proceed in a way which is appropriate to his or her role and the current situation as it develops.

Preparation

The trainer will need to prepare the room, information and roles before the exercise begins. Each role should be written on a sheet of A4 paper and placed in an envelope. An information sheet is needed 'Setting the scene'. The clock should be placed so that it can be seen clearly from all locations.

During the exercise

The trainer will observe and listen to individuals/groups as the simulation takes place. She or he will freeze the exercise at intervals so that participants can listen to a conversation or interview or telephone conversation which some participants are engaged in. The trainer will move the hands of the clock forwards at appropriate intervals and will depend on the progression of the action.

SIMULATION EXERCISE 1

Setting the scene

Three-year-old Eric arrives at the childminder's house at 8.30 in the morning. When she takes his coat off, she sees a burn on his right arm. She asks him what has happened. He says his daddy burnt him with a pan of water. Dad has been having Eric and his sister, Sharon, to stay over the weekend.

The following roles need to be allocated:

     Eric, three-year-old boy

     Sharon, eight-year-old girl

     Mum

     Dad

     General Practitioner

     Health visitor

     Childminder

     Nursery staff – principal, nursery nurse

     School staff – headteacher, class teacher, school nurse

     Duty Principal social worker

     Duty social worker x 2

     Under eights worker

     Child protection officer/custodian of the register

     Casualty staff – consultant paediatrician, sister, nurse

     CID officers x 2

Locations which need to be sited in the room:

>   Childminder's house
>
>   House where Eric and Sharon live with their mother
>
>   Mum's workplace
>
>   Dad's flat
>
>   Medical Centre where GP and Health Visitor are based
>
>   Nursery
>
>   School
>
>   Social Services Area Office
>
>   Child Protection Office in Social Services
>
>   Casualty Department, local Children's Hospital
>
>   Police Station

Information about roles to be played by participants. This information should be put on an A4 sheet and placed in an envelope:

ROLE: Eric (three years old)

You and your sister, Sharon, have spent the weekend with your dad in his flat. You like going to see your dad, but this weekend he frightened you because he kept shouting at you. Yesterday you got your arm burnt when your dad poured boiling water out of the pan. You were playing with your cars on the floor in the kitchen. You heard a scream and when you looked up you saw your dad throwing boiling water over your arm. He kept saying he was sorry, but all you can remember is that he hurt you and you do not want to go to stay with him anymore. You can also remember that he has started smacking you.

ROLE: Sharon (eight years old)

You are old enough to understand that your parents are divorced. Every other weekend, you and your brother, Eric, go to stay with your dad in his flat. You normally like going to see your dad but the last couple of times he has not wanted to play or go out with you. He has also been very bad tempered. He has smacked you and Eric on several occasions. This has upset you and recently at school the nurse found you crying in the toilets; you told her you were tired. Yesterday, you were watching television in the lounge when you heard your dad scream followed by Eric crying. Eric said your dad had thrown water over him; your dad said it was an accident. You do not know who to believe. Your dad has taken Eric to the childminder's this morning and you to school.

ROLE: Childminder

You look after Eric every morning and then take him to nursery for the afternoon session, after which his mum picks him up. This morning Eric's dad has brought him, because Eric and his sister, Sharon, have spent the weekend with their dad in his flat. Eric's parents are divorced. When you take off Eric's coat you find a severe burn on his arm. Eric says his dad threw water over him. You decide to ring your support worker, the Under eights Specialist at Social Services.

ROLE: Mum

You have been divorced for two years. You now live in a council house with your two children, Eric (age three) and Sharon (age eight). The children go to stay with their father in his flat every other weekend. It is Monday morning and you are at work. The children have spent the weekend with their father. He will have taken Eric to the childminder's at 8.30 and then Sharon to school. Eric goes to the childminder's every morning and to nursery in the afternoon, where you pick him up after you have finished work.

ROLE: Health Visitor

You have known this family since Eric was born. You have never had any concerns and were actually surprised when Mum and Dad got divorced. You do not see much of the family now as Eric goes to a childminder in the morning and to nursery in the afternoon. The last contact you had with Mum was when she asked you to support her application for a nursery place for Eric.

ROLE: GP

You have known this family for years. The parents are now divorced, but you are still the GP for all family members. There have never been any major concerns about this family. The children have suffered from the normal colds, earache, chickenpox and so on. However, you have been seeing a lot of Dad recently. Some months ago he started coming to see you because he was getting very bad headaches. You eventually referred to him to the local hospital. It has been diagnosed that he has a brain tumour which is inoperable. He only has a few months to live. He does not want any of his family to know. The headaches are getting worse; they come on very suddenly and cause excruciating pain. You are worried that Dad will not accept much help and have talked to him about the fact that his behaviour could alter in the future.

ROLE: Nursery staff – principal, nursery nurse

Eric has been attending Nursery every afternoon for the past three months. He is a very happy child and has settled very well. He talks openly about his family. You know that his parents are divorced and that Eric and his sister, Sharon, go to stay with their father every other weekend. You know Mum very well, but have never met Dad. During the past few weeks Eric has started to talk about his dad shouting at him. You have not discussed this with Mum.

ROLE: School staff – headteacher, classteacher, school nurse

Sharon is a very bright girl, who usually does not present any problems in school at all. The only time she has been really unsettled was when her parents divorced two years ago. Mum sometimes pops into school in the mornings and Dad brings Sharon to school on a Monday morning after the children have stayed with him, which happens every other weekend. The parents have always shown a keen interest in Sharon's education. Sharon's classteacher has noticed that Sharon has been very quiet after the last two weekends with her father. On one occasion the school nurse found Sharon crying in the toilets; when asked what was the matter, Sharon said she was just tired after the weekend.

ROLE: Duty Social Work Team – Principal Social Worker and two social workers

It is a busy Monday morning. It is only 9.00 a.m. and already there has been a phone call about an 86-year-old lady, who does not know who she is or where she lives, wandering the streets; and there is a 15-year-old girl in reception wanting to come into care, because her parents do not like her boyfriend.

ROLE: Under eights specialist

You work in a busy social services area office. It is Monday morning and you are just going through the applications you have received from people interested in becoming childminders. You receive a phone call from one of your experienced childminders, whom you have known for the past five years.

ROLE: Child protection officer

You are working in your own office trying to write an urgent report for ACPC. You may have to deal with several phone calls because nobody else is about in your section and the Child Protection Register is located in your office.

ROLE: Casualty department, local Children's Hospital – Paediatrician, sister and nurse

It is a normal working day in the Casualty Department.

ROLE: CID officers x 2

You are trying to catch up on some reports in your office.

SIMULATION EXERCISE 2

Setting the scene

Rachel is 13 years old and lives with her mother and father. During the summer holidays, Sam, a 19-year-old university student has been babysitting to earn some extra cash. Sam has been going into Rachel's bedroom after she has gone to bed and touching her. Rachel told her parents but they told her 'not to be so silly'. Last night, Sam had sexual intercourse with Rachel. Rachel told her mother this morning, but she would not believe her, so Rachel has now told her classteacher. It is 9.30 a.m.

The following roles need to be allocated:

> Rachel Glenning, 13-year-old girl
>
> Mr Glenning, father of Rachel, employed as a sales representative
>
> Mrs Glenning, mother of Rachel
>
> Sam Roberts, 19-year-old university student
>
> Mr Roberts, father of Sam and employer of Mr Glenning
>
> Mrs Roberts, mother of Sam
>
> General Practitioner for Rachel
>
> School staff – Rachel's classteacher
> Child Protection Liaison Teacher
> Headteacher
> School Nurse
>
> Duty Social Work Team – Principal Social Worker
> Social Workers x 2
>
> Child Protection Clerk
>
> Hospital staff – Paediatrician, sister, nurse
>
> Police – WPC (Abuse Unit) x 2
> CID officers x 2

Locations which need to be sited in the room:

> Rachel's house
>
> Sam's house
>
> Office – where Mr Glenning and Mr Cox work
>
> Factory floor – where Sam works
>
> General practitioner's surgery
>
> School
>
> Social Services Area Office
>
> Child Protection Office in Social Services

Casualty Department, Children's Hospital

Police Station

Information about roles to be played by participants. This information should be put on an A4 sheet and placed in an envelope:

ROLE: Rachel, 13 years old

Your mother and father go out a lot socially, because of your father's job. Normally, one of the neighbours comes in to sit with you or you stay overnight at one of your friend's houses. However, since the beginning of July your father has arranged for his boss's son, Sam, to babysit. Sam is a student and is currently home from university during the vacation. Each time he has babysat, he has come into your bedroom after you have gone to bed. At first he just looked at you, while you pretended to be asleep, but then he started lying on the bed and touching you underneath your night-dress. You have told him to stop it. You told your parents what he has done but they do not believe you and say that Sam 'is a lovely young man'. Last night, Sam got into your bed and had intercourse with you. You told your mother this morning and she told you 'not to be so wicked'. When you got to school you told your class teacher.

ROLE: Mr Glenning, Rachel's father

You are a sales representative, who works for a small firm run by Mr Roberts. You are very ambitious and are due for promotion. Your boss asked you if you would let his son, Sam, babysit for you during the summer months, because he needed to earn some extra cash. You felt you could not refuse, even though your neighbour normally babysits for your 13-year-old daughter, Rachel. Rachel does not like Sam and has made some ludicrous allegations that he has been coming into her bedroom and touching her. This morning you are in a business meeting with Mr Roberts.

ROLE: Mrs Glenning, Rachel's mother

You are married to a very ambitious sales representative, who is due for promotion. You go out socially a great deal because of your husband's work. Your husband's boss asked if his son, Sam, could babysit during the summer months, whilst he was home from university. You have known Sam for some time and have always thought him a very polite and pleasant boy. However, Rachel has said that he has been touching her after she has gone to bed. Your husband got very angry about what Rachel said and refuses to discuss it. You feel you have to stand by your husband and therefore will not talk to Rachel about it. Before she left for school, Rachel said Sam had had intercourse with her. You told her 'not to be so wicked'. This morning you are doing your washing and ironing at home.

ROLE: Sam, 19-year-old university student

You are home from university for the summer vacation. You want to earn some money so that you can travel round Europe before the end of the vacation. Consequently, your father has arranged for you to work in his factory during the daytime. He has also arranged for you to babysit for one of his sales representatives, who has a 13-year-old daughter called Rachel. You are lacking in confidence and feel very dominated by your father. You like Rachel and find her very attractive. Since you started babysitting at the beginning of July, you have been going into her bedroom and touching her. Last night you had full sexual intercourse with her. You are very frightened that she is going to tell her parents, but you will deny that anything happened. You are working on the factory floor this morning.

ROLE: Mr Roberts, father of Sam and boss of Mr Glenning

You are a very successful local businessman. You have one son, Sam, who goes to university, but is home for the summer vacation at the current time. Sam wants to travel round Europe before the end of the vacation, so you have arranged for him to work in your factory, and also to do some babysitting for one of your sales reps, Glenning, who has a 13-year-old daughter. You know that Glenning will do anything for you at the moment because he is due for promotion. This morning you are engaged in a meeting with Glenning in the office.

ROLE: Mrs Roberts, mother of Sam

You are married to a successful local businessman. You have one son, Sam, who is 19 years old. Sam has just finished his first year at university and is home for the vacation. Your husband has arranged for him to work in his factory but also to do some babysitting for one of the sales reps. Sam is hoping to travel round Europe before the end of the vacation. You are at home this morning.

ROLE: General practitioner

The Glenning family have only recently transferred to your practice. You have seen Rachel on one occasion when she came to the surgery about her spots. From the medical notes it would seem there have never been any real concerns. Rachel had her tonsils taken out when she was five years old and apart from that she has suffered from the usual childhood illnesses, namely chickenpox and measles.

ROLE: Rachel's class teacher

It is the last day of term before the summer holidays. When you took the class register this morning you noticed that Rachel Glenning looked very upset. She then asked to speak to you in private. You have a very close relationship with Rachel. Rachel said that the babysitter had forced her to have sex with him last night. You understand that a 19-year-old boy has been babysitting for Rachel during the past few weeks. You have no reason to doubt Rachel's story. You have informed the child protection liaison teacher and the headteacher. You are now discussing the matter with them. The school nurse is also present.

ROLE: Other school staff – child protection liaison teacher, headteacher, school nurse

It is the last day of term before the summer holidays. You are aware that Rachel Glenning has disclosed to her class teacher this morning that she has been sexually abused by a babysitter. You are currently discussing the situation. The liaison teacher is advising the headteacher to inform the local social services area office. The headteacher is reluctant to act hastily in case Rachel is making up the story. The school nurse has only met Rachel on one occasion and that was when she had started her period for the first time.

ROLE: Duty Social Work Team – Principal Social Worker, Social Workers x 2

It is a normal day on duty.

ROLE: Child Protection Clerk

You have only just started working in this section and it is all new to you. The Child Protection Officer is off sick and the Assistant Child Protection Officer is out of the office attending a case conference. So you will have to deal with any enquiries which come through this morning.

ROLE: Hospital staff – paediatrician, sister, nurse

You are on duty in the Casualty Department of the local Children's Hospital.

ROLE: Police – WPCs from the Abuse Unit x 2, CID officers x 2

It is a normal working day and you are working in the station this morning.

REFERENCES

Home Office and Department of Health (1992) *Memorandum of Good Practice*. London: HMSO.

Home Office, Department of Health, Department of Education and Science, Welsh Office (1991) *Working Together*. London: HMSO.

CHAPTER 6

PREVENTING FEMALE GENITAL MUTILATION
A PRACTICAL, MULTIDISCIPLINARY APPROACH

HILARY OWEN WITH LOLA BROWN

INTRODUCTION

Whilst many (if not most) Area Child Protection Committees' procedure manuals do not even mention female genital mutilation, *The Independent* newspaper reported in July 1992 that some 10,000 girls in the UK were feared to be at risk of being genitally mutilated. This chapter is intended to show how normal child protection procedures can be used effectively in dealing with this type of child abuse. First, we describe the practice of female genital mutilation. Second, we describe the health problems which it can cause, both in the short- and the long-term. Third, we indicate how certain professionals are well placed to recognise when children may be at risk of being genitally mutilated. Fourth, we suggest ways of working with parents and children which are acceptable to them to try and prevent it occurring. Fifth, we indicate how children who have already been genitally mutilated might be helped. Finally, we suggest ways in which communities may be assisted to give up this practice: the causes of female genital mutilation are different from the causes of other types of child abuse, as we understand them.

WHAT IS FEMALE GENITAL MUTILATION?

Perhaps the clearest description of female genital mutilation is that provided by Fran P. Hosken who, in 1976, was editor of Women's International Network News. She distinguished three separate surgical procedures which differ significantly in their implications for the victims' future health and happiness, but which had often, and still do, become misleadingly lumped together under the comparatively innocuous term 'female circumcision':

1. Sunna Circumcision: removal of the prepuce and/or tip of the clitoris.
2. Excision or Clitoridectomy: excision of the entire clitoris with the labia minora and some or most of the external genitalia;
3. Excision and Infibulation... This means excision of the entire clitoris, labia minora and parts of the labia majora. The two sides of the vulva are then fastened together in some way by thorns... or by sewing

with catgut. Alternatively the vulva are scraped raw and the child's limbs are tied together for several weeks until the wound heals...
The purpose is to close the vaginal orifice. Only a small opening is left (usually by inserting a slither of wood) so the urine or later the menstrual blood can be passed. (Hosken 1976 p.30)

Mutilation may be carried out on children from the first week of birth up to the age of twelve, and may be done with a variety of implements, including knives, razor blades or pieces of glass. These are frequently unsterilised. It is often carried out without anaesthesia.

It is difficult to be certain which cultures promote the practice, which is reputed to be widespread in parts of Africa, Asia and the Middle East. K. Sone (1992) reported it to be practised in more than twenty African countries, in addition to Oman, South Yemen, the United Arab Emirates and Indonesia. Western anthropologists have been reporting instances of it from around the world for many years, including in Australia and Peru (for example, Montagu 1945). In 1992, the Foundation for Women's Health Research and Development (FORWARD) were helping to protect children in the UK in cases involving parents from Nigeria, Sierra Leone, Malaysia and Somalia (FOR-WARD 1992). Female genital mutilation is not confined to black peoples and, in September of 1992, FORWARD reported having contact with five white victims (Corke 1992).

In Africa, the surgery is usually carried out by a woman who receives money and social status for doing so: Alice Walker, in her powerful and complex novel *Possessing The Secret of Joy*, explores the role a woman like this might play in one society, saying of her character, M'Lissa,

> ... among the Olinka, she was a prized midwife and healer, though to those Christianized ones who also turned to Western medicine, she was shunned. (Walker 1992 p.59)

If parents in the UK who want their daughters to have this surgery are unable to find anyone here to perform it, they may either send them out of the country for the purpose, or families may pay jointly to bring a midwife who is able to perform it to this country. Whilst there exist many justifications for female genital mutilation citing religious or cultural grounds, the compelling reason for many parents who want it for their daughters is that men in their society will not marry women who have not been mutilated, and marriage remains the main route out of poverty for most women. Indeed, in 1965, Jomo Kenyatta, President of Kenya, indicated that:

> ... no proper Gikuyu would dream of marrying a girl who has not been circumcised [because it] is regarded as the conditio sine qua non for the whole teaching of tribal law, religion and morality. (Kenyatta 1965 p.127–128)

Certainly, infibulation is regarded as a method of guaranteeing a bride's virginity and continued monogamy. In *The Guardian* (3.3.93) , Helen Pitt, reporting on the case of Teneng Jahate, recently imprisoned in Paris for voluntary mutilation of her daughters, pointed out that 'In the Gambian village she comes from, the operation is intended to ensure virginity, chastity and a dowry for girls.'

Whilst condemnation of female genital mutilation has led to allegations of racism in the UK (for example, see Sone 1992) , it has been illegal here since the Prohibition of Female Circumcision Act (1985) came into force. FORWARD are very clear about what this practice is:

> Removal of a normal functioning organ from a child constitutes a fundamental human rights violation. The practice of female genital mutilation, within the context of the Universal Declaration of Human Rights and of the Convention Against Torture, is an assault on the physical and moral integrity of women and children. The descriptions available of the reactions of children – 'panic and shock from extreme pain, biting through the tongue, convulsions, necessity for six adults to hold down an eight-year-old, and death' – indicate a practice comparable to torture. (1992 p.12)

They also point out incontrovertibly that:

> Under 'Categories of Abuse for Registration' as stated in Section 6.40 in 'Working Together Under The Children Act', female genital mutilation can be said unambiguously to constitute physical injury and an abuse.' (1992 p.12)

HEALTH PROBLEMS WHICH MAY RESULT FROM FEMALE GENITAL MUTILATION

Whilst the actual surgery involved is enough of an assault upon a child for us to do all we can to prevent it from happening, the short- and long-term health risks involved for those children who do suffer it are also serious. It is essential that professionals working with families in the UK are fully aware of these health risks so that the true impact of female genital mutilation upon victims can be appreciated and appropriate assistance given to them.

Helen Pitt reports that, in France, 'at least four babies are known to have bled to death' as a result of female genital mutilation. She indicates that

> Apart from psychological problems later in life, the serious health risks for the child include shock, urine retention, tetanus, blood loss, pelvic infection and even HIV. (Pitt 1993)

Sue Corke points out that it

> can often lead to blood poisoning and urinary infections, as well as infertility and complications during pregnancy and delivery, or the development of cysts... And on the level of day to day living and hygiene, infibulated women may take up to 45 minutes to empty a bladder and more than ten days to complete menstruation. (1992)

Sone notes the case of one victim:

> One teenager thought to be pregnant turned out to have a womb full of four litres of putrid menstrual blood, blocked up by her 'operation'. (Sone 1992)

Mary Daly points out the continuing pain of mutilated girls:

> What is certain is that the infibulated girl... can look forward to a life of repeated encounters with 'the little knife' – the instrument of her perpetual torture. For women who are infibulated have to be cut open – either by the husband or by another woman – to permit intercourse. They have to be cut open further for delivery of a child. Often they are sewn up again after delivery, depending upon the decision of the husband. The cutting (defibulation) and resewing goes on throughout a woman's living death of reproductive 'life'. (Daly 1978 p.157)

There is some suggestion that some couples resort to anal intercourse because vaginal intercourse causes the woman so much pain. Alice Walker, in her novel, explores the problems which could be associated with childbirth for an infibulated mother:

> The obstetrician broke two instruments trying to make an opening large enough for Benny's head. Then he used a scalpel. Then a pair of scissors used ordinarily to sever cartilage from bone... his head was yellow and blue and badly misshapen... Benny, my radiant brown baby... was retarded. Some small but vital part of his brain crushed by our ordeal.' (Walker p.55–58)

FORWARD (1989) indicate that, because of the keloid scarring, the anterior perineum sometimes tears during childbirth, causing bleeding which is difficult to staunch.

The psychological problems associated with female genital mutilation are not particularly well documented. However, such information as does exist suggests that the extent of psychological disturbance is closely related to the extent of physical trauma, not just at the time of the surgery, but in the long term. FORWARD indicate, for example, that

> In the mild form of simple removal of the prepuce of the clitoris, done under anaesthesia and within standard surgical conditions, and where the child is psychologically well supported, no adverse emotional or behavioural reactions generally took place. This may not be so in the case of infibulation, with all its known hazards. (1989 p.9)

In addition, it must be borne in mind that some of the 'secondary' effects of female genital mutilation may have detrimental influences upon mental health. Constant pain or discomfort, sexual difficulties and infertility may cause severe irritability, anxiety, depression or indeed psychotic illness (FORWARD, 1989).

RECOGNISING CHILDREN WHO MAY BE AT RISK OF FEMALE GENITAL MUTILATION

It can be seen that the implications of female genital mutilation for a child are extremely serious. When we usually speak of children being 'at risk' of abuse, or being 'likely to suffer significant harm', we are basing our judgment on the fact that there exists a consensus in our society that children should not be harmed. Parents who abuse their children in other ways know that what they have done is wrong: the abuse is perpetrated in anger or frustration, because of a loss of control; or the abuse occurs because an individual has a specific desire to hurt or humiliate a child, at the same time as knowing that what they are doing is offensive. However, as indicated earlier, those parents who wish their daughters to be genitally mutilated believe that it is very much in their interests, given the low status of women in their societies. Their history and culture confirm that it is the proper thing to do, and therefore they are behaving as good parents towards their daughters. When we speak of 'risk' of genital mutilation, therefore, it is a much higher risk than we usually associate with child abuse.

Professionals involved with children and in the health care of pregnant women are particularly well placed to detect risk of genital mutilation. Teachers may be approached for help by girls who are fearful of having the surgery. Midwives, nurses and doctors may treat women whom they notice have been genitally mutilated: the risk of these women arranging the same surgery for their daughters is very high. Any professional may come across families who come from a community which is known to practise genital mutilation extensively. Again, in these families, the risk is high, particularly if there is an elderly female relative present. FORWARD advise that 'any suspicion should be followed up' (1992 p.14). *Working Together Under the Children Act 1989* specifically states:

> In areas where there are significant numbers of children of particular ethnic minority or cultural backgrounds, workers will need to be alert to the possibility of female circumcision. Advice on this matter can be obtained from FORWARD... (Home Office *et al.* 1991 p.11)

Under the Children Act 1989, social services departments and the NSPCC have a duty to investigate suspected risk of child abuse: other agencies do not (Section 47). It is therefore imperative that anyone who does fear that a child is at risk of being genitally mutilated reports their concerns immediately to one of these agencies.

WORKING WITH FAMILIES WHERE THERE IS RISK OF FEMALE GENITAL MUTILATION

Before social workers make contact with families to discuss risk to their daughters, it will be essential for them to consider two issues which are fundamental to the Children Act 1989. First, local authorities have a duty to work in partnership with parents as long as to do so is consistent with the child's welfare. *Working Together Under The Children Act 1989* states:

Local authorities have, under the Children Act 1989, a general duty to safeguard and promote the welfare of children within their area who are in need and so far as is consistent with that duty to promote the upbringing of such children by their families. As parental responsibility for children is retained notwithstanding any court orders short of adoption, local authorities must work in partnership with parents, seeking court orders when compulsory action is indicated in the interests of the child but only when this is better for the child than working with the parents under voluntary arrangements. (p.1)

Second, there is a duty in multidisciplinary child protection work for professionals to address all issues to do with race and gender which might affect the way a particular child can best be helped. Again, *Working Together Under the Children Act 1989* indicates:

The basis of an effective child protection service must be that professionals and individual agencies work together... with a shared mutual understanding of aims, objectives and what is good practice. This should take into account the sensitive issues associated with gender, race, culture and disability.' (p.25)

There is an onus of responsibility upon social workers investigating risk of female genital mutilation to attempt to understand the life experiences the family has had so far: many families are refugees who have come to the UK after having frightening and damaging experiences in their own countries; some have suffered torture. Racism in the UK may well lead them to be very wary of contact with representatives of white authority. They may have reacted against the disorientating influences of white western society by attaching greater emotional commitment to their own cultural practices, of which female genital mutilation may be one.

FORWARD are clear that, in the last resort, legal steps must be taken to prevent a child being mutilated. Section 8 of the Children Act allows for 'prohibited steps' orders to be made if it is in the child's interests: it may be possible for a social worker to obtain one of these if the child's parents are intending to send her out of the country and it can be shown that mutilation is likely if she goes. Where the child appears to be in immediate danger of mutilation and parents cannot satisfactorily guarantee that they will not proceed with it, then an Emergency Protection Order should be sought. If, despite being offered clear, firm counselling and help, parents' intention to seek surgery is sustained, then application for a care order is a possibility. However, it may well be possible to work with the parents on a voluntary basis to prevent the abuse and, as indicated above, it is certainly a social worker's duty to look at every possible way that parental co-operation can be achieved.

Where initial interviews with family members (bearing in mind that where their first language is not English, it will be proper to involve an interpreter trained in social services business) and preliminary checks with those agencies who know the family, confirm that risk of mutilation may be present, then an initial child protection conference should be convened to discuss whether the child's name should be referred to the Child Protection Register (see

Chapters 10 and 11) and, if so, to formulate a child protection plan (see Chapter 12). Parents, and the child if she is old enough, will obviously be present at this conference, and it will be proper to ensure, again, that the services of an interpreter are available if necessary. The safety of every young female member of the household must be considered. It may well be that there are older children who have already been mutilated, and it will be the joint responsibility of the social worker and the police to investigate this possibility.

Where a child protection plan is being considered for a child at risk of mutilation, it might usefully be based upon two key principles. First, there will be a need to achieve close monitoring: doctors, health visitors, teachers, nursery staff and social workers can all be involved in this, depending upon the age of the child. If representatives of voluntary welfare agencies are in touch with the family and support the aim of preventing mutilation, they might also assist. Second, every possible means should be used to persuade the parents not to proceed. Many parents are unaware that female genital mutilation is illegal in the UK and that conviction carries a possible prison sentence. FORWARD quote the case of a Malian woman living in France, whose daughter died as a result of mutilation, and who said 'Had I known it was illegal in France, I would not have done it' (1992 p.15).

Parents may also be unaware of the existence of the African Human Rights Charter which, whilst endorsing traditional values, indicates that action should be taken to 'eradicate practices which are prejudicial to the child' (FORWARD 1992 p.13).

Health professionals are in a position to counsel parents on the proven detrimental effects of female genital mutilation upon physical and mental health, upon marital relationships, and upon the complications it may cause in childbirth. There is some indication that young men in communities which have traditionally practised mutilation are marrying women outside their communities, and are beginning to condemn it. It may be possible to talk to a mother who has herself been mutilated and support her strongly so that she can refuse to allow her daughter to go through the same pain. Older children can be given similar counselling and can be assured that, if they need direct help to escape mutilation, they will get it.

ASSISTING CHILDREN WHO HAVE ALREADY BEEN MUTILATED

As indicated above, where there exists a suspicion that a child has been mutilated, this should be the subject of a joint police/social work investigation, like any other allegation of abuse. Symptoms may come to the attention of general practitioners, teachers or health visitors. It may be that a child has bladder or menstrual problems unusually frequently, and stays away from school because of them. Teachers may become aware that a child has been away on holiday for a period of more than six weeks, and on her return her behaviour has changed. Alice Walker talks in her novel of 'the classic Olinka woman's walk, in which the feet appear to slide forward and are rarely raised above the ground' (Walker 1992 p.63), and one can well imagine that it would be difficult for girls who have been genitally mutilated to take part in any physical exercise.

Any police officer and social worker undertaking an investigation of suspected genital mutilation should seek medical advice from a senior paediatrician. An expert diagnosis and assessment of injury will be essential so that professionals and parents can provide the most appropriate help to the child. The consent of parents, and children if they are of sufficient age and understanding, must be sought for any medical examination or treatment beyond that required to save the child's life. Whilst it may be possible to obtain court orders for medical assessment if parents refuse to give their consent, great care must be taken to ensure that every possible method is used to enable parents to understand the precise nature of professionals' concerns and that they are given every opportunity to consent: again, this may include ensuring that an interpreter is available right at the start of the investigation. Parents must under no circumstances be disadvantaged by professionals because of their race.

If suspicions are not allayed in the course of the investigation then, again, a child protection conference must be convened to look at the information which has been obtained and to consider whether the child's name should be referred to the Child Protection Register. If it is found that the child has been genitally mutilated, there may well be medical treatment that can be offered to minimise the effects of the harm. A child protection plan may need to be formulated which ensures that parents co-operate with this treatment. The child may need counselling, either immediately or in the future. It may be that an application for Criminal Injuries Compensation can be made for the child, whether or not prosecution takes place, and legal advice should be sought on this issue.

Again, it is essential that risk to any other female children in the family is properly assessed, and protection plans put in place for them. The likelihood of parents arranging similar surgery for their other daughters will be extremely high.

HELPING COMMUNITIES TO CHANGE

There is a strong feeling in social work at the moment, as there may well be in other helping professions, that resources do not stretch to providing preventative services: rather, we are always responding to acute problems, to crises. Unlike other forms of child abuse, female genital mutilation is the sort of problem which would be ameliorated very quickly by health education and an improvement in the status of women in the communities in which it is practised. The help of community groups already working with families in those communities where it is thought to be practised might be enlisted to deliver health education: their advice is much more likely to be heeded than that of a professional from outside the community. Medics involved in health promotion work might ensure that they are fully aware of the problem and take it into account in their work when they know of communities in their area which have traditionally practised it. Information leaflets prepared for the general public by Area Child Protection Committees about child abuse might mention female genital mutilation and the fact that it is illegal in this country. Area Child Protection Committees might spend some time seeking information about the likely prevalence of the practice in the area of the country they are responsible for, and might co-ordinate a multidisciplinary response to health education.

To neglect the preventative work when it would help so many children and their families, whilst pursuing child protection procedures in respect of those few families where female genital mutilation, or risk of it, is detected is not in the spirit of the Children Act. It severely disadvantages children in communities which practise female genital mutilation.

EXERCISE 6.1

This is an exercise designed to stimulate thought, discussion and action on the problem of female genital mutilation. Participants will simply need a pen and paper on which to write down their ideas. Whilst the exercise can be done alone, or in single agency groups, participants will gain most from it if it is done in multidisciplinary groups and ideas shared. Participants must not be asked to undertake this exercise without having had plenty of opportunity to familiarise themselves with the problem of female genital mutilation and to deal with their personal responses to it.

Participants should write down their personal ideas in response to three questions:

1. What contribution could you make in your professional role to the recognition or investigation of female genital mutilation?
2. What contribution could you make in your professional role to a child protection plan formulated in respect of (a) a child at risk of female genital mutilation and (b) a child who has suffered it already?
3. How could your agency help to mount an education programme about the problem?

Where the exercise is done in a group, participants should be asked to share their responses and comments should be invited from other members.

REFERENCES

The Children Act 1989. London: HMSO.

Home Office, Department of Health, Department of Education and Science, Welsh Office (1991) *Working Together Under The Children Act 1989*. London: HMSO.

Corke, S., (1992) 'A Damaging Cult', *Nursery World*, 10.9.92.

Daly, M., (1978) *Gyn/Ecology*, London: The Women's Press.

FORWARD, (1989) *Report on the First National Conference on Female Genital Mutilation*. Conference Papers. London: FORWARD.

Hedley, R. and Dorkenod, E. (1992) *Child Protection and Female Genital Mutilation: Advice for Health, Education and Social Work Professionals*. London: Forward.

Hosken, F., (1976) *Women's International Network News 2, 1.*

Kenyatta, J., (1965) *Facing Mount Kenya.* New York: Vintage.

Montagu, M.F.A., (1946) 'Ritual Mutilation among Primitive Peoples' *Ciba Symposia 8, 7,* 421–36.

Nicholson-Lord, D. (1992) 'Fear that 10,000 girls face threat of circumcision'. *The Independent,* 7.7.92.

Pitt, H., (1993) 'A Knife in Any Language'. *The Guardian,* 3.3.93.

Sone, K., (1992) 'Sexuality, Abuse and Culture'. *Community Care* (11.6.92).

Walker, A. (1992) *Possessing The Secret of Joy.* London: Jonathan Cape.

CHAPTER 7

CHILDREN WITH DISABILITIES –
A CHALLENGE FOR CHILD PROTECTION
PROCEDURES

PHILIPPA RUSSELL

INTRODUCTION

> Children with disabilities are particularly vulnerable. They have the same rights as other children to be protected. (Children Act Guidance and Regulations, Volume 6, 1991)

> Myths are designed to allow secrets and denial to continue. For three years now I have been trying to explode a difficult myth which for years has suggested that disabled children are not abused. People feel that disability protects the child! Far from protecting the child, disability would seem to protect the abuser. (Margaret Kennedy, Overcoming Myths: The Abused Disabled Child, in Concern (Summer 1990), National Children's Bureau)

There are about 360,000 children with disabilities (aged 16 years and under) in the United Kingdom (OPCS 1989). These children form about three per cent of the child population in this country and many present major challenges to both their families and to statutory and voluntary services which provide support. All but around 5500 live in a family home. But those who have gone into residential care tend to have major health problems, significant behaviour disorders or to have experienced particularly severe problems at home. The OPCS studies of the lives of disabled people in the United Kingdom confirmed the findings of a range of studies about the lives of families with a disabled child. Few of the families knew of the full range of services which might have helped them. Despite the imminent implementation of the Children Act, only 12 per cent had a regular social worker and most relied heavily on child health and education services for information and advice. Only four per cent of families received respite care – although 50 per cent felt that their or other children's health was adversely affected by limited opportunities to go out or to give time equally to all family members. Of those children living in residential care, 15 per cent were known to have been abused. Thirty-three per cent had health or behaviour problems which it had proved impossible for the natural or foster families with whom they were living to cope with. A further 33 per cent had homes or family circumstances which were 'unsuitable' – and where the children concerned were presumably at risk.

The ability of families to cope appropriately with children with disabilities or special needs can be affected by many different circumstances. As already noted above, many families receive inadequate levels of support – and may find the competing interests of different family members hard to balance. But it is important that the OPCS studies found that disability imposed considerable additional costs on all caring families. Even when families had a member in employment, earnings were likely to be less than for similar families without a disabled child – often because of poor promotion prospects due to the competing demands of home care or because of lack of family mobility in search of new and better employment prospects. Single parents were significantly worse off, with 75 per cent relying wholly on state benefits.

The past decade has seen greater public (and professional) awareness of disability, with increasingly positive images about the capacity as well as incapacity of disabled people to make decisions about their own lives and to contribute to the planning and development of support services. But positive images are insufficient without a corresponding awareness of the increased vulnerability of disabled children and their families to abuse within a variety of settings (Westcott 1992) and the need for improved training opportunities for all professionals working in child protection services to ensure that they are aware of disability issues and, in particular, know how and where to locate expert advice when required.

CURRENT AWARENESS ON DISABILITY AND ABUSE

Evidence of the possible incidence of abuse and children with disabilities or special needs currently comes mainly from studies in the USA. Sullivan, Vernon and Scanlon (1987) found that out of 150 children with hearing impairments attending residential schools, 75 reported sexual abuse; 19 reported incest at home and 3 reported physical and sexual abuse. Kennedy (1990), in a UK study of deaf children, found 192 suspected and 86 confirmed instances of physical and emotional abuse, with 70 suspected cases of sexual abuse and 50 confirmed. She concluded that not only were disabled children more likely to be candidates for physical or sexual abuse, but that they were likely to be abused for longer periods of time than their non-disabled peers.

From 1977–1983, the Seattle (USA) Rape Relief and Sexual Assault Centre found over 700 reported cases of sexual abuse involving children and adults with learning disabilities from the Seattle area. This was considered to be significant under-reporting of the true incidence. Sexual abuse was defined in this study as rape, attempted rape or incest. Of the reported victims 99 per cent were sexually abused by relatives or care-givers.

In another study of 65 adults with learning disabilities, all attending a work activity centre, Hard (1986) found that 83 per cent of the women and 32 per cent of the men had been sexually abused. Abuse in this context was described as sexual contact caused by force, coercion or manipulation or otherwise entered into unwillingly or unknowingly. It included oral, anal or vaginal intercourse and touching breasts and genitalia. As in the Seattle study, the researchers found that in 99 per cent of cases, the abuse was carried out by someone known to the individual concerned. Sixty-four per cent of the women said they told someone about the abuse – but 55 per cent were not believed and no action followed. Of the 40 per cent of the men who told, all were believed.

Westcott (1992) has reviewed over twenty articles on the physical, emotional and sexual abuse of children with a range of disabilities. She notes that much of the current literature focuses upon *sexual* abuse (although children's vulnerability to sexual abuse may be greatly increased by emotional and physical abuse). She also notes that there has been little attention paid to the views and experiences of disabled people themselves – particularly with regard to *prevention* and *how* children and young adults might have been supported in disclosing abuse at an earlier stage. Westcott Study (NSPCC 1993) will contribute significantly to work in this area.

The existing literature on this subject clearly demonstrates the need for much greater vigilance in order to protect children and young people with disabilities and special needs and to ensure that these special needs are neither marginalised nor misunderstood within local child protection strategies. But it also provides some important messages about disability and child protection – and the myths which need to be dispelled in order to ensure that children with special needs do not experience a double jeopardy through misunderstandings and complacency about the quality of care and life experiences which are offered to them.

FAMILY FACTORS – FAMILY LIFE WITH A DISABLED CHILD

Motherhood has a single long-term goal – all good parents bring their children up to eventually do without them. But if a child has a disability or special need, there may be no long-term unemployment. The children can't get rid of their parents either! In effect the 'life plans' which all parents make for their children will be different for the child with special needs. Some parents – particularly if they have poor self esteem, low income, poor quality housing and little family support – may find the adjustment too difficult to cope with. They are not bad parents. They do care. But somebody has to care for them as people before they enter the wonderful brave new world of 'partnership' between parents and professionals that we all hear so much about. Our disabled children are not our burdens. But our lives have changed and things can go badly wrong. (Parent attending a Parent Workshop, Russell and Flynn 1992, National Development Team)

Parents of children with disabilities or other special needs are no more likely than other parents to abuse their children. But the additional responsibilities (and frequent lack of support) may make such families and children more at risk of abuse – and pressures of care may make families and professional carers hesitant to voice suspicions when there may be no obvious alternative source of help. A number of studies in the UK have shown the particular pressure placed upon families by the additional care needs of disabled children. A study by Glendinning (1986) found that out of 361 young children with disabilities, 50 children could not be left alone for even ten minutes in a day. A study by Wilkin (1989) of the lives of families of children with severe learning difficulties noted that they received little significant help from relatives, friends or neighbours in terms of day-to-day caring. Siblings (particularly sisters) frequently played an important role – other studies of disability in adults have shown a growth of young carers who may miss school or ordinary recreational activities in order to provide extra support at home. Quine (1989), looking at sleep disturbance in young children with disabilities, also stressed the depression and anxiety caused by disruptive behaviours – and the particular vulnerability of single parents with no extended family and limited social contacts for mutual support.

Pressures of care have to be put in the wider context of social and demographic change in UK society. Bradshaw (1991) has found that poverty is increasing sharply in families with children in the United Kingdom. The Office of Population and Census Surveys (OPCS) studies on the lives of disabled people (1989) found that families with a disabled member were *significantly* worse off than other families without disability. Additional costs for heating, clothing, laundry and food were particular strains on low incomes, with many women unable to work because of the care needs. Fifty per cent of parents interviewed in the OPCS studies said that they could rarely go out because of lack of sitters and felt that their own health had suffered because of the extra anxieties and physical care.

Parents under stress can, of course, receive support from a range of sources. Respite care is one obvious popular service – although currently only around four per cent of parents receive it. But the use of services such as respite care which remove a child from the family home may in turn create problems.

Many parents express great anxiety about their child's safety and care. Hubert (1992), in a study of respite care for young adults with multiple disabilities or challenging behaviour, found many parents desperately anxious about the quality of care available to their son or daughter. One mother described how her son always seemed to have been heavily sedated during his stay. Another was anguished by her son's poor physical care, sitting in a wheelchair wet and dirty – 'so lacking in any dignity'. A third mother told how she prayed that her son Callum would not die while he was away. She knew he hated going. The care was not good enough. But her husband felt they must have a break and she felt respite care was the choice that would keep the marriage together. A parent reading the study (personal communication) commented:

> If you have a disabled child, whatever you do is wrong. They (her relatives) are shocked that I could let my child use a respite care service run by social services. They think I must be abusing him – lots of parents think that now, everyone will think their child is on an 'at risk register' if they use services. Of course its not true. But we all try so hard and our children are all the time using new services, new people. Are they safe enough? I don't know. But then the professionals don't know if I am safe enough either! They won't ask, will they, when there is nowhere

local which could care for a fifteen year old who needs tube feeding, is doubly incontinent and has at least five fits a day.

Assessing risk for children with such complex disabilities will never be easy. But it can be done. Marchant (1993) in *Bridging the Gap* demonstrates the possibility of using the observations and skills of parents, staff and whatever communication aids the children use the assess the occurrence of abuse – and to identify potentially abusive behaviour early and avoid it if possible. Parents themselves can be supported and encouraged to join local parents' or support groups which in turn act as information givers, counsellors and advocates in getting appropriate services.

ASSESSMENT AND THE CHILDREN ACT

Assessment of potential abuse of a child with a disability should be assisted by the various assessments and reviews which the majority of children will already have experienced. *Working Together* (DOH 1991) identifies a number of different assessment procedures which children may go through. Although the definitions are not specifically linked to disability, many children with special needs will have experienced many of them. Indeed, many children will have become part of an 'assessment industry' which may (or may not) contribute significant knowledge to an investigation relating to abuse. An awareness of the multiple assessment processes is particularly important in the context of working directly with children. Children with disabilities (like other children) have new powers under the Children Act to refuse examination if they are judged to have sufficient understanding. But many will give consent (and will be able to communicate) if supported by a trusted and familiar professional. Teachers and paediatricians in particular (together with some therapists) may have long-term and detailed knowledge of a child and be readily able to identify uncharacteristic behaviour. Such familiarity is important not only for diagnosing actual abuse but for avoiding misdiagnosis when a child, for instance, self-abuses or where the cause of the child's disability predisposes the child to broken bones or bruising. Equally, parents may be willing to talk to trusted professionals and an honest and open working relationship may be achieved before actual abuse takes place.

ASSESSMENT – AN INDUSTRY OR A PROCESS?

Working Together (DOH 1991) lists the multiple assessment hurdles some children have to overcome in order to get services.

Assessment

In the context of *Working Together*, this term is used several different ways. Definitions are as follows:

INITIAL ASSESSMENT

An agreed multi-disciplinary composite report on the child's health and welfare in the context of his or her family which will enable participants at a case conference to plan the child's immediate future.

MEDICAL ASSESSMENT

A specific examination by a doctor for a definite purpose, e.g. a court request or as part of a child's health surveillance programme. The medical assessment may be more wide-ranging than a physical examination of the child and may in addition include comment on development and behaviour. The medical assessment may include recommendations for the ongoing care of the child within a medical context.

DEVELOPMENT ASSESSMENT

An objective assessment of a child, often to some agreed protocol, carried out by doctor, health visitor or child psychologist, for the purpose of determining the child's developmental level. Such assessments carried out in a serial way would provide information on a child's developmental progress. Development assessments are normally part of the DHA child health surveillance programme, but may be carried out at other times.

SPECIAL EDUCATIONAL NEEDS ASSESSMENT

A compilation of reports from various professionals to assist the local education authority to place the child in an educational setting compatible with his abilities. This assessment is carried out under the Education Act 1981.

HEALTH ASSESSMENT

An examination undertaken by the health visitor or social nurse to ascertain the child's health status. The health assessment will include information on height and weight, immunisation status, and vision and hearing.

COMPREHENSIVE ASSESSMENT

A structured time limited exercise to collect and evaluate information about the child and his family on which to base long term decisions. (See 'Protecting Children: A guide for social workers undertaking comprehensive assessment')

FAMILY ASSESSMENT

A report prepared over a period of time to assess the functioning of a particular family in relation to the needs of a child. The assessment is usually undertaken by a social worker but may be undertaken by a psychologist or family centre worker.

Precisely because the experience of disability may be disempowering for children (and families) and because the need for special care may mask inappropriate behaviour, the new Children Act procedures which include children with disabilities within a common legal framework for all children offer important new opportunities. Historically, children with disabilities received support through child health and education services. Social services' involvement was variable (although increasing with the development of services such as respite care and the growth in multi-disciplinary teams at child development centres and attached to generally all-age disability services). Divided responsibilities led to confusing variations in local management and many conspicuous gaps in services. Managing disability was often managing crisis. But the implementation of the Children Act has provided a new impetus to developing a common framework of services for all children, whilst simultaneously highlighting the challenges entailed in adopting an inclusive approach to disability in children.

The Children Act requires that every local authority 'shall have services designed:

(a) to minimise the effect on disabled children within their area of disability, and

(b) to give such children the opportunity to lead lives which are as normal as possible.' (Schedule 2, para 6)

Like the 1981 Education Act, the Children Act has a broadly integrationist principle underlying all its provisions. But defining integration has always been a challenge in terms of identifying positive support for children with special needs. 'An ordinary life' is not achievable by good will alone for the majority of children with disabilities, who need regular, practical and appropriate help in many aspects of daily living.

As the Fish Committee noted in 1985,

> The concept of integration as a dynamic process is difficult to grasp. It is often confused with physical location and discussed in terms of specific situations rather than the whole life-styles of children. Integration is about planned interaction between a child and his environment and is not about changing the concept of special provision but about its context.'

Volume 6 of the Guidance on children with disabilities and the Children Act stresses the crucial importance of looking at the whole lifestyles of children with disabilities in order to provide appropriate help. Misunderstandings about the abilities (as well as disabilities) of children can lead to major risks being taken and opportunities for early preventive intervention being missed. The Children Act does not specify specific procedures for the assessment of children with disabilities (or indeed for children in need). But as noted in Working Together and in Volume 6 of the Guidance, existing statutory assessment procedures – such as those relating to special educational needs under the 1981 Education Act and shortly to be amended under the 1993 Education Act – and section 5 and 6 of the 1986 Disabled Persons Act can be used as a basis for assessment of special educational needs (although they have legal rights to contribute to section five assessments). Particularly when children are living away from home – or where there are major or multiple problems relating to disability – educational assessment can contribute a unique (and inter- disciplinary) perspective on a child's total life experiences and correspondingly offers social services a chance to ensure that disability-specific services are aware of the risks of child abuse and collaborate closely when a child's welfare is in question.

However, education and other assessments may not be sufficient in many cases. Currently there is frequently a significant gap between the expertise of disability-specific services and the experience on child protection issues in local authority teams. This gap may lead to both under-reporting of actual or potential abuse – and also to inappropriate concerns about abuse because the management of a child with challenging behaviour may be misunderstood. There may also be a reluctance on both sides to acknowledge abuse when support services are scarce and when there are serious (albeit often inaccurate) assumptions about the inability of children with special needs accurately to describe their feelings and experiences.

The Children Act places considerable emphasis upon listening to children. But how can children with multiple disabilities or major communications be 'listened to'? The work of Margaret Kennedy and the Keep Deaf Children Safe project has demonstrated how positive outcomes can be achieved when there are realistic approaches both to reducing the vulnerability of children through specific training and support and awareness of how to communicate when communication seems problematic or even impossible. Both Marchant, in her work at Chailey Heritage (1993) has similarly explored strategies for listening to children with complex disabilities who can only communicate through Makaton or Bliss Symbol boards. Her work has demonstrated the importance of placing assessment for abuse firmly in the wider context of assessment of the whole child and listening to all relevant care- givers about the child's level of understanding and how best to listen to his or her views. Although major anxieties still exist about the acceptance by Courts of evidence given by child witnesses through some of the alternative or augmented communication methods, growing expertise in this area suggests that all local authorities should at least be aware of where to get expert advice in this area – and that staff working in direct services for disabled children should have shared training with their colleagues in generic services to ensure mutual understandings and to raise awareness of the importance of collective approaches to combatting disability. Whilst some local authorities may feel that they have few local sources of expertise in this area, all schools (including special schools) will have designated staff members with responsibility for child protection procedures. They (like relevant members of child development or community learning difficulty teams) are likely to have accurate information on the implications of a particular disability and to be able to advise both on communication and on a trusted individual who can support a child. Area Child Protection Committees and Teams similarly need to ensure that they have relevant disability expertise – and parents need to be aware of the importance of early discussion of any concerns that they have about their child's care and development. Assessment should be a corporate activity for all children. For disabled children, it is unlikely to be accurate or constructive without the close involvement of representatives from all three statutory services as well as families and any other services providers.

DEFINITIONS OF ABUSE IN THE CONTEXT OF DISABILITY

Children with disabilities are 'children first' and their experiences of abuse, neglect or disinterest will be similar to those experienced by all children. But disability may result in increased risk – and it may certainly expose children to greater risk of inappropriate care because of the likelihood of multiple care-givers and the increased dependency resulting from a disability of special needs. First, it is important to acknowledge the discrimination and disadvantage which many people with disabilities experience as part of their daily lives. The language of disability in itself demonstrates the negative connotations of incapacity and inferiority which may easily be attached to a disabled person. The language applying to 'learning disability' (mental handicap) shows the struggle which people with such disabilities have experienced in being recognised as people first. Educational subnormality, idiocy, feeble mindedness, learning difficulties have all in their time made attempts to create new and more positive images. But even contemporary media images – particularly those attached to charitable giving – perpetuate the notion of 'cripple' and 'helpless' and perhaps inadequate person or personality. In the past decade the majority of local authorities have confronted the need for equal opportunity policies which acknowledge and promote the diverse cultural and racial origins of their local populations. Although the rhetoric still often exceeds the reality, the majority of direct care staff – and those working in the education service – will be aware of the importance of anti-racism procedures and the need to provide care regimes which are appropriate to social, religious and cultural values. However, disability has historically not been part of generic social work practice – at least in children's services – and benign but dangerously inadequate idea about what disability means may abound. There may be reluctance to believe that anyone could abuse a disabled child (as if the disability confers some special protection). Disabled children may be seen as so 'different' that ordinary child care practices cannot apply to them. Equally parents (on whose care society depends very heavily) may be viewed unrealistically as 'super-carers' without needs (or problems) of their own. In purely practical terms, a family with a disabled child may find it difficult to use local children's services (such as daycare provision for under-fives; holiday play schemes and so forth) and will be simply unknown to local service providers. One mother of a six-year-old child with a rare genetic disorder commented (personal communication that parents caring for several disabled children form 'an invisible army', using statutory services only for emergencies because 'we are too difficult, too hard to understand the rest of the time.' This mother suspected a worker at a residential home which she used for occasional respite care of physically abusing her child. But, she said, 'we parents become part of the collusion that it's all right. There are so few places for disabled children to go... we all have to play the game of maintaining the status quo. I can't blame the social workers. I do it too – but I don's sleep at night when she is away.'

Physical, sexual and emotional abuse are all frequently inter-linked. In the context of disability it is worth redefining working definitions of abuse and in particular considering where they may overlap. Investment in tighter assessment procedures are unlikely to be effective unless all participants fully understood the 'add on' factors related to disability. For disabled children, therefore, working definitions of abuse may include the following

Emotional abuse

This may include: ridicule and rejection; humiliation (for example over problems relating to continuance of self-care skills); withdrawal from favoured activities such as leisure interests or activities with non-disabled children; inappropriate patterns of care (such as lack of privacy for intimate care).

Sexual abuse

Children with disabilities may be exposed to the full range of risks experienced by all children. Viewing or contributing to the production of pornographic photographs and videos; displays of sexual parts. Witnessing sexual activities are aspects of non-contact abuse. Children with disabilities may not only find it harder to remove themselves from such passive activities, but their limited social experience may not immediately indicate the inappropriateness of the activities in question. Contact sexual abuse, as with other children, may include a range of activities ranging from touching of parts of the body; masturbation or actual intercourse. Unlike other children, many children with disabilities may require personal care which involves undressing and physical assistance from another person. Furthermore, intimate contact (including access to a child in various stages of undress) may be considered quite appropriate by other family members or professionals. Because of poor personal and sex education, many children may also not only be unaware of the sexually explicit nature of some contacts, but may lack the necessary vocabulary in order to communicate what has happened.

Physical abuse

Physical abuse may also include non-contact abuse (such as threats of punishment or restraint). Contact abuse may range from actual bodily harm (such as slapping or shaking) through to force-feeding; physical restraint (such as tying up or chaining) and deprivation of heat, clothing, food or medication, often for the theoretical management of behaviour difficulty. Misuse of medication (often in combination with extreme exclusion diets) or force feeding have been cited in several recent court cases. They may occur in institutional settings (such as residential schools) as well as in private homes.

In some instances, the perpetrators may believe that the regime is right for the child or may be misapplying programmes which have been inadequately understood. Supervision of any behavioural programme is crucial – by an appropriately qualified professional and preferably through a multidisciplinary team such as a child development or community learning difficulty team. Although most disabled children in the community will be known to such teams, residential placements frequently mean loss of contact and inadequate supervision in the child's new place of residence, unless conscious efforts are made to ensure that such advice is available.

Racial abuse

This may occur in conjunction with any of the other forms of abuse. Because children with disabilities from minority ethnic backgrounds will be a small minority in any service (often because parents are unaware of possible sources of help), services may either not be offered at all because of false assumptions about families not wanting practical help such as respite care or the provision offered may be culturally insensitive, with poor communication, unsuitable diets and misunderstandings about any special health care needs such as those arising from sickle cell anaemia. Robina Shah (1992) has identified a number of potentially abusive situations for Asian families with disabled children together with positive recommendations for ensuring positive support and also avoiding under-diagnosis of abuse when a child has special needs and comes from a minority group.

Financial and property abuse

The National Development Team for People with Learning Disabilities (Russell and Flynn, 1992) has pointed out that people with learning disabilities may suffer adverse effects because of deliberate 'blocking' of access to monies, possessions or properties. People First, the self advocacy movement for people with learning disabilities, has cited a number of instances where benefits and allowances have been spent against the wishes of the actual recipient.

Systems abuse

Systems Abuse has been more widely documented in the USA and Canada and reflects growing awareness that people with disabilities may be directly abused – or made more a risk of abuse – because of the organisation of service systems which fail to take account of the special needs of disabled people. Clearly, children living away from home will be at particular risk of such abuse. As No More Victims (Allan 1992), a manual to guide Canadian Police in working with people with learning disabilities, notes

> Institutional life creates an ideal backdrop for abuse. Isolation and emotional deprivation make people who are institutionalised more vulnerable to abuse. While living in the community does not guarantee that people will be protected from abuse, the improvement of the quality of life and greater opportunity for the development of healthy social relations may lessen the likelihood of abuse.

Some 'systems' may fail disabled children because of complacency about their safety and over-confidence in good will rather than training and supervision for staff. Multiple service providers can cause fragmentation in care, with little attention being given to the actual wishes and feelings of children. Schools have probably been under-estimated in terms of their day-to-day knowledge of individual children and families. The growth of programmes such as those provided by Kidscape, to teach coping strategies and deal with bullying (frequently reported by children with special needs whether in mainstream or special schools) would appear to offer an important opportunity to maximum children' independence and confidence in avoiding abuse of any kind and in making strong representations when abuse occurs.

A special factor in systems abuse may relate to the lack of independent visitors (families, friends or appointees of the placing authority) to make certain that the child is well and happy and that there are no problems. The Castle Hill School enquiry found that the powerful personality and perceived credibility of the Head Teacher persuaded parents and professionals alike initially to disbelieve complaints from the young people. Because many lived several hundreds of miles from the school, informal visits by friends or families were unlikely.

Equally, within an institutional setting, abuse may become a collective activity with other pupils in turn seducing or abusing other children who may be too frightened to complain. Such an abusive environment will be particularly damaging to young people whose own life experiences and self-esteem are very limited – and who may have no coping strategies to 'whistle blow'.

In thinking about institutional or systems abuse, it is, however, still important to remember that good quality residential care or education may have a therapeutic as well as an educational role for some very damaged children and young people. The lessons from recent enquiries and from the Utting Report on residential care are that staff also need training, support and encouragement to be scrupulously honest about what they feel, hear and see within a residential setting. Equally, local authorities need to take greater responsibility for monitoring provision and for ensuring that there are independent visitors for all visited children.

A significant factor in 'systems' abuse may be the lack of contact with either independent visitors or with family or friends from a child's own community. If the school or residential setting is also provided as a solution to a crisis about the care of education of a child or young person who seems unmanageable at home, then independent scrutiny will be essential to ensure that the child's welfare is protected and that he or she is appropriately placed.

RISK FACTORS FOR CHILDREN WITH DISABILITIES

1. Limited life experiences and social contacts mean that many children with disabilities have had no chance to acquire the 'street-wise' behaviours and judgements which their non-disabled peers use in assessing the behaviour and attitudes of other people. Some children with disabilities may have had almost no contact with non-disabled people and are particularly at risk in terms of understanding inappropriate adult behaviour. In particular, children with high dependency needs may have learned from an early age that it pays to be pleasing and compliant and may be reluctant to challenge carers (family or professionals). Lack of experience together with a wider lack of control or choice over their own lives will be compounded if children with disabilities lack appropriate sexual education – including personal and social education. Craft (1989) and Middleton (1992) have found that lack of sexual and personal and social education creates problems which are further compounded if

isolation and rejection increase the need for affection and attention which makes such children particularly vulnerable to adults' attention and favours.

2. Children with disabilities are likely to use a much wider range of services than their non-disabled peers and, furthermore, to use services which are distant from their family home. 'Jason' – a young man with cerebral palsy and learning difficulties – attends a special school which he reaches by means of a local taxi service. He travels alone in the mini-cab which ferries him to and fro. He attends a weekly swimming club (again using special transport) together with a local scout pack (to which a neighbour takes him by car). He spends one weekend a month in a residential short-term care unit about 30 miles away. He spends a further two weeks in the summer in a residential holiday scheme. He is well known to the local child development team and to a specialist unit at a teaching hospital in London. He receives speech and physiotherapy; and is seeing a clinical psychologist regularly in an attempt to settle a sleeping problem. His parents' marriage has ended in divorce and he stays with both families (and new partners and children) together with periodic visits to grandparents. His mother is finding it difficult to cope and is talking about a residential school. Jason is not untypical of children with disabilities. Research tells us that he is most likely to be abused by someone he knows (few severely disabled children are out in the community unsupervised). But who does Jason know? And how well do the multiple professionals involved in his life and care 'know' each other and ensure that his wishes and feelings are fully recognised? In addition, with multiple carers, how does Jason learn appropriate and consistent models of adult behaviour? Children in Jason's position are known by a wide range of professionals. In theory they receive a balanced programme of therapy and support. They are certainly assessed and re-assessed continuously. But the danger lies in the complexity of the service arrangements offered – and in the absence of any child protection components in the training of many professionals working in the disability field. Jason's parents (however good the quality of parenting provided) are pressurised by care and may be reluctant to complain or to query the behaviour of any of Jason's carers or supporters for fear of losing a service.

3. Impaired communication skills may make disabled children appear to be 'safe victims' because they are unlikely to complain and may indeed lack the language skills in order to avoid the abuse in the first place. Communication skills may be obviously lacking, for example in a child who is profoundly deaf and can only communicate through sign language or when a child has a significant learning disability which restricts vocabulary and language. But they may also be lacking in children who theoretically can communicate but whose social skills and life experiences make it difficult for them to do so. A forthcoming study from the National Children's Bureau

(Wertheimer and Bargh, 1994) of young women with moderate learning difficulties found considerable evidence of bullying and emotional abuse (such as teasing) in families and the local community which was neither reported nor discussed. The young women in question needed considerable peer support in order to confront their difficulties and to think through strategies for dealing with them. Their own low self image and their awareness of their 'differentness' severely limited their own survival skills. The project concluded that all young people with special needs require positive discrimination in terms of assertiveness training – using role plays if necessary – and that parents may need help in really listening to what their children are saying.

4. Treatment or care may in themselves be abusive. The 'Pindown' Report (Levy and Kahan, 1992) demonstrated the dangers of young, inexperienced and unsupported staff carrying out treatment regimes which they did not fully understand. The past decade has seen a major growth in programmes for children with disabilities – in particular behaviour management programmes for challenging or difficult behaviour and a range of alternative treatments involving combinations of medication, diet and therapy for a variety of problems. Many programmes are effective, carefully planned and monitored and help to sustain children with very complex needs in their local communities. But others are not supervised; these may be implemented out of context and may result in: children experiencing loss of personal possessions; being confined to their room for long periods of time; suffering humiliation or ridicule or being denied a full diet or appropriate clothing. Guidance on the Children Act is quite clear that sanctions and treatment programmes should not interfere with basic human rights. But unless the care of children with disabilities is carefully planned and regularly reviewed – and children living away from home are visited and given the opportunity to communicate their feelings in private – inappropriate patterns of care are likely to continue.

5. The need for intimate care presents a major challenge. Many children with multiple disabilities require constant physical care and assistance with eating, dressing, toiletting and general mobility. Others require periodic intimate care (if – for example – they have to use a public toilet which has not been adapted for wheelchair use) but may manage very well in a suitable environment. Managing intimate care in a 'safe' and acceptable way means acknowledging a number of important preventive factors:

   (i) Environmental conditions – bathrooms and toilets need to be conveniently located, designed to permit maximum independence and privacy. As more children are integrated into mainstream services, environmental factors may become more problematic.

(ii) Staff training – practical help should be as unintrusive as possible. Staff need clear messages about acceptable and unacceptable approaches to personal care. Children can be asked what they want – and their ideas and perceptions incorporated into training. Training times need also to be seen as staff support. Anxiety about abuse can actually create emotional abuse if staff believe all personal contact must be strictly monitored. Many disabled children (particularly those living away from home) need friendship and affection – but may be indiscriminate in how they seek and give it. Prevention of abuse is most likely to occur when there are warm and open relationships between staff and children – rigid institutionalisation of care routines is unlikely to offer protection and may increase children's vulnerability.

(iii) Social skills and independence training – it can be easy to under-estimate a child's capacity to acquire self care skills. Positive encouragement to self-management of incontinence; dressing and so forth are crucial. Better partnerships between schools and parents or professional carers can produce major improvements – and greater protection.

(iv) Listening to children – 'listening' may mean 'observation' for some severely disabled children. Listening may mean using a range of communications, and asking key questions about the needs of particular children using a service. If a deaf child communicates through signing or cued speech, can at least one member of staff learn the same communication? Ruth Marchant (1992) has described how Chailey Heritage uses communication boards with children with multiple disabilities. Good record keeping by staff (including the use of video) can indicate when behaviour indicates that children are unhappy or having difficulty with a particular routine.

(v) Listening to parents – a number of studies have suggested that negative perceptions of disability (sometimes regarded as the Cinderella of equal opportunities policies) may apply to parents as well as children. Parents frequently feel themselves not to be believed – or regarded as trouble makers – if they complain about a service. As noted above, many families are multiple service users. Such services may involve a child staying away from home periodically (for example in respite care). One mother described (person communication) how she 'sat in the drive to the respite care home and cried' every time she left her child. Her father was seriously ill and she had been obliged to agree to her teenage son using a local residential respite care home. Because of his difficult behaviour, there had been no alternative, but she felt her son came home each time 'wearing someone else's clothes, dopey – too much medication' and desperate not to go back. She did not think her child was actually abused – but his personal neglect and her anxiety indicated the desperation she felt.

(vi) Crisis management – 'Peter' in the section above experienced major risks because of the over-riding necessity to ensure that he was cared for when his mother had other family commitments. For many local authorities, 'crisis management' when a child with significant levels of disability cannot be cared for at home is an increasing reality. The ending of admissions to long-stay hospitals has been widely welcomed. But the growing number of children and young people with multiple disabilities or challenging behaviour continues to provide major strains on local services. Increasing numbers of children are placed in private residential schools or homes, often in rural areas at some considerable distance from their family home. If the most vulnerable are to be placed the furthest away (with negligible prospects of telephone or other contact with home), then inspection arrangements and regular personal contact (perhaps through the use of the 'independent visitor') will be crucial. In addition, the needs of families for a package of support before the crisis arises should be carefully considered.

(vii) Listening to Colleagues: The enquiry into abuse at Castle Hill School (an independent special school) (Brannan, 1993) noted the importance of creating awareness of abuse amongst relevant professionals. He commented: 'The identification and awareness of organised institutional abuse is still in the early stages. A significant feature of our investigation was the disbelief of other professionals and their inability to accept and comprehend the volume and extent of the abuse. Within this setting the "disbelief factor" exacerbated the disempowerment, vulnerability and isolation of the victims. It is essential therefore that the professionals involved in this area of work be conversant with these issues. Only then are they in a position to accept "new systems" and take forward practice in relation to organised abuse. An open mind, and a preparedness to accept and objectively analyse improbable and sometimes unbelievable scenarios are essential'. In a special school or similar setting for disabled children, physical isolation, increased opportunity because of greater dependency and a reluctance by outsiders to accept abuse all necessitate teams as well as individual training on rapid responses to inappropriate behaviour or potential or actual abuse.

MESSAGES FOR THE FUTURE

The challenge for effective child protection procedures for disabled children is primarily that of reconciling the considerable expertise on disability issues in many professional services (with corresponding lack of awareness of child protection procedures) and the current local arrangements for child protection which frequently pay insufficient attention to the additional disability issues which may impact upon early diagnosis and effective intervention, and which may underestimate the contribution of disabled children to their own assessment and management.

Key issues for future discussion and development include:

1. Greater interchange between disability and child protection services, with common training and greater awareness of their respective contributions to protecting children with disabilities.

2. Utilisation of existing assessment arrangements for children with disabilities to avoid duplication and to ensure that any decision is made on the basis of the most up-to-date knowledge of child and family.

3. Improved personal and social and sex education for children with disabilities and special needs – over-protection will increase vulnerability as children become more independent in their local communities.

4. Particular attention to the welfare and safety of children with multiple or complex needs or challenging behaviour – the work of Marchant (1993) and others show that such children can be assisted in communicating their experiences – but that they are particularly vulnerable and plans for such children should include clear arrangements for monitoring and regular review.

5. Many parents caring for a child with a disability receive little support. Pressures of everyday caring may result in some families accepting help which is inadequate – or may result in recourse to inappropriate behavioural or treatment regimes. Children Act implementation of policies for 'children in need' should state clearly how the local authority in question will identify and assess parents' needs and the range of services which will be available to meet them.

6. Treatment may in itself be abusive – particularly if a child has very challenging behaviour. The recent court case in which a Lancashire head teacher of a school for autistic children was convicted of mistreatment of the children through totally inappropriate feeding and management regimes demonstrates the importance of regular inspection and audit of services for children with special needs.

7. Finally, and by no means least, we need to listen to the experiences of adults with disabilities who have ben abused (Westcott (1992a); Sinason (1992). Their stories remind us of the cumulative and negative consequences of disability and abuse – in effect a double jeopardy. Most worrying, they indicate considerable reluctance by professionals to believe that disabled people can be abused and lack of awareness of the particular isolation of those living in institutional care.

8. There have been considerable doubts expressed about the ability of disabled children (particularly those with multiple or learning disabilities) to act as reliable witnesses in Court. We need to further explore how such children can be helped to give evidence. Reluctance to prosecute because of anxieties about the achievable verdict may be valid in some cases. But in others the risks to disabled

children may be increased by blanket avoidances of court action which may in turn lead some potential abusers to consider that disabled children are indeed safe victims.

In conclusion, the Children Act has provided us with a legal framework within which children with disabilities can be seen as 'children first'. However, the principle of integration and inclusion should not be allowed to conceal the fact that many disabled children need considerable support in order to lead lives which are indeed 'as normal as possible'. As Butler Sloss (1988) noted in her introduction to the Cleveland Enquiry Report,

> There is a danger that in looking to the welfare of the children believed to be the victims of abuse, the children themselves may be overlooked. The child is a person and not an object of concern.

It is particularly easy to see a disability as separate to the child – if we see the person, our approaches to child protection and disability will become more effective.

REFERENCES

Allan, G. (1992) *No More Victims – a Manual to Guide the Police in Addressing the Sexual Abuse of People with a Mental Handicap.* Ontario, Canada: Roeher Institute.

Bradshaw, J. and Cooke, K. (1986) Child disablement, family dissolution and reconstitution. *Development Medicine and Child Neurology,* 28, 610–18.

Brannan, S. (1993) Castle Hill Report Practice Guide, Shropshire County Council.

Butler Sloss, Justice (1988) *Report of the Inquiry into Child Abuse in Cleveland.* London: HMSO.

Department of Health (1991) *The Children Act 1989 Guidance and Regulations, Volume 6, Children with Disabilities.* London: HMSO.

Craft, A. and Brown, H. (eds) (1989) *Thinking the Unthinkable: Papers on Sexual Abuse and People with Learning Difficulties.* London: FPA Education Unit.

Fish, J. (1985) *Equal Opportunities for All?* Report of Fish Committee's Review of Special Educational Needs. London: ILEA.

Glendinning, C. (1986) *Unshared Care – Parents and their Disabled Children.* London: Routledge and Kegan Paul.

Hard, S. (1986) The Sexual Abuse of the Developmentally Disabled: A Case Study. A paper presented at the National Conference of Associations of Retarded Citizens, Omaha. Cited in Mayer, P. and Brenner, S. (1989) 'Abuse of Children with Disabilities', *Children's Legal Rights Journal,* 10(4), 16–20.

Hubert, J. (1991) *Home-Bound: Crisis in the Care of Young People with Severe Learning Difficulties.* London: King's Fund Centre.

Hubert, J. (1992) *Administering Drugs to Young People with Severe Learning Difficulties,* Social Care Research Findings Number 18. London: Joseph Rowntree Foundation.

Kennedy, M. (1989) 'The Abuse of Deaf Children', *Child Abuse Review,* 3(1) 3–7.

Kennedy, M. (1990) 'The Deaf Child who is Sexually Abused – is there a Need for a Dual Specialist?' *Child Abuse Review,* 4(2) 3–6.

Kennedy, M. (1990) 'Overcoming Myths: The Abused Disabled Child', *Concern,* Summer 1990, 4–5. National Children's Bureau.

Levy, A. and Kahan, B. (1992) *The Pindown Experience and the Protection of Children: The Report of the Staffordshire Child Care Inquiry*. Staffordshire County Council.

Marchant, R. and Page, M. (1992) 'Bridging the gap: Investigating the Abuse of Children with Multiple Disabilities', *Child Abuse Review*, 1(3).

Marchant, R., Page, M. and Crane, S. (1993) *Child Protection Work with Children with Multiple Disabilities*, London: NSPCC.

Middleton, L. (1992) *Children First: Working with Children and Disability*. London: Ventura Press.

Office of Population and Census Surveys (1989) *OPCS Surveys of Disability in the UK. Report 3: Prevalence of Disability Among Children*. London: HMSO.

Office of Population and Census Surveys (1989) *OPCS Surveys of Disability in the UK. Report 5: Financial Circumstances of Families*. London: HMSO.

Office of Population and Census Surveys (1989) *OPCS Surveys of Disability in the UK. Report 6: Disabled Children, Services, Transport and Education*. London: HMSO.

Quine, L. and Paul, J. (1989) *Stress and Coping in Families Caring for a Child with a Severe Mental Handicap: a Longitudinal Study*, Institute of Social and Applied Psychology and Centre for Health Service Studies, University of Kent.

Russell, P. (1992) *Future Challenges to Family-based Short Term Care: Opportunities and Challenges for the 1990s*. London: Council for Disabled Children, London: National Children's Bureau.

Russell, P. (1992) *The Children Act 1989 and Disability*, Highlight 109. London: National Children's Bureau.

Russell, P. and Flynn, M. (1992) *Report of Parent Workshop for National Development Team* (unpublished).

Shah, R. (1992) *The Silent Minority: Children with Disabilities in Asian Families*. London: National Children's Bureau.

Sobsey, D. and Varnhagen, P. (1988) Sexual Abuse and Exploitation of People with Disabilities: A Study of the Victims. Unpublished manuscript.

Sullivan, P.M., Vernon, M. and Scanlan, J.M. (1987) Sexual Abuse of Deaf Youth, *American Annals of the Deaf*, 3, 256–262.

Sinason, V. (1992) *Mental Handicap and the Human Condition: New Approaches*. London: Free Association Books.

Wertheimer, A., Bargh, J. and Russell, P. (1994) *Something to Say*. London: National Childrens Bureau.

Westcott, H.L. (1992a) *Abuse of Children and Adults with Disabilities*. London: NSPCC.

Westcott, H.L. (1992) Vulnerability and the Need for Protection. In J. Gibbons (ed) *Family Support and the Children Act*. London: HMSO.

Westcott, H.L. (1991) The Abuse of Disabled Children – A Review of the Literature, *Child: Care, Health and Development*, 17(4) 243–258.

Westcott, H.L. (1969) *Abuse of Children and Adults with Disabilities*. London: NSPCC.

Wilkin, D. (1979) *Caring for the Mentally Handicapped Child*. London: Croom Helm.

Zirpoli, T. (1986) Child abuse and children with handicaps. *Remedial and Special Education*, 7, 39–48.

CHAPTER 8

ON BECOMING A TIGHTROPE WALKER
COMMUNICATING EFFECTIVELY WITH
CHILDREN ABOUT ABUSE

EVE BROCK

In 1800, in Aveyron, a wild boy was rescued from the pack of wolves that had been his family; he 'talked' only in the language of wolves. His story is told by Malson and Itard (1972), and the wild boy of Aveyron was graphic proof that humans are born biologically *able* to talk, but need to be taught *how*.

So, even doing 'what comes naturally' doesn't come naturally; especially, communicating effectively with children on a topic as difficult and sensitive as their (alleged) abuse requires a sophisticated set of skills that we, as professionals, need to learn.

First, what is meant by 'communicating effectively' in these circumstances? I would suggest that we succeed when the knowledge and understanding we acquire reflects the child's reality (as near as is possible), rather than being unacceptably skewed by the interview process – no easy definition and no easy task.

The communication task seems similar to that of walking a tightrope, where the professional needs to become a tightrope walker, balancing his or her performance between competing demands. This chapter aims to help professionals to develop the understanding and skills involved in negotiating that necessary balancing act. The aims are fourfold:

1. To clarify the competing demands upon you, when you are listening and responding to children who talk with you about alleged abuse.

2. To prompt you to assess your current skills and further training needs; and, because time, tide and children who are abused wait for no man or woman to be adequately trained, before they speak out.

3. To offer guidelines and suggestions for communicating effectively with children about alleged abuse.

4. To suggest a basic group training exercise you can use to develop or fine tune your skills.

CLARIFICATION: WHAT IS THE TIGHTROPE WALK?

The professional walks a tightrope when talking with children about their alleged abuse, balancing between the following demands:

- the balance between the rights of the child, the rights of the parents and the requirements of our legal system
- balancing within ourselves, between our professional responsibilities and our personal feelings, and even our rights (both as people and as professionals)
- the balance between finding out enough 'accurate' information about any alleged abuse and yet not further abusing the child by our attitude, speech or actions.

We need to be aware of these competing demands before we can attempt to balance them suitably; then, we may never achieve a perfect standard, but we can aim for what Aristotle called the 'Golden Mean' – a balance between excess and deficiency. Some pointers follow.

Generally, it is now recognised that children have the right to a childhood free from abuse and intimidation, and that the needs of the child are of paramount importance over the rights of parents and carers. Historically, that has not always been recognised. This recognition helps us as a principle for our decision-making, although it cannot make our decisions easy, for respect still needs to be shown for the rights and feelings of parents and carers. In addition, the requirements of our legal system need to be born in mind too, and this is discussed below.

The second balancing act concerns our own possible dilemmas between our professional duties and our personal reactions, doubts and fears. I would suggest that our professional responsibilities must take precedence; to deal with our personal fears, concerns and needs (especially if we are to be the 'whistle blower' upon a colleague whom we suspect of being abusive) we must recognise our own need for support, and assertively seek it. The topic of abuse is difficult, and our own needs are valid. The NSPCC offers an 'official' validation of such needs in its booklet 'A guide for Teachers on Child Abuse' (which is useful for all carers, not just teachers).

Finally, although we need enough information from the child to proceed appropriately, we need to keep in mind that the child must not be further abused by our conversation. This latter must take precedence over gaining information, and can be addressed by deliberate efforts to provide a patient and 'therapeutic' approach rather than that of an 'interrogation'. What do these demands mean in practice when communicating with children?

COMMUNICATING EFFECTIVELY WITH CHILDREN

Three fundamental principles to be kept in mind when communicating with a child about alleged abuse, are:

1. The child must not be further 'abused' by the conversation.
2. The adult must keep an *open mind* about any allegations made.

3. The adult must gather information without asking the child any 'leading questions', (because otherwise his or her contribution could ruin a potential court prosecution case).

The skill lies in translating these fundamental principles into practice, i.e., what do we say and do? There are the following practical approaches:

1. The child must not be further 'abused' by this conversation. This can be avoided or minimised by ensuring a number of factors, such as:

- By establishing a rapport with the child; this is essential and must be a deliberate process on the professionals' behalf. The process is reviewed in the 'Stage 1' of communicating with children below.

- By considering the environment where the conversation, (if not spontaneous), is planned to take place; the area should be as physically and atmospherically 'warm' as possible. Deliberate consideration of the obvious is helpful: avoid bare light walls and uncarpeted floors, stiff chairs, desks, and high tables; add plants and wall pictures that might appeal to children (but which are not too infantile).

- By using so-called 'counselling skills' when communicating with a child. Some professionals, particularly teachers, resist the idea of obtaining training in 'counselling skills', protesting that they are not counsellors. Perhaps the title 'counselling skills' is an unfortunate misnomer, for 'counselling' styles of thinking and interacting are not exclusively useful in counselling situations but benefit *every* human interaction (professional, personal and marriage relationships). Such skills can be acquired through courses. Any long course is best if accredited by the British Association of Counselling. The Central School for Counselling Therapy offer such courses – addresses on p.124. Useful books on the subject are listed on p.124 but reading always needs to be complemented by practice on a course or in-service training.
Communication skills that help avoid an 'abusive' style of encounter include:

  ○ active listening

  ○ sensitive questioning

  ○ questioning that stops at a minimal stage, and does not press for detailed revelations too soon or any more times than absolutely necessary.

So, it is useful to do a professional 'self-assessment' in which you clarify your own role in the 'chain' of professionals that may have to be involved, and clarify in your own mind how early you can stop asking for information. There is a human temptation to want to know details, out of concern for the child (or even natural curiosity) but this needs to be resisted; clarifying your own role and the limits of responsibility in advance, with your superior, helps you to avoid over-questioning the child unnecessarily.

Professional roles are outlined in the documents 'Working Together Under the Children Act 1989 (1991) and D.E.S. Circular 4/88. It is made clear in these documents that teachers do have responsibility for protecting pupils from abuse and for responding appropriately (*Working Together*, p.21); teachers *must* refer their concerns at an early stage to social services, without deep questioning of the pupil. There should be a 'designated person' in each school with responsibility for child protection issues. (If you are this designated person and have received no special in-service training, it is important that you acquire it; also, to best fulfil professional duties, some 'whole school' in-service training for all staff is recommended).

- By professionals 'desensitising' themselves to some extent about the nature of child abuse. The child is probably terrified enough without 'feeling' your terror to add to her or his tension.

  Also, if the child feels your embarrassment, disbelief, shock or recoil, he or she may withdraw from revealing more, either from her or his own discomfort or in order to 'protect' you. For the professional, it is another balancing act; to be desensitised enough to accept a child's account without showing a horror which incapacitates the child, but to remain sensitive enough to care about the child's suffering.

Such a balance can be achieved; this two-step process can be useful, first, by reading real accounts of survivors of child abuse, and persevering with the reading through your initial discomfort (see further reading list at the end of this chapter); and, second, by discussing the issues with a supportive, suitable colleague, counsellor or friend.

The topic of sexual abuse is a particularly sensitive and difficult one for most of us, especially as our society still fails to provide good sex education. Sexual mis-education in the form of innuendo, jokes, and pornography is plentiful: positive education which could help people to feel comfortable with sexuality and responsible about expressing it is, unfortunately, lacking. At the very least, we need to be comfortable with our own sexuality before we can be effective when receiving accounts of sexual abuse. Training can be acquired from the FPA (Family Planning Association, address on p.124) or from specialised training consultants.

Some knowledge of sexual abuse helps us to suspend any disbelief and also helps us to avoid holding unreal stereotyped ideas of abuse and abusers. For example, it is commonly known that men comprise the majority group of abusers (La Fontaine 1990), but we need to accept that women and mothers can be abusive too. Evidence is presented in a short article relating 'Cianne's story' of her childhood abuse by a woman relative, and 'When mother love can hurt' provided by Rosalind Sharpe (1992).

Finally, if a professional has a personal history of being abused that has not been at least talked over, that professional needs to explore such experiences with a suitably trained person before communicating with children on the subject of abuse.

2. Keep an open mind

The adult must keep an *open mind* about any allegations of abuse that are made.

From many studies of perception in psychology we know that, although it is our eyes and ears that receive 'factual' sensory information from the world, it is our brain that interprets it. As the philosopher Immanuel Kant showed in *A Prolegomena to Every Future Metaphysic* (1783) we see things not as they are, but as we are. There is too much information (and it maybe of a sort that we cannot comprehend) for us to process everything, so we are inevitably selective.

So, we recognise what we accept as possible – but we cannot recognise what we think of as impossible. We quickly recognise what we expect to recognise – but we may dismiss the unexpected. We notice what we are interested in – but ignore things that are not interesting. For example, in simple terms, if we have just bought a new red car, we probably suddenly start to notice how many red cars there are on the road, whereas before we simply never noticed.

These features of how we perceive the world in a 'selective' way, explain why professionals who have been on a training course about child abuse are more likely to recognise abuse soon afterwards. This is not because they have 'invented' the example of abuse, but because they are now more open to perceive it. However, there is a danger that our openness may spill over into such professional enthusiasm to care for children that it causes us to exaggerate or make unfounded assumptions about what we see and hear.

In the past, some professionals have been criticised for an over-zealous reaction to children's initial accounts of alleged abuse, later regarded as unfounded. So it is now emphasised that professionals should 'accept' and 'take seriously' rather than 'believe' a child's initial account of being abused. That is, have an open mind – neither closed to hearing of abuse NOR perceiving abuse where none might exist.

There are examples of professionals being accused of abuse by children in their care which have later been regarded as unfounded; Marion Bennathan and Robert Laslett air the pressures upon the accused in this situation, in a letter to the T.E.S. (18/12/92). Keeping an open mind is not easy, but necessary.

3. Gather information without leading questions

The adult must gather information *without* asking the child any 'leading questions' (because otherwise his/her contribution could ruin a potential court prosecution case).

This is a difficult demand but essential, for evidence given in a court session may be ruled inadmissible if it can be claimed that the questioning has 'led' the child's responses. A potential prosecution case of an abuser may fail on this issue.

So the principle of avoiding the use of 'leading questions' needs to be etched on the mind of every professional talking with children; also, an understanding of what is a leading question must be acquired and, finally, the skill needs to be practised.

A 'leading question' is one which, by its wording, may 'lead' the respondent towards a particular type of answer. For example: 'what did he do to you next?' includes a silent assumption that he did do something to the child next. This can be claimed to 'lead' the child to an affirmative response that may not be true. This issue is referred to again in Stage 3 of the communicating process below.

A child is a 'pleasing' creature (even if to a harassed adult it may not always seem to be so), and may try to please the questioning adult by answering in a way the child thinks the adult wants. Ironically, the better your rapport, the more possible the chance of the child wanting to 'please' you. Leading questions abet that process.

A local police officer, or solicitor, might well be a knowledgeable assistant to invite, to offer feedback, in a practical training session for a group of professionals practising questioning and recognising the 'leading' style.

STAGES OF COMMUNICATING EFFECTIVELY WITH CHILDREN ABOUT ALLEGED ABUSE

The idea of stages is introduced merely to assist our thought processes and is intended only as an approximate guide.

Stage one – establishing rapport and trust

- Be a suitable person to talk to children. If the child has chosen you, then you may assume that you are at least not unsuitable.

Rogers (1951, 1961) emphasised the idea of client-centred therapy where the client is empowered to talk (and to make choices), with the counsellor as a facilitator in the process rather than an expert who imposes her or his view. Rogers suggested that effective communication requires three factors: genuineness, respect and empathy.

Genuineness is about being 'real'; neither wearing a mask nor playing games in the ways identified by Berne in *The Games People Play* (1964).

Respect involves valuing all people as equally important. In this context, it includes regarding children as being equally as important as adults, and having rights as do adults. This implies that the child's views be consulted and that his or her wishes be regarded seriously, as of importance.

Empathy is about trying to see the world, and feel the world, from the other person's perspective.

First, we need to asses our own attitudes; then the skill lies in translating these factors into speech and non-verbal behaviour.

Sometimes we may need the courage to recognise that we are square pegs in round holes, re-assess our strengths and weaknesses, and even intimate to our superiors that talking to children about abuse is a particular duty that we are unable to fill adequately. Or, we might even recognise that we would be better to change professions completely.

- If you are the child's teacher, probably the process of rapport-building has already taken place. If you are a person new to the child, don't assume that rapport can be achieved in a single meeting. It may need gentle quiet periods together, playing or talking about things other than any alleged abuse. The child needs to feel that he or she can trust you before she or he can talk honestly with you. Patience and sensitivity (including observing the child's non-verbal reactions closely) are key approaches.

For preparing yourself, useful readings include the inspiring story of the troubled child called Dibs, in search of himself, (Axline 1964) and a short article about a teacher's 'defusing' of a six year old pupil 'timebomb' (MacKenzie 1992). For an example of one very articulate child's growing written revelations about her own abuse, refer to Elliott's *Kidscape Training Pack* for frontline carers (1992).

If the child has learning difficulties or other problems in communicating, this rapport-building will probably take longer, as will the interviews. It is essential that the professionals involved must be trained and experienced in communicating with children who have such difficulties, and be informed of the unique needs of the particular child. If the child is deaf and is accustomed to using sign language, no interviews must take place at all without a signing person or a suitable sign interpreter. Margaret Kennedy, who is a professional who is deaf and founded the Keep Deaf Children Safe Project, discusses alternatives to verbal interviews (1992). Marchant and Page (1992) discuss talking with children who have multiple disabilities, and point out the importance of the professional having high expectations of the child's communication potential. In practice, they found that such 'disabled' children communicated more than had initially been thought possible. Much previous educational psychological research has also suggested that the expectations of adults working with children can enhance or limit their performance.

- Rapport-building also involves decisions about who should be present besides the child and yourself; no one should be present whom the child specifically objects to (if practicable); on the other hand, if the child wants someone else present as a 'friend', (and/or a favoured toy), that must be considered seriously too, and accommodated if possible. That supportive person will need briefing beforehand about the situation and her or his role – its authority and its limitations. Bear in mind that he or she may possibly need support for her or himself afterwards, too.

Stage two – being open for the child to talk on in a free narrative way

- Ask for an account from the child, by saying something simple and using an 'open' question such as: 'would you tell me what happened?'

'Open' questions are those which invite a wide response, as opposed to 'closed' questions which tend to invite a more specific response. Closed questions generally begin with words such as did? are? was? were? is?

Open questions generally begin with words or phrases such as: what? where? who? how? when? tell me about: explain: describe.

- Use active listening techniques:
  - minimal encouragers; gentle verbal prompts such as 'uh-er'; 'mm'; 'any more?'; a non-verbal gentle nod of your head;
  - be very patient with silences; wait; the child may be re-grouping his or her thoughts. Accustom yourself to tolerate silences in conversations.
  - reflect back occasionally; if the child says 'I felt scared', reflect it back gently as 'you felt scared...'
  - clarify (only if needed at this stage); 'what do you mean by...?' The answer may involve a drawing if the child is unwilling or unable to verbalise the answer.
- Attend to the non-verbal messages that you are giving out in the way you sit and gesture. Sit at a similar height to the child, rather than towering above; do not sit behind a physical barrier such as a table or desk or you will present a psychological barrier too. Do not position your chair right opposite to the child's as it appears formal and confrontative, use a more informal arrangement. Helpful non-verbal reactions are gentle head-nods which signify acceptance. To avoid involuntary negative reactions to any 'shocking' content of the child's words, one helpful preparation has already been mentioned – in (to some extent) desensitising yourself on the topic of abuse.
- Keep your reactive sentences short, simple and delivered quite slowly, quietly and gently.
- To assuage any anxieties of the child, you could say: 'It's OK to tell me' (avoid saying 'it's good', or any adjective that's too enthusiastic, as this could be criticised as leading or inviting the child to make allegations to 'please' you).
- Avoid being critical of the alleged perpetrator(s); remember that the child probably loves him or her and suffers from ambivalent feelings, and that reconciliation may be possible.
- If the child asks you if the perpetrator will 'get into trouble', try to be both honest and re-assuring; for example, you could say: 'Maybe he or she will. But if they do get into trouble it's not your fault. If people do wrong things it is their fault if they get into trouble. I hope he or she will get some help to stop doing it.'
- Do not make any claims or promises that you may not be able to keep, particularly of confidentiality. If a child asks for confidentiality, you could respond gently: 'I am not able to promise that. But I will do all I can to help you.'
- Accurately record what the child says; see 'Recording Notes' below.

Stage three – asking for further information

This may or may not be needed at this point. It may now be your responsibility to refer your concern about the child's welfare to another appropriate professional. Teachers in particular have a duty to refer their concerns to social services, at any early stage. Use the same guidelines as before, using open questions and avoiding leading ones.

Stage four – acquiring more specific details

If this is needed, use the same guidelines as previously.

Stage five – closing the interview

- Remember that this needs to be managed by you in a sensitive and deliberate way.

- Aim to close the interview pleasantly, to show acceptance of the preceding content.

- Try not to close the interview abruptly but give notice that the two of you need to stop talking in a few minutes. This allows the child to prepare her or himself for the end of the interview, and if he or she has been procrastinating about telling you something, it allows her or him to be aware that there is not much time left at the moment. A simple phrase could be: 'we need to stop talking in about ten minutes… about ten minutes.' Then wait for the next response. Repeat when only about five minutes left.

- Avoid closing the interview in such a 'praising' manner that you could be accused of 'promoting' further revelations. Some youngsters can be very adept at telling us what they think we want to hear. So, avoid such closing comments as: 'I'm really glad you told me all this'; 'you are a very good boy or girl to have told me all about this'. Instead you could say something simple such as: 'OK. Let's leave it for now, shall we?'

- Explain briefly to the child what is to happen next, and check that she or he understands you; a good way to check is simply by asking him or her to repeat it back to you. If you merely ask: 'Do you understand?' you may receive a nod or a 'yes' that seems to indicate understanding but means very little. Children who have communication or learning difficulties especially display this response, but many children do. You could say: 'I'd just like to check I've explained that clearly to you; would you tell me what you think I said would happen next?' With this type of phrasing you are taking responsibility upon your shoulders for not being understood, rather than appearing to accuse the child of not understanding or not listening. It's a more sensitive and less patronising way of checking out understanding.

Recording notes

Make an accurate record, preferably at the time, on any handy scrap of paper/object that can be written on. Note the child's actual key words as far as possible. Use the child's own pet words if euphemisms for certain parts of the body are used. For example, if a boy mentions being touched on his 'willie', do not interpret 'willie' to 'penis' in your notes. Do not make assumptions; do not assume that 'willie' means penis to that child; check it out by asking what and where he means; allow him to point to a drawing (printed, or sketched by you) if he needs to.

Save your original notes, however scruffy or scrappy, in case they are required for any later prosecution case.

Clearly, suitable recording may be possible if the interview is set up in advance.

Walking the tightrope of communicating effectively with children about abuse is not easy – but then no-one ever promised that it would be. But it is possible. Guard against allowing yourself to feel overwhelmed by the task. Already, you have many skills, acquired both as a professional and as a person, that are transferable to this newer situation. So, allow yourself to feel some confidence, but realistically assess your weaknesses (maybe by asking for honest feedback from a colleague), and acquire appropriate training. Accept any need that you have for support, seek – and even demand it if necessary.

Finally, guard against aiming to be 'SuperSaviour' of the children's world, for you cannot. So, do what you can; accept what you can't – then sleep at night. For you would be unable to help another child if you became over-involved and incapacitated by the pain of one child.

The inspiring psychologist Abram Maslow suggested an aim as professionals working with other human beings; I invite you to adopt it, particularly when communicating with children about abuse: to be a 'therapeutic force for good'.

EXERCISE 8.1

Rationale

Learning by reading can often be adequate but, just as we cannot learn to ride a bicycle by reading instructions and without getting onto that bike and wobbling around inexpertly, we cannot learn how to communicate effectively without practising. Clearly, we wish to avoid the situation, if possible, where our first 'practice' is with a real child in distress.

Notes for the Facilitator

Some professionals avoid role play because of their (understandable) feelings of embarrassment. They may be encouraged if the facilitator points out that if we compare our feelings of horror of role play to the child's feelings of horror of telling us of abuse, we can probably 'feel our fear and do it anyway' (in the words of the helpful book on coping with our fears by Susan Jeffers, 1989) for the sake of children in our care.

The facilitator should also stress that the role play feedback is not in the form of a judgement or critical assessment, but a way of helping each person to recognise their strengths and build on their areas for improvement.

Some warm-up exercise should always be done before this roleplay is attempted.

Timing: 40 – 60 minutes (adjustable)

Role play: in threes, receiving a child's concerns about being abused

Participants A,B,C take the roles of child, adult, and observer.

The facilitator should set the scenario to suit the usual roles of the professionals involved, based on a child fairly reluctantly telling an adult about an abusive experience, either sexual or physical.

The observer should watch for:

- positive non-verbal body language (sitting position, accepting nods of the head)

- use of open rather than closed questions

- use of leading questions, which should be noted down and in the de-briefing, allow the 'adult' role player to re-phrase. These points could be displayed on a Flipchart, or an observer's sheet can be prepared and handed out.

The observer should offer feedback to the 'adult' immediately after the scene, giving specific rather than general comments, both helpful and unhelpful behaviours that were observed.

Each of the three participants should have a try at each role. After all the groups have finished, the group could reconvene, time permitting, for discussion of any difficulties and any positive points to be noted.

REFERENCES

Axline, V. (1964) *Dibs In Search of Self*. London: Penguin.

Bennathan M. and Laslett R. 'Adult victims of child abuse' in Letters to the editor, *Times Educational Supplement* 18/12/92.

Berne, E. (1968) *Games people play*. London: Penguin.

Elliott, M. (1992) *Protecting Children, Training Pack for Frontline Carers*. Kidscape.

Home Office *et al.* (1991) *Working Together Under the Children Act 1989*. London: HMSO.

Jeffers, S. (1989) *Feel the Fear and Do It Anyway*. London: Century.

Kennedy, M. (1992) 'Not the Only Way to Communicate: A Challenge to Voice in Child Protection Work' in *Child Abuse Review*, 1, 3, 169–177.

La Fontaine, J. (1990) *Child Sexual Abuse*. London: Polity Press.

MacKenzie, J. (1992) 'Stevie after the storm' in *Times Educational Supplement*, 19th June.

Malson, L. and Itard, J. (1972) *Wolf Children: the Wild Boy of Aveyron*. London: NLB.

Marchant, R. and Page, M. (1992) 'Bridging the gap: Investigating the Abuse of Children with Multiple Disabilites', *Child Abuse Review*, 1, 3, 179–183.

Neale, P. (1991) 'Men Trapped in a Spiral', *Community Care*, 27th Sept.

Rogers, C. (1951) *Client-Centred Therapy*. Boston: Houghton Mifflin.

Rogers, C. (1961) *On becoming a Person*. Boston: Houghton Mifflin.

Sharpe, R. (1992) 'When mother love can hurt' *The Independent On Sunday*, 29th March.

FURTHER READING

On Counselling

Egan, G. (1976) *The Skilled Helper*. Monteray: Brooks/Cole.

Nelson-Jones. (1991) *The Theory and Practice of Counselling Psychology*. London: Cassell.

On Sexual Abuse

Bass, E and Thornton, L. (1984) *I Never Told Anyone*. London: Harper and Rowe.

Bolton, F. *et al.* (1989) *Males at Risk: the Other Side of Child Sexual Abuse*. London: Sage.

Other

Miller, A. (1987) *For Your Own Good. The Roots of Violence in Child Rearing*. London: Virago.

Stewart, I. and Joines, V. (1987) *T A Today. A New Introduction to Transactional Analysis*. Nottingham and Chapel Hill: Lifespace.

USEFUL ADDRESSES

British Association for Counselling, 37a Sheep St. Rugby, Warwicks. Tel: 0788 7828.

BAPSCAN (British Association for the Study of Child Abuse and Neglect), 10 Priory St, York, YO1 1EZ. Tel:0904 613605. (Journal and conferences).

Brock, Eve., Training Consultant, PO Box 22, Gainsborough, Lincs. DN21 5PP. (Courses designed to suit on various topics, eg: sexuality, bullying, assertiveness, self-esteem, stress.) CareerTrack (UK) Drayton Rd, Newton Longville, Milton Keynes MK17 0DY. Tel: 0908 366544. (One-day seminars; assertiveness, self-esteem, and others)

C.S.C.T. (Central School for Counselling and Therapy), 56B Hale Lane, London. NW73PR. Tel:081 906 4833. Nationwide courses in counselling, approved by the B.A.C. F.P.A. 27–35 Mortimer St London W1N 7 RJ Tel: 071 631 0555E

Family Planning Association, 27–35 Mortimer Street, London. W1N 7RJ. Tel: 071 636 7866; Fax: 071 436 3288.

CHAPTER 9

PROMOTING INTER-PROFESSIONAL UNDERSTANDING AND COLLABORATION

TONY MCFARLANE

INTRODUCTION

Effective inter-professional communication requires related elements of attitude, knowledge and skill. Professional cultures are strong and often foster suspicion and stereotyping of other professions. Moreover, different professional groups have a different place in the child protection system. This may well result in conflicting definitions of the same situation (e.g. construing an episode involving physical punishment as 'correction' rather than 'abuse'). Most of us bring mixed feelings to working with the 'difference' of other disciplines. On one hand we recognise the distinctive expertise and powers of the other profession and their essential place in the partnership; but on the other hand, we are reluctant to accept that this comes with distinctive and sometimes 'awkward' manners and attitudes which can cause us discomfort. Yet the reality of inter-professional working is that difference comes of a piece.

Knowledge of other professions' responsibilities tends to be gathered 'on the move' rather than in a studied way, and is often as a result partial and superficial. Traditional professional development has resulted in the cultivation of high degrees of knowledge within well-defined boundaries. This is reflected throughout organisations, so that supervisory processes are often not very effective in broadening the horizons of practitioners. Hallett and Stevenson at the beginning of the 1980s wrote of 'widespread ignorance about the training, role and perspective of other professions, and linked with this a lack of congruence between the self-perception of particular professionals and the way others perceive them' (Hallett and Stevenson 1980, p.23). More than ten years on, the 'lack of congruence' persists, although there is a wider recognition of its existence, and a greater readiness to address it.

Skills are needed at many levels. Ability to explain role clearly and simply and ability to convey information and opinion orally and on paper in clear, well-organised, unambiguous terms, are two key skills; but there are many others to be developed from this foundation.

This chapter will focus on the understandings and attitudes which professionals bring to working together. This is not to be dismissive of specific skill development for inter-professional communication. The cultivation of such skills, however, depends upon foundations of knowledge deliberately acquired and perceptions which are self-aware. The chapter will look at ways in which staff from different disciplines can begin to develop these foundations. The experience from which the ideas have been drawn has been multi-disciplinary, and includes foundation training for less experienced groups, more specialist training for established professionals, and work with middle managers.

While training has an important part to play in improving professionals' ability to work together it does not provide of itself, 'the answer'. Some of the difficulties experienced are structural – some organisations have, built into their functions, a large investment in child protection; others have a marginal concern (Stevenson 1989, p.189). The move towards more developed understandings and skills will be constantly in tension with influences which run contrary to the achievement of more collaborative work.

ORGANISATIONAL ISSUES

For whom and where does it fit?

Training in relation to working together is relevant to staff at all levels in the child protection system, not just those at a foundation stage. Essentially, most staff at every level in their organisation will not have had the opportunity to step back from daily work, and reflect on how well or badly they work together across professional boundaries.

It is debatable whether it is preferable to establish particular training courses directed specifically at 'improving inter-professional collaboration', or whether it is better to include in each multi-disciplinary course a dimension which specifically addresses these partnership activities. Training directed at the former can appear nebulous while sounding worthy. The latter seems more natural, and enables staff to connect inter-professional work to specific themes of practice. It is difficult, moreover, to separate concerns such as the identification of abuse from collaborative processes.

So, for example, a Foundation Training course, as well as including information in relation to definitions, recognition of abuse, legislative powers and so forth, would include the opportunity to explore roles, responsibilities, expertise, and the relationships which bring these into collaboration. Or a training course on the subject of Emotional Abuse and Failure to Thrive would devote a significant part of its time to understanding the responsibilities, expertise, and dilemmas of each discipline.

Setting up the training

How training is organised and run plays a part in shaping inter-professional relationships. Complex and sophisticated exercises are likely to be less enduring in their impact than the messages given by the organisation and process of the training itself.

The key message of multi-disciplinary child protection training is that while different professions have greater or lesser levels of responsibility, there is collective ownership of the concern. That is the governing principle of inter-agency work, embodied in Area Child Protection Committees (ACPC). Training needs to be organised in a way which models collective ownership. While uni-disciplinary training has an essential part in the range of provision, attempts to provide inter-professional training from a single agency base is likely – however the trainers see it – to give the impression of that agency (inevitably Social Services) from a position of ownership, telling others 'how to do it'. This provides a poor model of working together, suggesting that child protection is a Social Services responsibility, the other professions having a more optional contribution. While staff may leave the training event better informed, for example in the area of recognition of abuse, the critical message of collective ownership is unlikely to have made an impression. For that reason, it is important that the organising source is inter-professional. The most obvious source is the ACPC or a special sub-group. From the outset this gives a very powerful legitimacy to the assertion of collective responsibility. Between the representatives of the different professions in the planning group, the training objectives and content can be negotiated and re-negotiated in the light of changing needs and new knowledge. Compared with the more straightforward way of organising a uni-disciplinary training programme, this will be a time consuming, and perhaps cumbersome process; it also runs the risk of producing a rather shapeless 'something for everyone' approach to training courses, where there are too many disparate elements. To guard against this possibility there is a need for a strong professional training input, so that what is planned represents 'good training' as well as multi-disciplinary perspectives. The hard work of preparation has its pay-off in the setting up and running of the training itself. Pre-course information can reflect the work of joint organisation. As the course runs, trainers can explain how the event has emerged from a process of negotiation. This can be re-emphasised at different stages of the training.

The structures which enable different groups to come together in a training experience are often fragile. Continuing participation often depends upon key individuals within organisations seeing such training as important and actively promoting it. Informal as well as formal contact with these 'fixers', as a way of recognising their value and ensuring their commitment, is an essential task for the trainer. Current organisational changes in health and education services are likely to pose difficulties here, as de-centralisation threatens established channels of access to some professional groups, most notably teachers. As well as the future challenges posed by these developments, there are past and present problems outstanding. Not all professional groups are equally motivated to engage in dialogue with others. The most obvious example is that of General Practitioners. The culture of isolation remarked upon by the Panel of Inquiry into the Death of Jasmine Beckford (Brent Borough Council 1985, p.235), seems no less strong now than in 1985.

GETTING THE MESSAGE RIGHT

Preparation

If the training is being jointly led by two or more staff from different professions, the training partnership should model the collaborative process expected in good child protection work. As with any form of co-work, there is a need for thorough preparation. Beliefs about abuse, family life, sexuality need to be discussed; the trainers each need to know if they can live with their differences. Groundrules for the partnership need to be worked out; trainers from different backgrounds will often have different rules for coping with common eventualities (e.g. absenteeism, disruptive or dissociative attitudes, conflict, distress). Before they start to train they need to arrive at a shared approach to handling these.

In addition, they need to consider the impact each will have on the other in the training process. Who will take responsibility for what, and what does 'responsibility' involve? As they rehearse all these issues, it is important for them to reflect on what they are learning about working with each other. Are they at ease with each other in the partnership; are they 'stuck' on any aspects of working together? Is their non-verbal communication – critical when the partnership is put to the test in training – clear and helpful to each?

If the multi-disciplinary training partnership works well it gives a powerful message to course participants. The training partnership should not be a 'bland front'. If it works well it is because it has had to face and resolve areas of potential conflict. It is useful to share this in an appropriate way with participants.

Introducing the training

Introducing a training course is always an important activity. For all, it is a point of both expectation and vulnerability. Restating the purposes and background, outlining some basics about content and process, establishing who's who, giving practical information, setting some basic ground rules, are all important activities for the trainer or trainers. Through all these, the leaders are giving messages about themselves, about accessibility, sensitivity to needs, and awareness of anxieties. In relation to training for working together there are particular considerations that it might be useful to emphasise. One might be a recognition that some participants may be more knowledgeable than others about child protection, and that this is inevitable, given the different responsibilities that participating agencies have. It is important that those who feel that they 'know nothing' are not disadvantaged. Another ground rule might be about the avoidance of jargon. A third might concern 'listening and explaining'; setting the expectation that the training will provide an opportunity to hear other professional groups describe their work, as well as to explain your own responsibilities and dilemmas. This involves respect for the views of others and in turn a right to be respected and listened to. As well as providing information about content, this sets expectations about the tone of inter-professional discussion within the course. It also provides a point of departure to return to in the event of conflict, or episodes of hectoring or defensiveness, which may surface later when participants feel sufficiently safe to raise awkward questions or voice grievances arising out of earlier experiences with professions represented in the room.

As before, this is establishing a 'modelling process'; in effect setting up an opportunity for and expectation of desirable inter-professional behaviour.

EXERCISES

Introduction

Having an inter-professional group together for learning purposes provides a rich opportunity for participants to learn from each other. There is a place for 'expert' contributions in any training event; particularly in inter-professional training, however, the resources of the group contain immense educative potential. There are some simple exercises which provide a means of using such potential to help develop knowledge of each other's responsibilities and expertise, and which help to reduce the gap between self-perception and the perception of others. An advantage of using the group's resources is that it gives a charge of energy to the exercise as different professional groups prepare among themselves, and present to their fellow participants. Group members sometimes struggle to grasp fully and explain their own responsibilities, but often the results will make an impact greater than the obvious 'expert'. The dialogue in the group can be more free, more direct, and more participative, and make a more lasting mark. There is always a risk of weak presentation, which leaves out crucial preparation and so forth. Course leaders need to be prepared for such an eventuality.

EXERCISE 9.1

Purpose

- To allow participants opportunity to explain their responsibilities and concerns to other professionals and to hear the responsibilities and concerns of others.

> No. of Participants   –   18 maximum
> Time needed   –   2 hours.

Instructions

Participants should divide into professional/agency groups, with a copy of Child Protection Procedures, flip-chart paper, pens. The trainer will ask group to consider three questions, and summarise their responses.

Groups will be given **one question at a time** so that trainers can ensure that groups keep in reasonable step with each other.

QUESTION I

What are the key responsibilities of your agency in relation to child protection? (20 minutes)

Participants should use the time to discuss among themselves and, with the assistance of Procedures, to respond, using the flipchart paper. (The use of the Procedures ensures firstly that staff read them, perhaps for the first time, and that their use provides some reasonable insurance against a group getting it too far wrong.)

In the course of the exercise the trainers are active leaders, visiting groups, clarifying, re-explaining, sometimes reminding a group of a point which they may have over-looked. Smaller groups, or individuals may feel particularly vulnerable and will need more time and reassurance. When groups have completed this part of the exercise they are asked to consider a second question.

QUESTION II

Identify a key difficulty/dilemma/anxiety you have which arises from carrying out this responsibility (10/15 mins)

In response to this question, groups will usually emerge with more than one point. It is important to encourage groups to make choices so that one, or at most two points are made. In this way there is greater force to the points made. Part of the rationale for this question, as well as allowing groups to express a concern, is that there will almost certainly be implications for the work of other agencies represented in the room. Thus, for example, teachers may express a fear of 'losing control' of a situation they refer to a statutory agency. In later discussion, this invites a response from staff in those agencies.

QUESTION III

Identify a way in which another profession (or professions) might help you with your dilemma (10 mins)

This question is designed to prompt thinking about positive responses to difficulties. Following the example given above, teachers would be encouraged to identify actions by Social Services or Police which would address their anxieties about referrals that 'run out of control'.

Presentation

Groups are then asked in turn to present their work to other participants. This needs to be a disciplined activity, involving both explanation and taking questions and so forth from other participants. Ten minutes per group would be a reasonable time, although there is a need for flexibility, since some groups will represent agencies with larger, more complex responsibilities.

Again, in the period of presentation, the trainer has an active role. First, it is important to 'keep the session moving'. Direction can be lost, for example by discussion straying into the general responsibilities of agencies. Some presentations can be overlong and presenters will need to be reminded about being disciplined. Second, it is important to help direct the responses of the other participants, for example posing the question 'How far does the presentation of the social workers correspond with your understanding of their job'? Third, on the rare occasions when presentations are weak or inaccurate, the trainer may have to add or correct information.

Comment

There are a number of points to be made about the outcomes of this exercise.

1. It generates a considerable volume of information about responsibilities and constraints previously unappreciated by participants from other agencies.

2. It helps to reduce fears; it also gives workers insight into the dilemmas of others. In this way, it influences perceptions of other agencies.

3. As well as generating sympathy, it is likely, where there are undercurrents of suspicion or antipathy, to provide a climate where these are expressed. It is an occasion for 'uncorrected experiences' to come home to roost. The dynamics in the room will reflect at least in part some of the dynamics of local inter-professional relations. It is important that conflict is allowed air, and that some time is available to allow exploration of the source of hostility. Two points are worth remembering. First, it may be useful to recall participants' attention to the practice of listening and explaining and the principle of respect implied therein. Second, a useful way of 'moving on' from conflict to possibility is again to pose Question III to an individual or a group in another form such as 'Can you identify one thing which would help you with the difficulty you have experienced'?

4. Unlike using experienced staff, chosen by the trainer both for their quality of practice and ability to present, in this exercise the trainer has, even with the active role identified above, given a large measure of control to the group. A poor presentation by an agency participant (which for example describes the use of power in an insensitive way) may influence others' perceptions of the agency, perhaps reinforcing a stereotype. This risk is

present in the exercise. In my own experience this is off-set by the potential of the learning process, whereby groups educate each other, and in doing so establish a sense of community in the room.

EXERCISE 9.2

Exercise 9.1 tackles the issue of inter-professional and inter-agency understanding through the clarification of function. There are, of course, other ways of understanding the different contributions of professionals and their relationship to each other. Exercise 9.2 is designed so that course participants approach the area via examination of the kinds of information and expertise needed in order to determine risk, and assess protection needs.

Purpose

- To promote understanding of the range of information required in order to assess protection needs, and identify the different possible sources of this.
- To demonstrate the inter-dependence of different areas of information in carrying out this task.

No. of Participants	–	18 maximum
Time needed	–	1.25 – 1.5 hours approx.

Instructions

Provide participants with a brief case study outlining some presenting concerns. Below is an example of a case study in relation to suspected physical abuse and neglect.

Andrew is four. He attends nursery class in infant school. In the three months that he has been there his teachers have been concerned about a number of things. On several occasions he has appeared hungry in the mornings; this, it has been established, is because he has had no breakfast.

His hygiene is poor. He wets himself a lot and his clothes go mostly unwashed. On a number of occasions, staff have spotted bruises on his legs and forearms; these seem accidental, such as any child might have. On one occasion a teacher spotted what might have been grip-marks on his upper arm. Today a member of staff notices two sets of red 'loop' marks on his lower legs. In reply to a question, he says that his father hit him because he had wet himself. Andrew has a younger brother James aged 2 years and 6 months.

Group members staying in the large group are asked to identify the different kinds of information needed in order to establish the nature of the harm being suffered by the child/children. (Time 20 minutes approx.)

This will generate a lengthy list of different kinds of information needed (e.g. about the injury, the explanation, the children's growth pattern) which should be written down on a flip-chart by the trainer. It is possible that the spontaneous responses of participants will omit certain important areas, and the trainer will have to give direction on these.

When the information has been fully listed, it will require some sifting and reorganising by the trainer in order to 'group' the material into manageable headings (e.g. marital/family dynamics, children's level of development, history of injuries).

When the 'grouping' has been completed, it would be useful for the trainer to provide the participants with a visual representation of the summarised areas of information. A 'jigsaw' motif is the most powerful because it so graphically illustrates inter-dependence in child protection work. This is difficult technically to produce quickly within a training exercise, so a segmented circle will suffice. The information which has been organised and given visual representation provides the trainer with significant teaching opportunities to underline the importance of putting the pieces alongside each other. One point which might be well made here is that relatively minor physical injuries do not equate with lesser harm, and that the true significance of such injuries can only be understood in the context of a wider process of information gathering.

This brief teaching episode might take 15/20 minutes. On the basis of the visual representation, participants are asked to identify the different possible sources of information needed. In order to achieve this, the trainer might divide the task between a number of small groups each given different areas on which to work. (Time 15 minutes approx.)

The group will report back, the trainer writing into the relevant segments, the sources identified. Again, depending on the level of experience, there may well be gaps in knowledge, where the trainer will have to prompt or 'fill in'. A very important feature of this part of the exercise is that in most segments, there will be more than one profession/agency identified, so that while different pieces of information may interlock, like the 'jigsaw', the work of different agencies and disciplines will continually overlap. For example in the area of 'parent/child attachment', there will almost certainly be a number of different possible sources identified, for example play-group leader, teacher, health visitor.

Comment

1. Akin to Exercise 9.1, this example helps to broaden and deepen participants' knowledge of the sources of information and expertise which are vital to 'building the picture' in child protection work.

2. As well as encouraging participants to use their own resources, it provides good teaching opportunities for the trainer. Using the metaphor of the 'jigsaw', for example, helps to advance understanding of inter-dependence because of the clarity it offers. We know, however, that piecing together information in child protection work is not nearly so detached and clear-cut a process. Depending on the level of the group, the trainer may wish to explore the impediments to good accurate 'picture-building'.

UNCORRECTED EXPERIENCES

One of the features of professional life is that agencies and disciplines are constantly working on each other's boundaries without really having or taking opportunity to examine how they are working together. Structured opportunities to examine how such unacknowledged partnerships work are rare. We often meet each other in crises, when 'things are going wrong'; in other words at exactly the point when the possibilities of misunderstanding and mistrust are at their height. We rarely have time to recognise what we are doing well together and what we appreciate about other's contribution, or express dissatisfaction when we believe an assumed partner has acted in an unhelpful way. Negative experiences in this mode of working remain in the consciousness and inform the next encounter.

Inevitably, professionals bring such experiences to training. Many participants will have had such experiences, or been influenced by colleagues' stories. It is important to hear these and to acknowledge that they are part of the reality of inter-professional life. Common statements, drawn from a range of localities and professions are:

- I don't hear back. I have never heard.

- Being identified as a source of information made me feel very vulnerable.

- I know the child better than anyone but no-one bothered to ask.

- It was taken right out of my hands.

- Some professions don't want to take responsibility for the information they pass on.

- Some groups hold on to information too long.

In those training events where there is a major focus on inter-professional understanding (e.g. in Foundation Training courses), it is important that space is given to airing experiences both positive and negative. Opportunities may arise out of the kind of exercises outlined above. Equally, the trainer might consider devoting a specific session to group members' experiences of working together. A number of points need to be borne in mind, in planning such an exercise:

- It should be scheduled for a place in the course when participants will feel sufficiently safe to be frank and undefensive.

- It is useful to have some additional ground rules (e.g. participants do not have to answer for their agency/profession, though they may be able to offer some information or clarification, which might set the experience in context. This frees participants to listen to critical comment).

- The trainer's introduction is important in setting the tone of the discussion. It is useful, for example, to refer to the likely range of experience that participants will have had, in a matter-of-fact way, and the usefulness of using those experiences to learn about what helps or hinders good interprofessional working.

- It is important to have good leadership (e.g. being able to encourage balance, use the ground rules to discourage aggression/defensiveness, being able to contain the occasional professional malcontent).

- It is useful to have a fixed-time session, and a concluding phase which offers participants some positive directions (e.g. brainstorming a list of behavioural 'do's and don'ts for good inter-professional working).

My own experience is that participants welcome frank exchange, even if this involves some discomfort. It is important for those with a negative experience that they are heard. It may be that some information provided by other participants or the course leader will put the experience in a context which helps the aggrieved professional make fuller sense of what happened; or it may be that other professionals listen, recognise the grievance, and identify what in their own practice needs to change to meet the concern.

CONCLUSION

The trainer is in the privileged position of hearing in a way in which few others do, about the fears and uncertainties involved in inter-professional working. That, in turn, places responsibilities with the trainer to ensure that managers and policy makers are aware of where the distances are greatest, or the tensions more acute. Trainers, as well as having their defined responsibilities, are also players in the system, and need to recognise their place in developing its more effective operation.

REFERENCES

Brent Borough Council (1985) *A Child in Trust*. London: London Borough of Brent.

Hallett, C. and Stevenson, O. (1980) *Child Abuse: Aspects of Inter-Professional Co-Operation*. London: George Allen and Unwin.

Stevenson, O. (1989) 'Multi-Disciplinary Work' in O. Stevenson (ed) *Child Abuse: Professional Practice and Public Policy*. London: Harvestor Wheatsheaf.

CHAPTER 10

DEVELOPING SKILLS IN CONTRIBUTING AT CHILD PROTECTION CONFERENCES

HILARY OWEN AND LINDSEY SAVAGE

This chapter clarifies the function of each of the different types of meeting professionals may hold in the process of protecting children, and indicates which are governed directly by government guidance. It offers straightforward advice on how professionals from all agencies can improve the way they make their contributions at child protection conferences. Finally, it looks in detail at the one decision initial child protection conferences are required to make: whether the child's name should be referred to the local Child Protection Register. Exercises are included which are designed to allow professionals to practise making judgments about registration.

Professionals involved with families have many different types of meetings about their clients. They may attend statutory reviews of children who are looked after by a local authority; they may attend case discussions convened by education social work staff or by teaching staff to discuss a child's progress at school; they may attend case discussions about babies born with health problems who are about to leave hospital to go home for the first time. Many professionals attend so many different types of meetings that it is easy for them to become confused about the status and purpose of them. Since 1988, however, with the publication of the first *Working Together* document, child protection responsibilities have, thankfully, been much more clearly defined. For the first time, for example, it was clearly indicated that it should only ever be the social services department or the NSPCC which convenes a child protection conference. Usage of the specific term 'child protection conference' was not introduced until 1991, with the publication of the document *Working Together Under the Children Act 1989:* until then, the non-specific 'case conference' was used.

However, the situation is not completely clarified by this as, within the child protection process itself, several different types of meeting are possible. It is helpful to think of the child protection process in chronological terms in order to see what distinct purposes these meetings have and how they assist in protecting a child. In doing this, professionals in all agencies with responsibilities towards children can see clearly where their particular contributions will fit in. This is the first step in learning to contribute well.

DIFFERENT TYPES OF MEETING IN THE CHILD PROTECTION PROCESS

1. Strategy meetings

The first meeting professionals may have following an allegation or suspicion of child abuse is a 'strategy' meeting. This sort of meeting has a very specific and practical purpose: to plan the details of a joint investigation by social workers and police officers so that all action is co-ordinated and no-one is replicating the same task. This is particularly important when an allegation of sexual abuse is being investigated because repeated medical examinations and interviewing of the child should be avoided to minimise further distress. It may be that professionals who are in possession of important information about the suspected abuse will be invited to attend, in addition to social work and police staff. Parents and children are not invited to attend strategy meetings, indeed, are not even told about them taking place as, in some cases, it is possible that evidence vital to a criminal prosecution may be destroyed by the perpetrator should he or she find out about the planned investigation. For example, in a case of sexual abuse, the child may describe the adult ejaculating onto a particular item of clothing and the police may find the item in time and send it away for forensic testing to establish the presence of semen. It is essential that details of a child's statement like these remain open to verification, and that perpetrators are not alerted and items destroyed. In addition, it is most important that a child who is being abused is not intimidated by the abuser into remaining silent before the full extent of the abuse is known.

Not all allegations of abuse will be followed by a stategy meeting, as many straightforward investigations may be planned satisfactorily over the telephone. However, where the situation appears complex or unusual, for example where there appears to be a high level of risk to the child, or where there are many individuals to be interviewed, either suspected perpetrators or suspected victims, a meeting may well be more appropriate. Situations where strategy meetings are likely to be called are, for example, where foster parents or residential social workers appear to have abused children in their care, or where an unusual type of abuse is involved, like Munchausen Syndrome by proxy.

2. Initial or 'incident' child protection conferences

The next meeting which is likely to be held in the protection process is the initial child protection conference. For the first time, specific guidance is given, in *Working Together Under the Children Act*, about the timescale to which agencies must work:

> The time between referral and the initial child protection conference will vary according to the needs of each individual case. The pace should not slacken once the protection of the child is ensured but sufficient time should be taken so that the conference does not result in premature or disorganised action. Initial conferences should take place within eight working days of referral unless there are special reasons why information from the investigation which will lead to a better

decision is not available. Normally a maximum of 15 days should be set. If court action is underway the timing of the conference will be determined by the Court Rules. (Home Office *et al.* 1991 p.31)

These conferences are really the key to the whole child protection process in as much as it is on the basis of the information presented at these conferences that the major decisions are made about the child's immediate future. It is at these meetings that, for the first time, all the information known about a child and her/his family, the allegation of abuse, and the subsequent medical, police and social work investigations will be available to all the professionals involved. It is hoped that significant questions about the nature of the abuse the child has experienced, how it was caused, what the parents think about the harm that was done and how safe it will be to return the child home will be answered by the information available at this meeting. It is not a surprise, therefore, that for many years, some organisations (for example, the Family Rights Group and Parents Against Injustice) have argued that parents should be allowed to attend these conferences and, indeed, *Working Together Under the Children Act* asserts for the first time that parents and children will be allowed to attend them.

The only decision that an initial conference can make as a body (as opposed to recommendations to its constituent agencies) is whether or not to place the child's name and the names of her/his brothers and sisters on the local Child Protection Register. The CPR is a register of all those children in the area who have been abused, who have been harmed and abuse it thought to be the likely cause, or who are deemed likely to be abused; and for whom there are current concerns about abuse which have not yet been resolved. If, therefore, the meeting you attend does not consider whether a child's name is to be placed on the CPR, then it is not an initial child protection conference.

There may well, during the time that a child's name is on the CPR, be cause to convene further 'incident' child protection conferences if the child is injured again or there are grounds to suspect that the child is being subjected to risk of a kind not identified previously.

3. Core group meetings

Whilst an initial child protection conference may only make the one decision, if it decides that a child's name should be placed on the CPR, it is then required by *Working Together Under the Children Act* to formulate a child protection plan (for further discussion, see Chapter 12). This plan, simply, is the action which the conference feels the agencies directly involved with the family need to take in order to ensure the child's continued protection and wellbeing. Those workers carrying out this work are known as the 'core group', and it may well be that this group needs to meet to discuss particular issues of immediate concern to one or more of its members which arise in the course of their work with a family – issues which are not so significant that they necessitate a more formal response.

For example, the child protection conference may make broad recommendations about contact arrangements between a child and members of her/his family. The social worker named as the child's keyworker may then wish to meet residential social workers and school staff to work out the fine details of those arrangements: who should supervise the contact, if supervision is necessary; where the contact should take place; what time it should take place; who will prepare the child for the contact and ensure that all is well with her/him after the contact; whether family members should be given assistance with transport and who should provide it; whether a meal will be available for the family to eat together.

In general, a core group may meet on a regular basis to exchange information about a family's progress and ensure that all is well with the child. In the first few months of registration, the work of the core group may be intensive because of the necessity to carry out a comprehensive assessment (see Chapter 12) and therefore they may meet frequently. Core group meetings themselves have no defined role in the child protection structure developed by the government, although the work of a core group will always be governed by government guidance, local Area Child Protection Committee procedures and in certain cases by court orders.

4. Child protection reviews

The final type of meeting, thinking in chronological terms, which takes place in the child protection process, is the child protection review. *Working Together Under the Children Act* indicates that these should take place at least every six months, and their purpose is stated very clearly:

> The purpose is to review the arrangements for the protection of the child, examine the current level of risk and ensure that he or she continues to be adequately protected, consider whether the interagency co-ordination is functioning effectively and to review the protection plan. Every child protection review should consider whether registration should be continued or ended. (Home Office *et al.* 1991 p.42)

Child protection reviews should bring to light any failures by involved agencies to carry out action recommended to them as part of a child's protection plan. It is only at these meetings that a decision can be made to remove a child's name from the CPR.

It is essential that this clarity of purpose is kept firmly in mind as far as this type of meeting is concerned because, where the child involved is also being looked after by the local authority, *Working Together Under the Children Act* indicates that it is acceptable to combine the child protection review with the statutory review of the child's progress whilst away from home. Obviously, combining the two meetings like this is very convenient for all participants, and no doubt the issues to be considered by one will inform the other. However, care needs to be taken that all the proper tasks of both types of forum are fully addressed: the different functions of each cannot be elided.

Like the initial child protection conference, parents and children should be invited to attend this type of meeting.

CONTRIBUTING AT INITIAL CHILD PROTECTION CONFERENCES

Having clarified the purposes of the different types of meeting held in the process of protecting a child, it is most helpful to concentrate on the initial child protection conference when attempting to develop skills in contributing, because it is at these meetings where by far the most demands will be made on the professionals involved in a case, and where they will undoubtedly feel the most anxiety. Whilst acknowledging that, in these days of curtailed public spending, many professionals feel they are too busy to spend much time planning ahead, responding instead to one urgent need after another, it has to be said that the key to contributing effectively at child protection conferences is preparation: child protection work is far too complex these days for anyone to do without it. In addition, the presence of parents and children is a sharp challenge to poor practice. Most of the professionals attending an initial conference have to address themselves to three separate tasks in contributing:

1. giving information to the conference, both from personal knowledge and from agency records;
2. developing an opinion on whether or not the child should be registered;
3. thinking about whether they should be contributing to a child protection plan and, if so, how best to do it.

Formulating a child protection plan and monitoring its continued effectiveness should be regarded as the most important task agencies undertake in child protection work. In some cases, it will mean making difficult decisions which are distressing for the professionals to implement, and which will involve parents in hard, challenging work which questions some of the most intimate areas of their lives. This central task of child protection work is addressed fully in Chapter 12. In the present chapter we shall therefore concentrate on the first two of these tasks.

Whilst proper preparation results in a better standard of work, it also means that a great deal of anxiety is taken out of the situation. As Hallett and Stevenson (1980) found in their research on conferences:

> The uncertainty of those who are not familiar with the procedures, as one respondent who was not sure whether to place a child on the at risk register meant his removal from home and another similarly unsure about the consequences of a place of safety order, added to the anxiety and doubt about playing a part in conference decisions. (p.75)

The first step which any professional attending an initial child protection conference should take in preparation is to ensure s/he knows what the agenda is. It can normally be expected to proceed as follows:

- A chronological account of how the abuse or concern about likely abuse came to light and was investigated, given by those personnel directly involved

- The sharing of other relevant information about each member of the family

- Discussion leading to a decision about whether or not the child and her/his siblings should be registered, based on local Area Child Protection Committee criteria for registration
- Formulation of a child protection plan, including any necessary legal action.

In addition, professionals should assume that parents and children (if they are of sufficient age and understanding) will be attending for most of the conference, in accordance with local Area Child Protection Committee procedures. Precise details of how family members will contribute at the conference should be available from the person who is to chair the conference or from the social worker involved in the investigation. It should, however, be born in mind that some children's situations are so complex, involving several adults with parental-type relationships with them, all of whom may have to be contacted about the conference and their views sought, that it may not be until, perhaps, the day before the conference is to take place that details of their involvement will be available.

Knowing how the conference is to be run will enable each professional to judge at what points her/his contribution will be required and, in turn, knowing this means s/he need not be anxious about making sure her/his views are heard: 'butting in' with snippets of information when someone else is speaking is unhelpful and confusing for other participants, not least the minute-taker.

Giving information to the conference

It is extremely important that basic information about a family is accurate, for many different reasons, the most obvious of which is that it is irritating and offensive to family members if it is wrong: it implies a lack of care on the part of agencies who may later ask those family members to trust them with their most private feelings. It is also important that individual professionals do not assume that everyone at the conference has the same level of knowledge about family members as themselves. It is a good idea, therefore, for professionals to check their records against colleagues' for correct spellings and pronunciations of names, correct dates of birth, and correct family relationships before the conference.

Where the family relationships appear complex and there is a need for all conference members to understand them, then social workers or any other professional with detailed information about this, such as a health visitor, might prepare a family tree for distribution at the beginning of the conference. In any event, Chairs of conferences can assist by ensuring that all family members who are significant in the situation are named and their relationships to each other clarified.

The way information is given needs to be well thought-out, and it is often helpful to write out beforehand which points you feel you must mention. Other participants need to be left with a clear idea of your involvement. For example when the child involved is too young to speak and cannot give an account of how s/he sustained an injury, parents may well take advantage of this and offer several different, but unfeasible, explanations to professionals and other family members whilst the investigation is in progress. Which explanation was offered, to whom, and when, may be extremely relevant in making a judgment about how parents regard what has happened, and how safe it will be to return the child home. It is, therefore, extremely unhelpful to present events without the dates and times that they occurred.

It is important, so as to avoid misleading participants and distressing parents, that any medical details are checked carefully before being presented: weights, heights, measurements of areas of bruising or lesion, number and location of fractures must all be correct, and you must ensure that other participants are made fully aware of any conclusions which need to be drawn from them.

When it comes to presenting information about your previous knowledge of the family, it is helpful to have made a note of information already presented at the conference so that you do not simply repeat it and waste time. Finally, it is helpful to participants and minute-taker if you speak slowly, clearly and loudly enough, even if the information you are giving causes embarrassment or is upsetting. Technical information may be particularly difficult for others to understand, and the minute-taker is going to have to record it, correctly spelt, in the minutes.

Deciding whether or not to register a child

Child Protection Registers in different areas of the country operate in different ways and, before attending a child protection conference, it will be helpful to you to read about the one in your area in your local Area Child Protection Committee's procedure manual so that you know how, in practice, it assists in protecting children. The minimum that a CPR does is prescribed by *Working Together Under the Children Act,* which states:

> The purpose of the register is to provide a record of all children in the area for whom there are unresolved child protection issues and who are currently the subject of an inter-agency protection plan and to ensure that the plans are formally reviewed every six months. The register will provide a central point of speedy enquiry for professional staff who are worried about a child and want to know whether the child is the subject of an inter-agency protection plan. (Home Office *et al.* 1991 p.48)

This means, for example, that a junior doctor at the accident and emergency department of a hospital, on seeing a suspicious injury to a child, will check the CPR. If s/he discovers the child to be registered, s/he will exercise much more caution in the action s/he takes, requesting that the senior doctor available examine the child. The examination the child receives will be much more thorough, checking that there are no additional injuries. The CPR is particularly helpful where parents present a child they have abused at different hospitals in an effort to avoid detection.

The reqirements which need to be fulfilled before a child can be referred to a CPR, again, differ slightly from area to area, but are based closely on the Department of Health's definitions of child abuse, which are:

Neglect:

> The persistent or severe neglect of a child, or the failure to protect a child from exposure to any kind of danger, including cold or starvation, or extreme failure to carry out important aspects of care, resulting in the significant impairment of the child's health or development, including non-organic failure to thrive.

Physical Injury:

> Actual or likely physical injury to a child, or failure to prevent physical injury (or suffering) to a child including deliberate poisoning, suffocation and Munchausen's syndrome by proxy.

Sexual Abuse:

> Actual or likely sexual exploitation of a child or adolescent. The child may be dependent and/or developmentally immature.

Emotional Abuse:

> Actual or likely severe adverse effect on the emotional and behavioural development of a child caused by persistent or severe emotional ill-treatment.

(Home Office *et al.* 1991 pp.48–49)

Once the conference has established that one or more of these categories of abuse apply to a child, then a judgment has to be made about whether harm, or further harm, is likely in the future, and therefore whether the child is in need of a protection plan. This judgment can be made either on the basis of the findings of the investigation, or on the basis of research evidence. Judgments about registration are often difficult for professionals to make.

Parents who attend conferences are at liberty to express their views about registration and, where they have strong objections to it, perhaps on the grounds that it 'labels' them formally as child abusers, professionals may find it even more difficult to make a proper judgment. In this respect, it is salutary to bear in mind the research carried out by Dingwall *et al.* described by Morrison *et al.* in the NSPCC's Occasional Paper No. 8 (1990):

> ... powerful evidence about the tendency for all professionals to operate a rule of optimism in favour of parents comes from Dingwall *et al.*'s extensive research. They concluded, 'In all cases the workers preferred the least stigmatising interpretation of the child's condition and the least coercive form of intervention possible.' (Dingwall, Murray and Eekelaar, 1983 p.21)

Whilst *Working Together Under the Children Act* indicates that Chairs of child protection conferences should seek parents' views about registration, this guidance is equally clear that the decision lies only with the professionals at the conference. It must always be dangerous practice to allow considerations other than the child's welfare to influence this decision. It may be helpful to professionals to consider that a decision to register a child, made properly, may assist that child in making a successful claim for Criminal Injuries

Compensation in the absence of a criminal conviction, where the abuse is serious enough. This may be particularly important in cases of sexual abuse, where it has been notoriously difficult to obtain convictions (see Chapter 13).

Given the difficulty of making this decision, and the anxiety all professionals feel about expressing their opinions about it in conferences, the following exercises have been designed to allow professionals to practise this decision-making process and become familiar with the factors which often influence it. Participating in these exercises, through private study, in single agency discussion groups or, most usefully, in multidisciplinary groups, will help professionals to make better judgments with less attendant anxiety.

EXERCISES

It is essential that professionals participating in these exercises have to hand a copy of their local Area Child Protection Committee procedures manual detailing how, in their area, children may be referred to the Child Protection Register. Where the exercises are done through group discussion, individual participants will need their own copies of the exercises to read through and think about before the discussion begins. It will be helpful to appoint a Chair as a consensus must be achieved: disagreement must therefore be talked through in detail, and the reasons for it fully explained.

EXERCISE 10.1

Samantha Wood is two months old. Four days ago, her mother and maternal grandmother brought her to the Accident and Emergency Department of the hospital, saying they were worried about bruising on the side of her head. On preliminary examination, the Senior Registrar became immediately concerned because the area felt 'boggy' and was suggestive of an underlying fracture. She asked Samantha's mother, Mrs Wood, how the injury had occurred. Mrs Wood said she did not really know how it had happened, and she had not noticed it until her own mother, Mrs Butler, had pointed it out to her that morning and said they had better take her to the hospital.

The Senior Registrar referred Samantha immediately to the Consultant Paediatrician on duty, Dr Thompson. Samantha was admitted to the children's ward and Dr Thompson arranged for her to have X-rays of her whole body, after examining her thoroughly. When the results were ready, they showed that Samantha had an unusually large skull fracture. She had no further injuries. Dr Thompson at that stage explained the seriousness of the injury to Mrs Wood and Mrs Butler and asked if it was really the case that neither of them knew how it had occurred. Mrs Wood said she recalled Samantha rolling off the settee onto the living room carpet two days previously when she herself had been the only adult in the house and she had gone into the kitchen for a moment to make herself a cup of coffee. Dr Thompson explained that it was not possible for a young baby to cause that much damage to herself, even by falling onto the floor. She said it would have taken a very hard blow indeed to cause the injury and Samantha would have been extremely distressed and crying for some time afterwards. It was not at all likely that the injury was accidental. She indicated to Mrs Wood and Mrs Butler that she would have to contact the social services department and the police to look into the matter further.

Every member of Samantha's immediate family was interviewed by either the social worker or the police officer, or both. The only other explanation offered for the injury in the course of the investigation was from Samantha's father, Mr Wood, who suggested that Samantha might have banged her head on the bars of her cot as she moves about so much when she is asleep.

The social worker reports that both parents appear very caring towards Samantha. Mrs Wood has stayed with her in hospital and Mr Wood has visited every day. They have been interviewed separately and both refuse to countenance the assertion from Dr Thompson that the injury is non-accidental.

The health visitor reports at the incident child protection conference that Samantha has been developing more than satisfactorily, and has always been clean and beautifully dressed whenever she has seen her.

The police indicate at the conference that they have insufficient information to think about a prosecution.

ISSUES FOR DISCUSSION:

1. Are there grounds to refer Samantha to your Child Protection Register?
2. If there are grounds, under what category of abuse would the referral be made?
3. Would the referral be made because of actual or likely harm?
4. Should Samantha be referred?
5. If Samantha is not to be registered, is an alternative course of action necessary?

EXERCISE 10.2

Martin Holmes is 12 years old and he lives in a children's home. Last week, he told his class teacher, Mr Ash, that his keyworker at the children's home, Ken, has twice grabbed him by the genitals when play-fighting. He said he did not mind, because 'boys will be boys' after all, and he does get on with him very well. However, he asked whether Mr Ash thought it was okay for this to happen. Mr Ash said that he thought it was wrong for Ken to do this, that he was taking advantage of their good relationship.

Mr Ash contacted Martin's field social worker and Martin was interviewed on video at the police Special Investigations Unit about what had happened. He confirmed that both incidents had happened at bed time when he had just got into his pyjamas. Ken has been suspended whilst the joint investigation takes place and Martin is extremely unhappy about this. Martin was not examined by a doctor, as he was sure he had not been hurt. When Ken was interviewed by the police, he denied knowing anything about it.

The police have submitted a file to the Crown Prosecution Service who have not yet decided what to do, as there were no witnesses to what happened. The social services department manager responsible for making a decision about whether or not disciplinary action should proceed against Ken is waiting to hear the decisions and recommendations of the incident conference before taking any further action. The field social worker, the police officer and Mr Ash all believe that what Martin said was true, as he has been consistent throughout, despite being upset at Ken's suspension and the fact that Ken now appears to be calling him a liar.

ISSUES FOR DISCUSSION

1. Are there grounds to place Martin's name on the Child Protection Register?
2. If there are grounds, under what category of abuse would the referral be made?
3. Would the referral be made because of actual or likely harm?
4. Should Martin be registered?
5. If Martin is not to be registered, is an alternative course of action necessary?

EXERCISE 10.3

Staff at Elm House school have requested a child protection conference in respect of 6-year-old John Carter. John recently came into school with a badly cut hand, saying he was opening a tin of beans when it slipped. His mother was persuaded to take him to the hospital for a tetanus injection. He did not need stitches.

John's behaviour at school has been causing concern for some time. He seeks attention from the teacher all the time by being very noisy, swearing, running around the classroom, and spoiling other children's work. Last week, he hit another child in the face with a large book, causing a bruised eye and a nosebleed. Whilst he is physically healthy, he soils himself regularly and the other children avoid him and reject him.

There has been a social worker involved for some time, who reports that the boy's stepfather is very controlling and punitive with him, locking him in his room for hours on end, depriving him of toys for days at a time when he thinks he has been particularly naughty, and not allowing him to have the light on at night: he has taken out the lightbulb in his room, saying he only gets into mischief if he can see.

It was John's birthday recently, and his parents bought him a new coat, saying he could wear it when he had managed to be good for a whole week: so far he has not managed it. He did not receive any other presents. The Education Department has just referred him to a special school for children with behavioural problems, and this school provides psychiatric and psychological assessment.

ISSUES FOR DISCUSSION

1. Are there grounds to place John's name on your Child Protection Register?
2. If there are grounds, under what category of abuse should the referral be made?
3. Would the referral be made because of actual or likely harm?
4. Should John be registered?
5. If John is not registered, is an alternative course of action necessary?

EXERCISE 10.4

Eighteen months ago Tracy Goldman, at that time only 5 weeks old, sustained bruising to her face. She had 2 fingertip bruises to her left cheek and one to her right cheek, and in addition had bruising and petechiae on and behind both ears. She also had a bruise in the centre of her forehead. Her parents always denied knowing how these injuries had occurred, but the investigation established that only they had had care of Tracy over the time the consultant paediatrician thought the bruising had occurred. Tracy was registered, care proceedings were instituted and a supervision order was obtained. This order has now lapsed. Tracy's parents, Ann Green and Terry Goldman, were prosecuted for the injuries but were found not guilty at the trial.

Ms Green and Mr Goldman had their second child, Emma, last week, and they were outraged when the social worker told them that a child protection conference needs to consider whether to place their new baby's name on the Child Protection Register along with Tracy's. They say that Tracy has thrived in their care, they have co-operated with the social worker by allowing her into their home, and now they want to be allowed a new start, free of Tracy's supervision order. At the conference, the health visitor confirms that there have been no further concerns about Tracy; however, she is worried that young babies may be at risk in the household. The social worker indicates that, in all the time she has been working with Ms Green and Mr Goldman, they have never been able to accept that Tracy had been assaulted, maintaining that her injuries were accidental. Mr Goldman says at the conference that he and his partner will simply refuse to let the social worker in if their new baby is registered.

ISSUES FOR DISCUSSION

1. Are there grounds to refer Emma's name to your Child Protection Register?
2. If there are grounds, under what category of abuse should the referral be made?
3. Would the referral be made because of actual or likely harm?
4. Should Emma's name be referred to your Child Protection Register?
5. Should Tracy's name be removed from the Register?

REFERENCES

Hallett, C. and Stevenson, O. (1980) *Child Abuse: Aspects of Interprofessional Co-Operation*. London: George Allen and Unwin.

Morrison, A., Blakey, C., Butler, A., Fallan, S. and Leith, A. (1990) *Child and Parental Participation in Case Conferences*. NSPCC Occasional Paper Number 8.

Home Office, Department of Health, Department of Education and Science, Welsh Office (1991) *Working Together Under the Children Act 1989*. London: HMSO.

CHAPTER 11

CHILD PROTECTION CONFERENCES
MAXIMISING THEIR POTENTIAL

MARIAN CHARLES

Child protection conferences play a crucial role within the framework of a co-ordinated multidisciplinary approach to the protection of children. In common with other parts of the child protection process, conferences face the characteristic difficulties inherent in interagency work, such as inadequate communication or role confusion. Although these problems in multidisciplinary working and co-operation are well recognised, surprisingly little attention has been focused upon the effectiveness of conferences in protecting children. Much of the available literature offers descriptive (Jones *et al.* 1987; Stainton Rogers *et al.* 1992) rather than analytical information about conferences and, although now over twelve years old, the work of Hallett and Stevenson (1980) continues to be the most extensive and substantial text about the background, purposes and processes of conferences. Yet, in order to make effective contributions, participants need a thorough grasp and understanding of the purposes, functions and special characteristics of conferences and how these impact upon its members. Whilst it is impossible to explore all aspects of child protection conferences in a single chapter, I will briefly consider each of the above areas in turn and offer some suggestions as to how individual participants might ensure that the potential of their contributions is maximised. The contents are based on the author's experiences as a conference participant, conference observer and as a trainer with multidisciplinary groups of actual or potential conference attenders. Emphasis will be given to initial conferences, usually arranged following an allegation and subsequent investigation of abuse, in the belief that these early conferences frequently set the pattern for later conference behaviour.

WHY HOLD CONFERENCES?

Working Together Under the Children Act 1989: a guide to arrangements for inter-agency co-operation for the protection of children from abuse (Home Office *et al.* 1991) states that:

The initial child protection conference brings together family members and professionals from the agencies which are concerned with child care and child protection to share and evaluate the information gathered during the investigation, to make decisions about the level of risk to the child(ren), to decide on the need for registration and to make plans for the future. If a decision to register is made, it will be necessary to appoint a named keyworker and make recommendations for a core group of professionals to carry out the inter-agency work. (p.42)

This would suggest that the purposes of child protection conferences fall into four broad areas: sharing information, assessing the level of risk, deciding on registration and co-ordinating future intervention.

Sharing the information available to the individual disciplines and participants about family members is an important conference task, encompassing an examination of any existing concerns about the family as well as their strengths. Any gaps in the current information need to be identified alongside an analysis of any precipitating factors leading to the allegation/incident of abuse. Detailed information about men in abusive situations is often lacking: perusal of the statistics of Social Services Departments, for instance, will show that social work is an activity chiefly undertaken by women with other women. This lack or low level of contact with men, many of whom will be perpetrators, frequently requires acknowledgement when building a picture of the family.

Assessing the risk of further or continuing abuse to the child(ren) is obviously a key task facing the conference, and may encompass consideration of any legal action necessary to protect the child(ren). Once the conference has discussed the above, then a decision is made as to whether or not a child(ren)'s name(s) should be placed on the Child Protection Register. This is the only decision-making function of child protection conferences. If this happens, a keyworker for the family – a social worker from either of the two agencies holding statutory powers, the NSPCC or the Social Services Department – will be appointed. The keyworker is responsible for co-ordinating future work, thus avoiding different people visiting with different approaches and purposes and adding to the stress within the family. This intervention will be discussed at the conference, with recommendations for the multidisciplinary plan for the protection of the child being outlined. Individual agencies can only be advised as to their future involvement, as the conference has no power to compel agencies to co-operate with the protection plan. In reality, it is unusual for conference recommendations to be totally ignored.

Although the current government guidance indicates that the purposes of child protection conferences fall into the categories described briefly above, Hallett and Stevenson (1980) propose an additional purpose, namely the sharing of anxiety: 'So far as conference purpose is concerned, it should be said that the conference may, quite properly, increase or decrease anxiety as information is pooled.' (p.78) They argue that the feelings generated by abusive situations and evidenced in conferences must be acknowledged if professionals are to function effectively without constantly feeling overwhelmed.

On paper, the reasons for holding child protection conferences would seem to be fairly straightforward and clear cut, yet practice demonstrates that conferences are often far from that. Much depends on whether the most appropriate people attend – for instance: is the person who has observed the child closely at the conference? (many schools, for example, are represented by·headteachers rather than class teachers). Do participants have a clear understanding of why a conference is being held? My own experience indicates that conference participants, especially those who are not regular attenders, are frequently confused as to why conferences are convened. This confusion is compounded by the special characteristics of conferences, some of which will be considered in the next section.

THINGS TO LOOK OUT FOR

Child protection conferences are difficult meetings. In Corby's (1987) study they are described by social workers as:

> over populated uncertain gatherings likely to reach rather unpredictable conclusions about families. At their best they were seen as well co-ordinated responses to complex problems where the responsibility for important decisions regarding the protection of children and the rights of parents could be sensibly shared. (Corby 1987 p.130)

So what makes conferences so problematic? To begin with they take place in a highly charged emotional atmosphere. Child abuse raises powerful emotions, particularly so when a child's wellbeing has been endangered by parents/carers to whom the child is emotionally close and trusts. Conference participants may well be faced with having to admit to the potential within themselves to be aggressive towards and harm those they love and care for: 'a frightening reminder of aspects of ourselves that we would prefer not to acknowledge' (Hallett and Stevenson 1981 p.81)

For some individuals, accepting the occurrence of abuse, especially child sexual abuse, is too painful; they will deny the abuse has happened, even in the face of overwhelming evidence such as pornographic polaroid photographs. Others may overreact rather than underreact, anxiety leading them to believe abuse has always taken place. If abuse has been going on for some time, anxiety will be fuelled by worries about why 'I', as a particular professional, did not spot the indicators, or by concerns about the possibility of having to give evidence in court.

Conference participants can find themselves having to confront personal beliefs and attitudes about the value of family life or why abuse occurs – issues perhaps not deeply thought about previously. Some may experience a sense of voyeurism as intimate details of someone else's family life and relationships are revealed, raising in the process a host of questions about the privacy of family life and the degree of acceptable state intrusion. Consideration of what constitutes 'good' family life, 'adequate' parenting or 'normal' sexuality within families are areas likely to produce conflict in conferences. For instance: 'No society condones incest, but whether certain other activities, such as allowing children to watch 'soft' pornographic videos, constitute sexual abuse is frequently a matter of dispute and personal views' (Charles with Stevenson 1991 p.94).

Opinions will vary, reflecting individual views of family life and expectations of parental behaviour. Some may attribute great importance to physical conditions, financial stability and household management while others concentrate on the quality of family relationships or the family's reaction to professional intervention. Yet there is no time available in the conference setting for participants to share their attitudes and values and become mutually aware of the bases on which they make their judgements.

The group meeting together may have had little or no experience of working together before; participants will not share any common background in terms of 'race', gender, class, sexuality, professional training or agency structure; some may have no previous experience of child abuse situations or child protection conferences. An understanding of individual roles and skills may not be detailed, resulting in the use of stereotypical images of particular professionals. The family under discussion is also at risk of being stereotyped, assessed as falling way below dominant societal expectations about family norms. Despite the fact that recent census figures show wide variations in the composition of family units, perceptions of families, for the most part, are still based on a traditional model of the working man who supports his partner and children; a household which is a: 'secure, stable, sexually exclusive, internally harmonious unit of law abiding and responsible citizens' (Dingwall, Eekelaar and Murray 1983 p.67).

Those professionals who are regular conference attenders may well have forged some working relationships within the group, evidenced to 'outsiders' by the use of first names or by casual references to other family situations. Infrequent attenders often attribute a greater degree of knowledge about and experience in dealing with child abuse situations to frequent attenders than is the reality. The status ascribed to individuals within the conference may bear little relation to their knowledge of and involvement with the family. Hallett and Stevenson (1980) suggest that inexperienced and infrequent attenders perceive themselves as of lower status, only speaking when spoken to and having little expectation of influencing any decisions or recommendations. Professional status may well be reinforced by the use of jargon, which can be employed, wittingly or unwittingly, to exclude and strengthen some participants' feelings of inferiority.

Some people will come to conference having already made a firm decision as to what they believe the outcome should be. These preferred outcomes stem from a variety of sources: fear of violence from families for whom registration and consequent longer term intervention is to be avoided at all costs; belief that children's names should always be placed on the Child Protection register to protect professionals; desire to avoid further damage to the family by certain sorts of intervention (some social workers, being aware of the dangers of the care system, will not want children to be looked after by the local authority). Overstretched workers may wish to avoid continuing involvement and extra work knowing they are not able to offer an appropriate service. If the outcome is not preferential, individual commitment to and co-operation with any proposed action may be doubtful. Those who disagree may distance themselves from the plan, choosing not to be involved, whilst others, like social workers, over whom the conference holds greater power in terms of future activity, are obliged to implement action with which they are not fully in accord.

The conference facets briefly outlined above clearly have implications for the dynamics and communication patterns of the meeting. The emotional impact of discussing the details of abuse has the potential to hamper rational discussion, and may even induce 'paralysis' in some participants, who, overwhelmed by their own feelings, find themselves unable to speak either to proffer information or express their views, thus possibly withholding important data. Some may regard themselves as 'unprofessional', particularly if others appear to have the ability to talk about the abuse in a detached, more objective manner. From my own research, I vividly recollect a teacher recalling how her difficulty in coming to terms with the idea that children she knew were being sexually abused was increased by the way the social worker calmly described the abusive incidents. It was only later on that she had an opportunity to learn that her colleague struggled equally with her feelings, but had devised strategies to enable her to carry out her professional duties.

Lack of knowledge about signs and symptoms of abuse or a low level of understanding of some of the language used in conferences can inhibit participants, unwilling to display their ignorance, feeling they are the only individuals not *au fait* with the terminology. They may be reluctant to question or challenge others' statements and picture of the family, or feel they are obliged to support contributions offered by higher status members of their own profession.

Ideas proposed by participants perceived to be of high status may be concentrated upon, leaving crucial information from more peripheral conference members unheard. In the Beckford report (Brent Borough Council 1985), the Panel of Inquiry considered insufficient attention had been paid to the information supplied by the health visitor. The Panel were hesitant to conclude this was due to: 'the inferior status accorded to health visitors by a doctor. But we cannot help feeling that throughout our Inquiry the worth and status of health visitors are not always given the credit they deserve' (p.82).

The status linked to professional roles is inextricably tied to issues of gender. Peace (1991) states: 'the field worker may be the person most in touch with the circumstances of the case, but her gender combined with the low status of her position in the eyes of some might diminish the value of her contribution' (p.56).

My own experience demonstrates that women are often talked over and/or interrupted – usually by men of higher status and power. I witnessed a softly spoken school nurse make three efforts to contribute information that would have plugged a huge gap in a family's history. After the third attempt, she simply gave up. This clearly had a detrimental effect on the conference proceedings and decision making.

Ferguson (1987) argues that masculine values prevail at meetings such as conferences. She suggests this causes women to question their own feelings and alter their judgements in deference to others. Issues of power and status – male versus female, one profession versus another, one ethnic group versus another – inevitably have the capacity to make conference participants feel uncomfortable and ill at ease. Such discomfort will mean certain individuals hang on to personal beliefs, theoretical stances or courses of action at all costs, whilst others move to agree with those who are more persuasive or seemingly more knowledgeable. Relevant information may be withheld or not given in full, so as to avoid conflict with other participants, or to honour misguided agreements of confidentiality. Alongside the interplay of the other factors alluded to above, what implications does all that hold for key conference activities such as risk assessment and formulating recommendations?

Brian Corby's (1987) work, borne out by my own experience, suggests that it is often difficult to say why and how conference decisions are reached. He points to the lack of explicit criteria for assessing the level of risk even though this is a stated conference function. The absence of formal discussion for estimating degrees of risk is also pertinent. Assessing risk assumes there is agreement as to what constitutes abuse and what is adequate parenting, but as has already been pointed out, these issues are frequently a matter of contention. So what does the assessment of risk involve? For the majority of conference participants, risk relates to the possibility or probability of continuing or future harm to the child(ren) in question. That is likely to be discussed during the conference and will entail the forming of moral judgements about parental behaviour. Have parents/carers broken the rules of 'adequate' parenting; did they intend to abuse or consider their actions abusive; do they show any remorse or distress; do they have the capacity to deal with current and/or future stresses?

Risk, however, refers not only to families but also to the professional network and professional practice – aspects often ignored in conferences. A lack of shared values between agencies, oversensitivity to the needs and feelings of parents, excessive compliance with the views of particular professionals or poor interprofessional communication can all directly or indirectly add to the risks for the child.

Part of the innate value in holding multidisciplinary conferences is the bringing together of a rich diversity of skills, knowledge, expertise, talent and resources. Yet in terms of risk, these differences are likely to reduce the probability of child abuse being identified. The research undertaken by Dingwall et al. suggests a 'rule of optimism' comes into play, eliminating 'the overwhelming majority of potential cases by providing justification or excuse and allowing front-line workers to prefer an optimistic reading of client behaviour' (Dingwall et al. 1983 p.82).

The most favourable interpretation is placed on parental behaviour; anything questionable is re-interpreted or ignored via two institutionalized devices, natural love and cultural relativism, both pertinent to risk assessment. In terms of 'natural love', parental behaviour is excused on the basis that they instinctively love their children so are incapable of abusing them. Cultural relativism on the other hand is an assumption that all cultures are equally valid in their ways of formulating human relationships. Hence members of one culture have no right to criticize members of another by using their own cultural standards of judgement. In other words, abuse is redefined as appropriate rather than deviant parental behaviour for that culture. Cultural relativism has significant implications for Black children, who are at risk of not being protected as agencies hesitate to intervene (Ahmad 1990, Dingwall *et al.* 1983, Driver and Droisen 1989, Violence against Children Study Group 1990). Explanations of injuries and abuse are too readily accepted. This has the effect of elevating the cultures of minority ethnic groups to a status where non-intervention is the norm and emerges from racist beliefs and expectations.

The rule of optimism links closely with the stereotyping of families and parenting behaviour and the subsequent moral judgements forged. Dingwall *et al.'s* (1983) work illustrates how respectable upper, middle and working class parents, those with learning disabilities and African-Caribbean and Asian parents are less likely to be labelled as abusive. In contrast, lone mothers and 'undeserving' families in poverty are left as the groups disproportionately represented in recommendations for compulsory measures to protect children. The combination of the rule of optimism with the lack of explicit risk criteria suggests conferences are prone to making 'risky' decisions.

In spite of the contentious nature of the subject matter, most decisions and recommendations appear to be made in an atmosphere of professional consensus. Corby (1987) argues that conferences work on a no-conflict norm, with disputes being minor. Any person challenging the no-conflict norm, by questioning what others accept or by offering alternative perspectives, is usually allowed to have his or her say, and then is ignored. Thus the conflict disappears. Studies on how groups work indicate that the larger the group, the more acceptable differences become (Kane 1975 cited in Hallett and Stevenson 1980). There is some suggestion (Brown 1965) that group decisions tend to be bolder and riskier than individual ones, although they become more conservative if there is any sense of an important factor(s) being overlooked. Perhaps conferences tend to operate on a consensus model because child protection itself is a risky business for professionals. Conference participants feel 'safer' going along with the majority view even if the opinion is not shared.

Child protection conferences have always been perplexing professional meetings. The recent change in practice of involving parents and children has added a new dimension to an already difficult forum. This warrants specific attention and will be discussed in the following section.

THE INVOLVEMENT OF PARENTS AND CHILDREN

Involving parents and/or children in child protection conferences is a relatively new phenomenon, although arguments about their participation have persisted for some years (Phillips and Evans 1986). The shift in practice from non-inclusion to attendance throughout initial and review conferences has been swift. The draft of the *Working Together* document in 1987 stated quite categorically that parents were not to be included, but by the time of publication in 1988 parents were to be 'invited where practicable to attend part, or if appropriate the whole, of case conferences' (*Working Together* 1988 para 5.45 p.29) unless in the opinion of the chair, their presence would preclude total consideration of the interests of the child. The revised version of *Working Together*, published in 1991, shows an expectation of parental involvement 'with reasonable opportunities for parents, the children themselves and others to present their points of view' (*Working Together* 1991 para 1.7 p.2).

This change in attitude stemmed from two chief sources: first, the messages from Inquiries such as those held in Cleveland (Butler Sloss 1988) and Rochdale (North West Social Services Inspectorate 1990), criticizing the degree of family involvement in the chiid protection process; second, the general trend towards increased openness about information and enabling individuals to participate in planning and decision making about their own lives.

In principle, many professionals agreed with this change of practice, but the prospect in reality produced ambivalence, uncertainty and anxiety. Four key areas of concern were generated: relationships with the family; the effects on the parents; the impact on the child; communication within the conference.

A common anxiety focused on the potential difficulties of maintaining a continuing relationship with family members post conference. Professionals were fearful that working with the family could prove impossible once doubts had been aired publicly about parenting skills and/or family life style. Concern was expressed as to how parents/children would cope in the meeting itself, although there were indications that:

> most parents felt strongly that they should be invited... For most parents the exclusion from the case conference increased their anxiety and lack of trust, and left them feeling frustrated and powerless. They wanted to be able to meet people, hear what was being said and put their views forward. (Brown 1986 p.99)

Questions were raised about the effects on children: would they be re-abused by the process? would they be made more vulnerable? would they be able to express their views and feelings if parents were present too? Professionals were worried that the presence of family members would inhibit their ability to contribute, causing discussion and speculation about the family's functioning to be lost.

A growing body of literature (McGloin and Turnbull 1986; Shemmings and Thoburn 1990) suggests that these initial concerns were unfounded; child/parent participation can be beneficial and positive for both the family and professionals involved, providing the process is well managed. Parents are more likely to be committed to working with future plans and value being given time and opportunity to express their views.

A good deal of the responsibility for the conference process lies with the chairperson. He/she has an onerous and unenviable task, ensuring all participants have a chance to make contributions, checking that the information is 'heard' in a similar fashion, and clarifying issues. The chair, however, does not own total responsibility for the meeting. Participants can do much to facilitate the effectiveness of conferences by giving detailed thought to their contributions and performance. Some suggestions as to what needs to be addressed in order to be effective conference members are given below.

GOOD PRACTICE POINTS

Child protection conferences have three distinct stages: preparation, execution and aftermath. For ease of discussion, these will be looked at in turn.

It would seem that participants in conferences rarely give much detailed attention and thought to their contributions (Hallett and Stevenson 1980). Advance preparation might tighten and focus the actual conference, easing the management of problematic areas. On receiving an invitation, potential attenders would be well advised to familiarize themselves with their local Area Child Protection Committee agency procedures to ensure that they have some understanding of the child protection process as a whole and an awareness of the role of their particular agency. Certain questions should be posed: am I the most appropriate person to attend? whose views will I be representing? what information do I/my agency hold that might be relevant? what is the best way of presenting my contribution? If a more suitable candidate exists, his/her attendance should be negotiated. Whoever attends should be clear as to whether the information to be offered is his/her own or that of the agency. Some participants may be contributing information on behalf of others: health visitors or practice nurses may offer the GP's perspective; teachers can represent other teaching staff with whom the child has contact. Clear briefing and instructions from such absent members is crucial. A decision, as to what is relevant, must be reached. Individuals should collate factual data, as well as gathering together any concern-raising incidents relating to the family. Patterns of behaviour may be significant: for example, a child with a regular attendance record overall, but repeated school absences on Mondays; a child who continually becomes distressed when the time to leave the nursery approaches. The status of the information should be identified; is it fact, opinion or speculation? Opinions must be substantiated. It is simply not adequate to describe a child as 'unhappy' or a parent as 'immature' without providing evidence to support the statement. Nagging 'feelings' that something is 'not right', should be acknowledged as such, if of sufficient strength to warrant inclusion.

Those unused to presenting information to groups may prefer to write a report. If so, this should follow a logical sequence. A suggested format might begin with the details of the child who is the subject of the conference, followed by information about other family members. Areas of concern must be delineated and, if possible, an opinion expressed as to the level of risk. Attention to detail is important. Isolated incidents or concerns often take on a different significance when put alongside others' information. Any recommendations need to be couched in terms of being possible options. Definite statements about future action early on can overinfluence the conference, which then fails to consider alternative courses. Diagrams, flowcharts or other visual aids can be useful to convey information effectively. A graph, revealing the number and duration of separations a child has endured, can have far more impact than the written or spoken word.

Participants may find it helpful to rehearse their written or oral contributions with colleagues beforehand. Practise increases confidence and skill in giving information in a sensitive manner. For instance, families may well be offended if their home is described as a 'pigsty', but may agree that their dislike of household chores is reflected in their surroundings.

Prior to the meeting, participants should engage in some self analysis, focusing on personal attitudes to family life, definitions of abuse, theoretical stances subscribed to and reasons behind a particular preferred outcome. Mentally asking these questions helps reduce punitive stereotyping of less conventional families, or the abuse being divorced from the context in which it happened. Conference members will undoubtedly have opinions as to why abuse occurs, yet may feel ignorant of theoretical bases relating to child abuse. Beliefs that abusers are 'mad', needing treatment, or 'bad', requiring punishment, can block consideration of pertinent factors. For instance, children brought up in Black families are more likely to experience poverty and environmental deprivation. Conference members need an awareness of their attitudinal positions if such relevant factors are not to be overlooked.

Parent and/or child involvement in conferences must be in the child's interests. Any individual, who considers that a child's interests will not be served by their own attendance or that of their parents, needs to voice this to the chair before the meeting. The chair usually holds responsibility for any decisions concerning exclusion. These views also need to be shared with families, along with the detail of individual contributions. This aids the family's preparation for the conference and allows for resolution of issues of confidentiality. Openness and honesty is usually appreciated by families and enhances the spirit of partnership.

Participants should allow sufficient time to arrive at the conference venue punctually. At least an hour and a half should be allocated for the meeting. Late arrival or early departure of conference members can have implications for the decision making process. If significant people intend to leave before the meeting concludes, decisions may be made too early without all the missing pieces of information being identified. Tardy arrivals, on the other hand, can result in the risk assessment and discussion of future action starting too late for all the options to be fully explored. It is worth noting that conferences which fail to start on time are a source of stress to families, who may assume that conference members will be hostile and unwilling to listen to them.

With adequate preparation, attendance at the conference should be less anxiety provoking. Conferences usually begin with the agenda being outlined, giving participants a clear idea of when they will be expected to contribute their information. During the introductory round, individuals should state precisely who they are and in what capacity they have contact with the family. Information should be presented as clearly and concisely as possible and be free from jargon. Opinions need to be given openly and honestly, with concerns not being 'watered down' out of an oversensitive regard for the child or parents. Participants should be prepared to seek clarification on issues, say they do not understand or disagree. Others' statements must be challenged if evidential support for them is missing or if they conflict with personal knowledge of the family. Stereotypes and prejudiced comments also need tackling. If the rationale behind the decisions or recommendations is muddled or illogical, this too should be queried.

Evidence gathered from studies of conferences (Horton and Robson 1992, McGloin and Turnbull 1986, Shemmings and Thoburn 1990) involving parents shows that their presence has reduced both the amount of jargon used and the number of unsubstantiated value judgements made. Communication has improved with greater clarity and improved precision in the sharing of information. Parents appear to be quick to spot when professionals are not being totally honest and straightforward in their comments (McGloin and Turnbull 1986).

All participants share some responsibility for the process of the conference, which reflects the multidisciplinary ownership of the child protection system. Indicating to the chair that someone out of his/her line of vision is trying to speak, is being talked over or not being heard, can all help to facilitate the process. Summarizing and interpreting information is a useful device to check one's own and others' understanding.

At the end of the meeting, conference members are advised to check their understanding of the decisions and plans reached, and who has agreed to do what. Individuals should be clear of their future and/or continuing role with the family, and of the core group membership.

Post conference, a period of reflection is necessary. Individual performance should be evaluated with different approaches or training needs being identified for the future. Anxieties or stresses generated by the conference require sharing with colleagues and/or line managers, hopefully sympathetic to the conference's emotional impact. Feelings, as to what was or was not achieved, should be analysed. Any dissatisfactions with what has taken place should be aired and not allowed to 'fester' until the next conference. These should be taken up with the chair or the conference colleague responsible for the offence. Differences with other participants or family members need to be addressed to ensure they do not block future working relationships.

Details of decisions and recommendations may have to be given to relevant colleagues. For those with continued involvement, contact patterns of others will need checking so as to avoid the family being swamped by various professionals visiting at the same time. Communication channels need to be established for keeping in touch with family and core group members. This avoids duplication of work and allows for regular monitoring of progress and practice, essential if children are to be adequately protected.

The complexities of child protection conferences illustrate how the protection of children is never a straightforward task. Children can only be safe if the protection system is well constructed, with agencies fully accepting their role within it and individuals exercising appropriate professional judgement. The uniqueness of each child and his/her family defies the production of a single 'recipe' for maximising the potential of conferences, whilst simultaneously highlighting the necessity of achieving this. Conferences can and do help to protect children if participants give time and thought to their contributions. The following exercises are designed to stimulate and trigger thoughts about individual and group performance in that particular setting.

EXERCISES

EXERCISE 11.1

Participants begin this exercise on their own, but can choose to take their learning further by sharing their initial activity with a colleaugue, from either the same or a different discipline.

The aim of the exercise is to offer an opportunity for professionals to consider the selection of material for their conference contribution.

Stage 1:

Individuals are to imagine that a child whom they know in a professional capacity has made an allegation of physical and/or sexual abuse by his/her parent(s).

Details of their knowledge of the child and family are to be written down. Participants then decide which pieces of information they would present to a conference. Reasons behind their choice should be noted. Any of the following should be identified: the status and source of data (fact, opinion, speculation, gossip); jargon; unsubstantiated, prejudicial or stereotypical views. The factors on which opinions or speculative comments are based should be listed. Finally, participants need to think of which is the most effective way for them to present their information, then practise their chosen method.

Participants may wish to consider whether or not their selection would have been different, had the child been disabled, of the other gender or from another ethnic group.

Stage 2:

If desired, individuals can choose to share the above with a colleague to check if he/she agrees with the selections made and shows a similar understanding of the information. Feedback from the colleague should then be incorporated into both the content and method of the contribution.

EXERCISE 11.2

This exercise is for a group of at least 12 people. It aims to explore the factors which hinder or facilitate the making of an effective group decision.

Copies of the individual scripts will be required for the participants. Everyone in the group is involved in the exercise: 8 members are party to the group discussion; the remaining 4 (or more) act as observers of the group process.

The exercise follows the steps outlined below:

1. Participants are given their individual scripts to read with instructions not to share the contents with any other person. Those who are acting as observers may discuss this role with the other observers.

2. The person holding the 'chairperson' script begins the discussion by introducing the group task. The task is to reach a group decision as to what colour the room they are working in should be painted. A decision must be arrived at within 20 minutes.

3. At the end of the discussion, participants need to share their experience of arguing from their particular prescribed position and how they perceived other participants during the process.

The observers should follow this with their views of the process, and whether in their opinion, the group succeeded in making an effective decision collectively. Comments about the position of dissenters to the colour choice would be particularly helpful.

4. Finally the entire group needs to transfer the experience from the above exercise to the child protection conference setting, through the debate of questions such as:

- Were participants reminded of any experiences they had witnessed in conferences?

- What impact would taking a particular stance have on the conference?

- Which particular presentation styles are effective and why?

- What effect would holding different viewpoints have on conference functions of risk assessment and decision making?

- What factors would have helped or hindered the conference process?

Individual scripts

1. You are to act as the chair for this meeting. Your task is to ensure that a decision is reached within the time limit and that everyone is given a chance to voice their views. Introduce and support the colour GREY. Oppose GREEN. Present your view as clearly and logically as possible, but listen to others' reactions

and consider them before you press your point. Confidently and persistently press for GREY.

2. Introduce and support the colour YELLOW. Oppose WHITE. Avoid changing your mind only to reach an agreement and avoid conflict. Only support solutions with which you are at least able to agree with in part. Only give way to views that have objective and logically sound foundations. Seek out differences of opinion and encourage participation of all group members.

3. Introduce and support the colour GREEN. You know something about colours and see yourself as having some expertise. You offer facts, opinions and expect to be listened to.

4. Introduce the colour WHITE. You are worried about conflict in the group and fear it will be impossible for agreement to be reached. You will be happy to abandon your chosen colour if it avoids any tension and keep changing your mind to be in line with the majority. You are quick to point out any areas of agreement in the group and suggest compromises.

5. Support the colour YELLOW. You try to make the task fun and light-hearted in order to reduce tension in the group.

6. Oppose the colour GREEN – quietly! You dislike GREEN intensely, but are anxious about expressing your views, being the newest member of the group and wondering what the possible consequences could be if you appear too forceful.

7. You really do not care which colour is chosen. You offer no suggestions, but disagree with everyone else's. If challenged about a personal choice, you withdraw from the discussion psychologically.

8. Introduce and support the colour BLUE. You are not interested in anyone else's views and intend to talk as much as you can to get what you want. You try to get other group members to communicate with you and reinforce your view. Be persuasive.

You are an OBSERVER.

Consider what factors facilitated and/or hindered the making of an effective group decision. What did group members do to be heard? Comment on the styles and techniques employed.

Who did and did not influence the decision? How was influence determined (expertise, gender, loudness of voice etc.)? Did everyone participate?

REFERENCES

Ahmad, B. (1990) *Black Perspectives in Social Work*. Birmingham: Venture Press.

Brent Borough Council (1985) *Report of Panel of Inquiry into the circumstances surrounding the death of Jasmine Beckford*. London Borough of Brent.

Brown, C. (1986) *Child Abuse Parents Speaking*. Working Paper 63. Bristol University: School for Advanced Studies.

Brown, R. (1965) *Social Psychology*. New York Press.

Butler Sloss, Justice (1988) *Report of the Inquiry into Child Abuse in Cleveland*. London: HMSO.

Charles, M. and Stevenson, O. (1991) *Multidisciplinary is Different Part 2: Sharing Perspectives*. Nottingham: University of Nottingham.

Corby, B. (1987) Working with Child Abuse. Milton Keynes: Open University Press.

Department of Health and Social Security and Welsh Office (1988) *Working Together*. London: HMSO.

Dingwall, R., Eekelaar, J. and Murray, T. (1983) *The Protection of Children: State Intervention and Family Life*. Oxford: Blackwell.

Driver, E. and Droisen, A. (1989) *Child Sexual Abuse – Feminist perspectives*. London: Macmillan.

Ferguson, M. (1987) 'A feminist interpretation of "Professional Incompetence" in the Beckford case'. In G. Drewry (ed) *'After Beckford?' Essays on Themes Related to Child Abuse*. Social Policy Papers No1. London: Department of Social Policy Royal Holloway and Bedford New College.

Hallett, C. and Stevenson, O. (1980) *Child Abuse: Aspects of Interprofessional Co-operation*. London: George Allen and Unwin.

Home Office, Department of Health, Department of Education and Science, Welsh Office (1991) *Working Together under the Children Act 1989*. London: HMSO.

Horton, M. and Robson, K. (1992) 'Open Secrets' *Social Work Today* 17. September 1992.

Jones, D.N., Pickett, J., Oates, M.R. and Barbor, P. (1987) *Understanding Child Abuse*. London: Macmillan.

McGloin, P. and Turnbull, A. (1986) *Parent Participation in Child Abuse Review Conferences*. Greenwich Social Services Department.

North West Region Social Services Inspectorate, (1990) *Inspection of Child Protection Services in Rochdale*. Manchester: NWRSSI.

Peace, G. (1991) *Child Sexual Abuse: Part 2 – Interprofessional Collaboration*. Cheadle, Cheshire: Boys and Girls Welfare Society.

Phillips, J. and Evans, M. (1986) *Participating Parents – An Examination of the Issues For and Against Parental Participation in Child Abuse Case Conferences*. Bradford: Bradford Family Service Unit.

Report of the Inquiry into Child Abuse in Cleveland 1987 (1988). London: HMSO.

Shemmings, D. and Thoburn, J. (1990) *Parental Participation in Child Protection Conferences*. Norwich: University of East Anglia.

Stainton Rogers, W., Hevey, D., Roche, J. and Ash, E. (1992) *Child Abuse and Neglect*. London: Open University/Batsford.

Violence against Children Study Group (1990) *Taking Child Abuse Seriously*. London: Unwin Hyman.

CHAPTER 12

CHILD PROTECTION PLANS
PROMOTING CONSISTENCY AND ACCOUNTABILITY

JACKI PRITCHARD AND HILARY OWEN

INTRODUCTION

The events in Cleveland in 1987, as most professionals are now aware, caused the government to issue the first 'Working Together' document (DHSS 1988) which, for the first time in the history of child protection work, provided a comprehensive structure within which multidisciplinary work could be carried out. It brought together in one place all the statute, Department of Health guidance, Department of Education and Science guidance and Home Office guidance governing the responses of all statutory agencies to the problem of child abuse. It ensured that Area Child Protection Committees were set up to provide constant monitoring of child abuse and responses to it, particularly where, in individual cases, those responses entailed the close co-operation of several agencies. One particular aspect of the child protection process received most of the government's attention at this time: the investigation of child abuse.

Additional guidance was issued in 1989 by the Home Office (Home Office Circular 67/1989) in an attempt to ensure that police officers and social workers were selected, on the basis of their experience, existing skills and personal attributes, to undertake good quality training in the joint investigation of child sexual abuse. This emphasis was, obviously, not surprising, given that this was the aspect which had been so fraught with difficulty in Cleveland. However, it caused concern amongst some practitioners in many agencies who were struggling to do longer term work with victims and indeed perpetrators to prevent further abuse: they felt that they were receiving no guidance or resources in what is just as important an area of work.

RECENT DEVELOPMENTS

In 1988, the Department of Health also published its document *Protecting Children: a guide for social workers undertaking a comprehensive assessment*, indicating in Section 2 that:

> During the preparation of the Guide there has been healthy debate about the danger on the one hand of being too prescribed and detailed or on the other of being too vague and general. It is hoped that social workers will use the guide in differing ways, reflecting their own training, experience and style. The inexperienced may welcome the detailed phrasing and ordering of questions, whereas more experienced and specialist workers may wish to modify, change and experiment with the format. (HMSO 1988 p.5)

This publication, whilst becoming known almost everywhere as the 'orange book' because of its cover, was referred to, it seems fair to say, only occasionally by social workers because actually to carry out such an assessment involves a great deal of work. It necessitates looking, potentially, at every aspect of a child's life, including: the precise causes for concern; parents' perceptions of their child; how they care for him or her; what has happened in the child's life; the child's physical and emotional development; the child's perception of his or her life; family composition; personality and attitude of each of the child's carers; personal history of each of the carers; the carers' relationship; relationships between other family members; the social and professional networks of which the family is part; the physical conditions in the home; and the family's financial position (see HMSO 1988 pp.29–64).

Our impression is that workers began to undertake comprehensive assessments in what they perceived to be the most dangerous cases they were dealing with, but it did appear that they did this very much in isolation, rarely discussing how helpful they felt it had been with colleagues, and not knowing whether they had carried out the assessment in the same way as their colleagues.

This situation is beginning to change radically now with the implementation of revised Area Child Protection Committee procedures based on *Working Together under the Children Act 1989* (Home Office *et al.* 1991) which provides much more detailed guidance than the original 'Working Together' document on how child protection plans should be formulated, implemented and reviewed (see Chapter 10 for information about the circumstances in which child protection plans must be formulated). Perhaps more important, the role of the guide to comprehensive assessment is clarified and substantially strengthened. Rather than the guide being a tool to be used by social workers as they feel necessary, *Working Together under the Children Act 1989* indicates clearly:

> On registration of a child, the initial plan should include a comprehensive assessment. Its purpose is to acquire a full understanding of the child and family situation in order to provide a sound basis for decisions about future actions. (HMSO 1991 p.31)

Not only has a comprehensive assessment become an essential part of an initial child protection plan, but it has to be carried out with clear reference to other agencies and the contributions they can make:

> The assessment has to be planned and structured and decisions have to be made in respect of each of the following questions:

- who will undertake the assessment?
- where will it be undertaken?
- what is the timescale?
- how should it be recorded?
- how to involve the family?
- what is the legal status of the child?
- how will it fit in with any court action, and have the necessary steps in relation to this been taken?
- how will it fit in with other action, e.g. by the Police in respect of the offender?
- what is the social services department's position regarding parental responsibility?

Such an assessment should include contributions from all relevant agencies to cover social, environmental, medical and developmental circumstances (pp.31–32)

It is clear that the government intends the formulation of child protection plans to be a much more detailed, lengthy and careful process than professionals have been accustomed to, involving two different stages: the initial plan which ensures the child is protected in the short term; and the full plan which is based on a deeper knowledge of all risk factors present in the child's situation, a judgement about whether these can be addressed and, if so, identification of the appropriate means to alleviate them.

It is also clear that the government intends all agencies involved with children to ensure that any helpful services within their control are provided. In addition, it intends that parents and children should be involved as much as possible in the process. Indeed, it would not be possible in practice to undertake a comprehensive assessment without ensuring family members are appraised of the task, as it involves them committing a considerable amount of time, thought and memory to the process. *Working Together under the Children Act 1989* indicates:

A written plan will need to be constructed with the involvement of the carers/parents and in the light of each agency's statutory duties... will identify the contributions each will make to the child, to the other family members and the abuser. It will make clear the part to be played by parents, what expectations they may have of agencies and what expectations agencies may have of them... it will be the responsibility of individual agencies to implement the parts of the plan relating to them and to communicate with the keyworker and others as necessary. The keyworker will have the responsibility for co-ordinating the contributions of different agencies. (HMSO 1991 p.32)

The way in which child protection plans are to be implemented and reviewed is also clarified and strengthened by *Working Together under the Children Act 1989*, so that specific aspects are examined with all agencies involved in the 'core group', and with family members at least every 6 months (see Chapter

10 for more detail about review conferences). Whilst it will be essential that each practical element of the plan is looked at in terms of whether any progress has been made, in addition the level of risk is to be assessed at each review conference, as are the adequacy of the protection offered, and the quality of the co-ordination between the agencies. Finally, a judgement has to be made about whether or not the child's name needs to remain on the Child Protection Register.

IMPLICATIONS FOR PRACTICE

Having appreciated these new developments, it is easy to understand when professionals who have just read *Working Together under the Children Act 1989* say 'Well, it's a very good model of perfect practice, but our resources, particularly in terms of having sufficient workers, fall far short of what would be needed to provide such a comprehensive service'. Certainly, for those social services departments already failing to provide keyworkers for registered children, it seems like a standard of practice which is impossible to achieve.

Increasingly, it seems that work can be carried out to an improved standard, but only at the cost of the volume of cases which can be dealt with: staff cannot 'spread themselves thinly' to meet more families' needs in child protection work and to attempt to do so is to put the children one works with at greater risk, as well as one's professional position. Managers need to be very frank about cases their staff are simply unable to take on.

Nevertheless, it is possible to learn from the guidance and improve the quality of the work we are doing, particularly where several agencies are involved and all are aware of the full part guidance indicates they should play. The following suggestions about practice and exercises are intended to assist all agencies to improve the work they can do.

WAYS OF IMPROVING PRACTICE

Preparation

Obviously at the present time child protection plans need to be given much more attention by all professionals. From our own experience, we have seen workers talk in depth about a particular child or children in a case conference, then suddenly become very quiet when a child protection plan has to be formulated. Professionals should think about how an initial child protection plan should be formulated *before* a case conference takes place.

It could be argued that this is pre-judging the outcome of the conference, but it is good practice to plan work and set objectives. In some cases, it is essential to have already done some work with family members on an initial plan to enable the children concerned to live with relatives in the short term because of unacceptable risk at home, thereby avoiding unnecessarily long stays in hospital or having to live with foster parents who may well be strangers to the children, albeit caring ones. Even if the outcome of a conference was that a child protection plan was not needed, the worker would still have focused on his/her own objectives in working with the child/family.

However, it is not just social workers who should be thinking ahead in this way: *all* professionals who are involved in a case should be functioning in a similar way. If a core group is already in existence then it is easier to get together to prepare and review the child protection plan before the review case conference. However, if an incident case conference is to take place, then individuals should prepare themselves by liaising as fully as possible with other professionals.

So how should a social worker prepare for an initial child protection plan?

A social worker may find him/herself in two different situations: either where there has been no social work intervention before or alternatively where the case is already open. There is one simple rule to begin with – **get as much information as possible about the family**. This is achieved by liaising with as many people as possible who may be involved with the family (health visitor, nursery, school, school nurse, education welfare officer, general practitioner, hospital staff, psychiatrist, psychologist, community psychiatric nurse etc). By doing this, the worker will prepare him/herself for the conference, but also it will help to plan work for the future.

Social workers should use their line managers to discuss future work and plans for a case and this should be done through regular supervision (for more detail see Chapter 16). However, if there is to be an incident case conference, the line manager and worker should spend time together beforehand to discuss the crucial issues which will arise in the conference.

It is also very important to discuss matters with family members, both adults and children. It is a waste of time making plans if the family are unwilling to work in a certain way. For example, in one case a mother preferred to see the family support worker more regularly than the social worker because she said 'I can talk to her. She understands me'. The mother felt the social worker was 'a snob'. Therefore, in this case, the social worker visited once a week, but the family support worker visited more frequently and helped the client with all the practical matters. For example, she took the mother to the Housing Department about getting rehoused; she liaised with the gas and electricity boards to arrange weekly payments to clear arrears. In terms of the child protection plan, it may well be appropriate in circumstances like these to name a 'primary' worker (in addition to the keyworker), who will in fact have most direct contact with the child and other family members. The keyworker, however, retains all other normal duties in relation to the case.

Workers should not make plans for families without finding out how family members perceive their problems and how they think they could be helped. Obviously workers can suggest ways of helping and may have some creative ideas which the family may not have thought of, but the clients (and this includes children too) can also have ideas.

The Guide to comprehensive assessment is useful inasmuch as it draws attention to the fact that *all* family members have to be considered in formulating plans, and this includes fathers, stepfathers and co-habitees. Many male perpetrators of child abuse have managed in the past to avoid being involved in plans to protect children simply by withdrawing from discussion, by being aggressive, or by being out when professionals visit. Agencies will have in their records a large number of copies of conference minutes which do not even record the date of birth of male adults in the household in question.

Often a particular adult in the household will have abused a child, and an essential element of the initial child protection plan will be to ensure that any contact between alleged perpetrator and child is controlled. Police officers can assist by ensuring they bring to the conference accurate and full information about any bail conditions imposed on the alleged perpetrator by the court. Magistrates can assist child protection agencies greatly by ensuring they do not bail alleged abusers to reside at other addresses where there are children. Often, however, it is not possible for the police to charge an alleged perpetrator, (particularly where the child is too young to say what has happened), and in these circumstances, where serious abuse has occurred, it may be necessary to find an alternative placement for the child.

The Children Act advocates that when a child is at risk, it is preferable to place a child with family members rather than the local authority having to accommodate the child. Therefore, it is crucial for the worker to know the family structure and who is important to a child. Grandparents, aunties and uncles, or older brothers and sisters may be able to help in the child protection plan for the future.

Focusing on practical considerations

As indicated earlier, it is our impression that not enough time is spent on formulating a child protection plan and often people are vague when putting forward ideas. Any professional could benefit from using Exercise 12.1

EXERCISE 12.1: FOCUSING ON A CHILD

Objective

To make participants think about issues which should be considered when formulating a child protection plan.

Participants

Exercise to be done in small groups.

Equipment

Flipchart and pens.

Task

Each group is given a question, which is written at the top of the flipchart paper. The group is asked to write down their immediate responses to the question.

Time

10 minutes for group exercise Feedback – 5 minutes for each group, followed by general discussion in large group.

Some possible questions

- Who are the important people in a child's life?
- Where does a child go?
- Who does a child mix with?
- What does a child like doing?
- Who can influence a child?
- Who knows a child best?
- Who does a child trust?
- Who does a child confide in?

This range of questions should be asked in relation to children of different ages.

All professionals need to think about the following areas when formulating a child protection plan:

- visiting by professionals
- contact with parents/other family members
- ways of monitoring situations
- resources

How many times do we hear professionals use the words 'visiting regularly'. What does regularly mean? To a social worker working with the elderly it might mean once every three months. To a social worker working with a family it might be every day when there is a crisis, or in other situations once a week, or once a month. To a health visitor who has concerns about a small baby it might be once or twice a week. To an education welfare officer it might be every couple of months.

The word 'regularly' will not do in a child protection plan. Details must be more specific. It needs to be spelt out exactly *who* is visiting *when* and what activities or work will be carried out. If there are concerns about a family it is unhelpful if all the professionals are visiting at the beginning of the week, and then no-one sees the family from Wednesday through to the following Monday. People must take into account that some professionals only work part of the week or they may have other commitments.

If a child is being looked after by the local authority or is living elsewhere because s/he cannot live with his/her parents, then contact with parents and other family members must be included in the plan. Again specific details and arrangements need to be noted. For example, supervision of contact may be necessary; if so, whose responsibility will it be – social worker, residential worker, foster parent, other professionals, other family members?

Often, magistrates will impose a bail condition on an alleged abuser allowing him/her no contact with the child. This may well not meet the child's needs, particularly where the alleged abuser is a natural parent. If, after some work with the child it is apparent that s/he desires continued contact, then it may well be possible to support the alleged abuser in an application to change the bail condition, perhaps to one allowing supervised contact.

'Monitoring' is yet another word which is bandied about by professionals, but again what does it mean? And how can monitoring take place? Professionals need to be clear about what they are looking for. The most obvious method of monitoring is by visiting either in the home, school or institution. Each core group member needs to know precisely what the nature of the contacts made by the other members is so that work is co-ordinated and efficient. For example, a health visitor may be addressing several different issues with a family, like the importance of hygiene in caring for a baby, ensuring the baby is weighed every fortnight and offering firm guidance about feeding routines. A family support worker may not wish to go through the same issues actively with parents, but may need to follow the health visitor's work closely, so that her own involvement can be consistent with it and she can note and act to rectify any failure to follow the health visitor's advice. At the same time, it may be possible for professionals to be a little more imaginative and perhaps get to know a child and the family better by varying the nature of their contacts; for example, giving parents and children a lift to clinic or nursery from time to time.

It is important for professionals to build relationships and trust with a client. A five-year-old child is going to open up more to the person who takes them out to do 'nice things' like playing in the park, rather than to the person who comes to the house every week to have a chat and cup of tea with mum. Children need to be engaged in activities where they feel relaxed and at ease. Workers need to consider the age of a child and what may be appropriate for that child. For example, it may seem obvious, but it is not unknown to happen, that it is not appropriate to sit a three-year-old child in an armchair for a talk. The worker should be getting involved in play, even if it means getting dirty because of painting, or having to sit in a sandpit.

The people who have frequent contact with a child will get to know a child and family more quickly than a worker who visits weekly or fortnightly perhaps for an hour. This reminds us that childminders, nursery staff and schoolteachers may know more about a child than the social worker. Also, children are more likely to confide in these people whom they see every day of their lives.

In a time of scarce resources it is important to use existing resources imaginatively. We need to think about people and places. As well as all the professionals who might be involved, who else could help a child? Where could a child get help/support/advice/stimulation/security?

EXERCISE 12.2: WHO WOULD HELP ME?

Objective

To make participants think who might be involved in helping a child other than professionals and family members.

Participants

This exercise is to be done by individuals. Therefore, it can be carried out in group settings or perhaps in supervision sessions.

Equipment

Trainers need to prepare a card in advance for each person. Participants need sheets of paper and a pen.

Task

Each person is given a card which states the age and sex of the child (trainers can give more details about the child if they wish to do so). The participant is asked to imagine that they are that child and to list who might be in their lives, apart from family members, who could help them if they were in trouble.

Time

Participants have 10 minutes to complete the task. Feedback to group/line manager/supervisor.

Range of people who could be involved

Childminder

Foster parent

Youth worker

Leader of a group e.g. brownies, guides, cubs, scouts, youth club

Volunteer

Vicar/priest

Neighbour

Parent of friend

Professionals also need to think about places. The exercise above could be repeated asking individuals to list places rather than people.

All aspects of a child's life have to be considered in formulating a child protection plan. People need to be reminded that the objective is to *protect* a child and, as the Children Act states' 'promote and safeguard the welfare of the child'.

Written records

Often, the main components of child protection plans are written down in case conference minutes. However, there are often problems in minuting conferences, getting them typed and circulating the final document. There are often long time delays. Detailed child protection plans should be written out separately in accordance with the guidance contained in *Working Together under the Children Act 1989* (HMSO 1991 p.32), placed on the case file and circulated to each professional who is to help implement the plan. It is also crucial that the family (and particularly the child if of an appropriate age to understand) have a copy of the plan, which will act as a 'working contract' between the professionals and family members.

Achieving closer co-ordination between agencies

Once the comprehensive assessment has been completed, professionals should be in a position to identify sources of risk to a child; to have in place safeguards to prevent the child being exposed at all to serious risks; and to have identified ways in which other risks can be reduced over time. In addition, professionals and family members should all have a clear idea of what needs to be achieved before the child's name can be removed from the child protection register. All this will form the basis of the full child protection plan.

For workers in any agency, contributing to a child protection plan is obviously a piece of work which needs to be closely co-ordinated with other professionals involved, both at the initial stage when a comprehensive assessment is being undertaken and later when the full plan is being implemented. It is an area of work which would be greatly improved through multidisciplinary training and Exercise 12.3 could usefully be included in such training.

EXERCISE 12.3: MAKING A PLAN

Objective

To increase participants' knowledge of the services other agencies can offer; to make participants think about service delivery; and to enable participants to practise formulating child protection plans.

Participants

This exercise to be carried out in multidisciplinary groups containing representatives of all agencies involved in child protection work.

Equipment

Flipchart and pens.

Task

The group will be asked to consider a case study and then to perform two tasks:

(a) each member of the group in turn should be asked what service their agency would be able to provide as part of the initial protection plan. Other group members may wish to ask questions after each contribution and discussion should be encouraged.

(b) the group should then be asked to write out a suggested detailed protection plan.

Both these tasks should be carried out with reference to the 9 issues to be addressed as part of a comprehensive assessment, identified in *Working Together under the Children Act 1989* (HMSO 1991 pp.31–32)

Time

(a) 30 minutes
(b) 45 minutes

CASE STUDY 1

A child protection conference has been convened in respect of Tim, aged 7 years, Marcus aged 12 years, and their baby brother Sandy, aged 18 months. It is accepted by all involved, including family members, that Marcus has been sexually abusing Tim. There has been a joint police/social work investigation, and Tim was medically examined by a Consultant Paediatrician. The police are considering prosecuting Marcus for 2 offences of indecent assault. Neither Marcus nor Tim are particularly distressed by what has happened and have continued to play together like any brothers. Marcus has remained at home and his mother and stepfather have been supervising him closely.

The father of Tim and Marcus, who lives with his new family in another part of town, attends the conference, in addition to their mother and stepfather. This is the first time any of the professionals have met him.

The conference decides to register Tim because of actual sexual abuse, and also to register Sandy because of likely sexual abuse. The interests of all these children have to be considered when an initial child protection plan is being formulated.

CASE STUDY 2

Rory is a mixed race child who lives with his maternal grandmother, Mrs Matthews. The local authority has a Care Order on Rory because a year ago his mother beat him about the head and he was bruised very badly. He is on the Child Protection Register because of actual physical abuse.

Rory's mother, Juliet, has three other children and is pregnant again. She usually visits Rory at the weekend. Mrs Matthews is 58 years old and recently widowed. She also cares for two other grandchildren, Clinton and Leroy, who are twins, aged 6 years. Clinton and Leroy's mother, Lydia, works as a prostitute and comes and goes as she pleases.

Recently, the staff at the nursery which Rory attends every morning have been worried about Rory's behaviour. They have described him as being 'aggressive', 'violent', 'out of control', and 'a danger to other children'. Two days ago Rory was seen to have several linear bruises on the back of his legs. When asked how he got them he said 'Gran hits me with a belt'.

Rory was taken to the local Children's Hospital, where the medical evidence confirmed non-accidental injury. Mrs Matthews has said in interview with the police that she had hit Rory with a belt, because he had opened a bag of sugar and thrown it all over the living room.

Nursery staff say that Mrs Matthews cannot control Rory at all and they are questioning whether he should be moved to a foster home. A review case conference was due to take place next week, but now it will have to be redesignated a 'new incident' conference.

REFERENCES

Department of Health (1988) *Protecting Children: A Guide for Social Workers Undertaking a Comprehensive Assessment*. London: HMSO.

DHSS (now Department of Health *et al.*) (1988) *Working Together: A Guide to Arrangements for Inter-Agency Co-Operation for the Protection of Children*. London: HMSO.

Home Office, Department of Health, Department of Education and Science, Welsh Office (1991) *Working Together Under the Children Act 1989*. London: HMSO.

Home Office Circular 67/1989. *Joint Training for Police Officers and Social Workers Responsible for Investigating Child Sexual Abuse*.

CHAPTER 13

VICTIMS OF CHILD ABUSE GIVING EVIDENCE
HELPING TO REDUCE THE TRAUMA

ISOBEL TODD

> Which is the worse ordeal for a child; being sexually abused or being forced to retell the trauma in intimate details under cross-examination from seven successive barristers? (The Guardian Comment 22.12.90.)

This editorial described the harrowing experiences of children giving evidence in a case of an alleged sexual abuse network in Kent. Seventy-five children were involved and there were nine separate trials. Seventeen defendants faced serious allegations and only five were finally convicted. On a number of occasions children 'crumpled in the witness box' and the stress and revictimisation of these children exemplified the trauma the criminal justice system imposes in such trials.

I have seen children similarly traumatised and humiliated by their court room ordeals during eight years as a court social worker and in July 1990, with my colleague Hilary Owen, wrote in *The Independent* (6.7.90) about the poor facilities for children in the Sheffield Crown Court – we wrote in anger and frustration at what seemed to be a complacency and total disregard for much needed changes in the procedures for hearing evidence from child witnesses.

Following the Pigot Report (Home Office 1989) and the implementation of the Criminal Justice Act 1991 in October 1992 progress is at last being made – we hope this is the beginning of more radical reforms.

Children are called to give information to courts in many different proceedings. For example, they may testify in the Family Proceedings Court, in Wardship or Adoption Hearings or as witnesses to accidents or crimes. In civil proceedings the burden of proof and evidential rules make it easier for the child's viewpoint to be heard and safeguards to ensure that the child's interests are paramount have been built into the system. The *Guardian Ad Litem*, the Court Welfare Officer and the Official Solicitor all play a part in this. In criminal proceedings many of the obstacles to securing a conviction to offences involving child victims arise from the procedural and evidentiary rules whose purpose is to protect the rights of the accused and are safeguards against wrongful conviction.

I shall be concentrating on the issues surrounding the criminal courts, where increasing public and professional awareness about the physical and sexual abuse of children during the last few years has lead to growing concerns over the difficulties faced by child witnesses in these courts. At present there are no centrally collected national figures about the total number of offences committed against children, although it is acknowledged that cases which do reach the official statistics are only the tip of an iceberg. NSPCC research looking at the period 1983 to 1987 suggested that where abuse did come to light prosecutions were planned in only 9 per cent of physical abuse cases and 28 per cent of sexual abuse cases (Home Office 1989).

There are a number of reasons why prosecution may not be considered appropriate. For example, the police may consider cautioning; a caution can only be given when an offence is admitted. The police may refer a case to the Crown Prosecution Service for consideration for prosecution, who in turn will consider whether there is a sufficient evidence and if there is a realistic prospect of conviction. They will also consider if prosecution is in the public interest and *Working Together under the Children Act 1989* (Home Office 1991) additionally requires the Crown Prosecution Service to consider whether or not it is in the interests of the child.

By its very nature abuse frequently occurs where there are no witnesses except the child involved, and a case will rest on the word of the child versus that of the abuser. This means that without an admission of guilt conviction is remote. NACRO (1992) estimate that the conviction rate following a child's disclosures of abuse is only one in five in some areas, that the 'child's experience following disclosure is more likely to be one of being disbelieved than vindicated', and 'Where there is a conviction, any sense of vindication is likely to be overshadowed by guilt and upset about the break up of the family' especially where the case involves inter-familial abuse.

It is clear that up to now the criminal justice system has failed abused children; evidence from all professionals working in the area of child protection suggests that the 'recorded growth in the number of offences committed against children has not been matched by a corresponding increase in prosecution because a high proportion of the crimes now coming to light are committed against the very young who are unable to testify in the criminal courts' (Home Office 1989). If we believe that small children are not capable of giving evidence then it follows that their testimony should be excluded and changes to enable them to give information to any tribunal should be disregarded. However, recent research does not support such a view.

RESEARCH FINDINGS REGARDING CHILDREN'S RECALL OF INFORMATION

Spencer and Flin (1990) point out that resistance to changing the way children give evidence to the courts is based on longstanding suspicions and mistrust by lawyers of children's fitness as witnesses. They quote an English lawyer, Heydon, whose words summarise this distrust.

> First, a child's powers of observation and memory are less reliable than an adult's. Secondly, children are prone to live in a make-believe world so that they magnify incidents which happen to them or invent them completely. Thirdly, they are also very egocentric, so that details seemingly unrelated to their own world are quickly forgotten by them

completely. Fourth, because of their immaturity they are suggestible and can easily be influenced... a fifth danger is that children often have little notion of the duty to tell the truth... Finally, children sometimes behave in a way evil beyond their years' (Heydon, quoted in Spencer and Finn 1990)

Spencer and Flin have collected together much of the current research focusing on the debate as to the competence of children to give evidence in court and their book is essential reading for all professionals involved in this field. Overall the findings support the view that children can recall accurate information and can make reliable witnesses, refuting views such as Heydon's. However, a central theme throughout the research findings confirms that the quality and reliability of a child's evidence is dependent on the skills of the interviewer.

In tests of recall with children there will be a wide range of ability even within a single age level and factors such as motivation and emotional state can greatly affect memory. In experiments to test memory, using staged scenarios, results show that younger children typically report less information later in a free recall interview than older children and adults. However, the information they do recall is accurate – the difference is one of quantity not quality. In interviews using more specific questions younger children tended to be less accurate and found particular difficulty in gauging time, distance and speed. Again the important element in eliciting correct information was dependent on the communication skills of the interviewer (Spencer and Flin 1990).

Looking at skills of identification, Spencer and Flin found that children recalled limited but accurate information and that the amount and accuracy of the information increased with age: again children find specific details such as age, height, weight especially difficult. It is important to remember, however, that adults too frequently have difficulty in these areas of identification.

In assessing how stress impacts on memory, they summarise that there is increasing scientific evidence which indicates that children can remember a significant amount of information about traumatic events and there is no evidence that their reactions are essentially different from those of adult witnesses. They found that delay affects both adults' and children's memories, and this is a crucial factor for witnesses waiting many months between their involvement in a crime and the case finally coming to court. This factor has not escaped the notice of defendants and their legal representatives who can use tactics to prolong proceedings, such as unnecessary adjournments. These deliberate tactics aside, the system of bringing cases to court can be extremely slow. In 1988 the Home Office announced a policy to speed up progress in the handling of child abuse cases by the police and Crown Prosecution Service and strongly recommended a system of 'fast track' prosecutions, but despite this cases can still take from six months to eighteen months to reach a final trial date. Long delays will reduce the likelihood of children remembering details and thus reduce the possibility of conviction.

I accompanied a nine-year-old girl to Sheffield Crown Court in February 1990. The girl alleged that her uncle had sexually abused her on Bonfire Night in 1988 and on three subsequent occasions. She had waited fifteen months for the case to come to court. She was able to recount the abuse in great detail, but after skillful questioning by the defence barrister, she became confused over times, dates and details of clothing. Finally, the Judge stopped the trial. Spencer and Flin conclude that there is clear evidence that memory will fail over time in all ages but the initial interview can 'help the witness to consolidate his or her memory and this may help to inoculate it against the ravages of time' (Spencer and Flin 1990). It is crucial that cases involving children be brought to court as soon as possible, not only to ensure that information is not forgotten, but to enable treatment or therapy to commence when the trial is over.

Children and adults are suggestible and children do fantasise – make-believe is part of their play. Spencer and Flin point out that 'there is certainly no psychological research or medical case study material which suggests that children are in the habit of fantasising about the sort of incidents that might result in court proceedings', for example physical or sexual abuse.

With regard to the question of false allegations, it is pertinent to bear in mind that adults sometimes make false allegations on behalf of children, but overall, false allegations by children are rare. Rather than false allegations, a major risk in the investigation of child abuse is that children will frequently retract initial allegations; this particularly occurs in cases involving older children who may become more aware of the full implications of disclosures during an investigation.

In assessing how truthful children are and their appreciation of the duty to tell the truth, Flin conducted a survey with a group of children who had given evidence in a criminal trial (Flin *et al.* 1988). The children were asked why it was important to tell the truth in court. Their replies included 'You might get the wrong person', 'You must get the right account', 'You would get into trouble'. Another survey of children between six and ten years asked the children what would happen if they lied in court. The children said they would expect to be punished and most thought they would go to prison (Flin 1989). Such misunderstandings of the consequences imply that children are far more likely than their adult counterparts to tell the truth in court. The research also suggests that children as young as six do appreciate the importance of telling the truth.

In summary, the evidence supports the view that children can recall information accurately and, if interviewed skillfully, can provide the courts with a crucial source of evidence. So how has legislation changed to make it easier for child witnesses to appear in the criminal courts?

Legal Changes to Improve the Position of Child Witnesses

Legislation in England has changed over the past few years, recognising how advances in technological equipment can be introduced into the court process to reduce the trauma for children called to give evidence.

The Criminal Justice Act 1988

The first major change was introduced in the Criminal Justice Act 1988. Prior to this courts had started to allow a child to give evidence from behind a screen in the courtroom, but this change enabled a child under fourteen years of age, in a trial on indictment, to give evidence to the court via a live television link. The offence must be one of the following, listed in Section 32(2) of the Act:

(a) any offence which involves an assault on, or injury or threat of an injury to a person

(b) an offence under section 1 of the Children and Young Persons Act 1933 (cruelty to persons under 16)

(c) any offence under the Sexual Offences Act 1956, the Indecency with Children Act 1960, the Sexual Offences Act 1967, Section 54 of the Criminal Law Act 1977 or the Protection of Children Act 1978

(d) any offence which consists of attempting or conspiring to commit, or of aiding, abetting, counselling, procuring or inciting the commission of, an offence falling within (a) (b) or (c).

The child would no longer have to go into the courtroom and face the accused person. However, the television link could only be used with leave of the court on application from the prosecution. Certainly from my experience the limited number of centres equipped with the television link, even up to 1990, meant that it was not always possible to take advantage of this change in the legislation. An application to transfer a case to a centre with appropriate equipment could add considerable delays to the cases and Prosecution Agencies frequently did not apply for such transfers.

In June 1990 in *The Independent* I described how a nine-year-old boy was to be a witness in a trial of sexual abuse inflicted by his father. When he arrived at court with his foster mother, there were no screens in the courtroom and the witness box was approximately five feet from the dock. On behalf of the Social Services I complained, as did the police. The Judge asked for the case to be transferred to another court, but this was not possible. Eventually, the police constructed a screen, using a display board from a nearby police station covered with brown paper and sellotape. The trial then proceeded.

This case could have been heard at a Crown Court with television link facilities as the legislation was introduced specifically with this type of case in mind. No application had been made to transfer the case. It is still possible for a child to give evidence in open court with or without screens – a decision has to be made in each individual case. It is hoped that that decision is made after consultations with social services, the police and the Prosecution.

Report of The Advisory Group On Video Evidence (Pigot Report)

This Advisory Group was set up in June 1988 following pressure for more far-reaching reforms and was asked to consider the use of video recorded interviews with children that could be used as evidence. The Group strongly supported the use of such interviews for use at trials for violent and sexual offences and offences of cruelty and neglect involving children under fourteen years of age. They recommended their use to be extended to child witnesses under seventeen years if the offences were of a sexual nature. The Group also recommended keeping children out of the courthouse altogether and that the cross-examination of a child by the defence should be conducted away from court in informal surroundings at a preliminary hearing excluding the press and public. The Group recommended this to be extended for all vulnerable witnesses.

The Group put forward proposals that interviews with children should be conducted within a statutory code of practice and that the trial judge should take account of this code when deciding whether to admit the video-interviews in evidence. They recommended training for all those involved in investigating child abuse offences to enable these codes of practice to be implemented stringently.The Group examined the issue of age and the case of Wallwork (1958) which had led to a policy of not admitting the evidence of very young children in court. They concluded that all children, including very young children below the age of eight, should be regarded as competent witnesses unless the contrary is proved. They also recommended that children under fourteen should not take the oath or affirm.

Many of the recommendations have been incorporated into legislation, but regrettably the more child-centred proposals have not. In my own discussions with barristers, many felt that it was preferable to keep the child out of the courthouse and the idea of preliminary hearings prior to the trial was widely supported.

The Criminal Justice Act 1991

The provisions of Sections 52 to 55 of the Criminal Justice Act 1991 followed the recommendations of the Pigot Report. They provide for the evidence of children under fourteen years of age to be given unsworn and removes the special competency tests for these children. Section 53 allows committal proceedings to be by-passed following a certificate from the Director of Public Prosecutions in certain cases involving child witnesses. The defence will therefore no longer be able to require a child witness to appear in two separate court hearings, one at the magistrates court and a second at the crown court trial. Section 54 provides for the admissibility of video recorded interviews of child witnesses to violent or sexual offences. However, it will still be necessary for a child to attend court for cross-examination by the defence, although this maybe conducted by live television link.[1] The use of the television link is extended to the Youth Court and the Appeal Court and where a court does not have these facilities cases can be transferred to one that does. Section 55 makes further changes including the removal of the right of the accused in person to cross-examine a child witness.

The age limit of the use of video recorded interviews to replace the giving of evidence in chief to the court by a child is extended to under fifteen years of age if the child attains fourteen before the case comes to trial. In the case of sexual offences, video evidence can be used for cases involving children under seventeen years of age, or under eighteen if the case comes to trial after their seventeenth birthday. All video recorded interviews must be conducted in

---

1   Under the Prisoners and Criminal Proceedings (Scottish Bill), due to come into effect in 1993, children in Scotland will not have to appear in court for cross-examination either in the witness box or via the video link. The court will appoint a 'Commissioner' who will preside over a pre-trial hearing. All Parties will be present. This hearing will be recorded on video and may then be used at the full trial.

accordance with guidance which has now been published by the Home Office in conjunction with the Department of Health in the *Memorandum of Good Practice* (1992).

The use of the television link

The use of television links has been in use since 1988 and I have seen this system working well; children adapt surprisingly well to the technology and children as young as six years of age can give their evidence via the television link with considerable skill.

The child gives evidence from a specially equipped room within the courthouse. These rooms can often be small, cold and stark. In the main courtroom large screens show the child's face to the jury. The judge has a small monitor in front of him showing the same image and counsels for the prosecution and the defence have similar monitor screens beside them. It is the judge who operates the system and acts as editor of the television link technology. In a recent trial a girl of twelve was giving evidence against her stepfather via a live television link. She gave her evidence clearly and confidently. The accused man began to sob loudly and the sound system, ostensibly to enable the court to hear the child, relayed this sound back to the child. The judge had not anticipated this and the child, on hearing the sobs, also began to cry. Judges, therefore, need to be familiar with the technology and be able to cut off microphones speedily when appropriate.

Research carried out for the Home Office on the use of live links has shown that there is now widespread acceptance of the system and evidence from children using the link was more consistent and audible; the children were happier testifying in this way and felt safer and less pressured (Davies and Noon 1992).

It is hoped that the use of video evidence will show the court how the child was initially interviewed, and that an accused, seeing such evidence, may plead guilty rather than put the child through the ordeal of coming to court. There are likely to be initial problems in its use: trials may become much longer and minute details of the tapes may be queried in cross-examination of the child. There may be long arguments on interviewing techniques and if more than one video tape has been made, cross-examination may involve detailed analysis if one tape contradicts another. However, it is too early to speculate on how video evidence will be received by the courts and how successful this way of presenting evidence will be.

In 1987 I accompanied three young girls who had been sexually abused by a parent. They all entered the Crown Court where they each had to stand alone in the witness box and give their evidence without screens. They faced the jury, judge, barristers, the press, the public gallery and the accused. The details they recounted were shocking and each girl was questioned in the witness box for over four hours. The new legislation means that this type of ordeal should no longer be commonplace in our criminal justice system.

The Process and Practice of Taking Evidence from Children

The legislation has set up a new structure for the court proceedings but the process of taking evidence begins as soon as an allegation is made that a possible offence has been committed. Traditionally, different agencies have had the responsibility of evidentiary or therapeutic concerns in child abuse cases, but now the need for much closer cooperation between the police and child protection agencies is imperative. If the judiciary are to be convinced of the validity and credibility of the new procedures then *Working Together* (Home Office 1991) and *The Memorandum of Good Practice* (Home Office 1992) will need to be adhered to by those agencies.

The Cleveland Inquiry (Butler Sloss 1988) was set up to examine the reception of one hundred and twenty children into care and the breakdown of communication and trust between the police, medical and child protection agencies. The Report by Lord Clyde was critical of the lack of appropriate interviewing skills demonstrated by social workers investigating child abuse in Orkney and now a report by Her Majesty's Inspectorate of Constabulary has severely criticised the methods used by the police in interviewing suspects.

All these reports call for more training and, in particular, inter-agency training if we are to avoid the mistakes and poor practice revealed in these various inquiries. Conroy, Fielding and Tunstill (1990) found that four-fifths of police forces and three-quarters of social services departments were conducting joint interviews with children, however much of the interviewing of the children's families and alleged offenders was likely to be undertaken separately. NACRO published information suggesting that in 1990 only one-third of police forces had specially trained and designated officers to investigate child abuse cases and only two-thirds used video-taped interviewing techniques. With the implementation of *Working Together* this situation should have altered and all areas should by now have joint-investigation teams. However, there is clearly a need for extensive training and resources to be made available for ongoing inter-agency training if we are to be able to marry up the balance between ensuring the child is protected with the strict demands of evidence for the criminal courts introduced by the Criminal Justice Act 1991.

Memorandum of Good Practice (Home Office and Department of Health 1992)

The *Memorandum of Good Practice* is an attempt to set out procedures which will make good practice consistent in the making of video recorded interviews with child witnesses. This guidance is voluntary. It recommends that the interview should be conducted by jointly trained police and social work investigation teams in order to replace the examination in chief of a child by an advocate in open court.

The system will only work if there are sufficient trained teams and appropriate facilities for conducting joint interviews.[2]

At some point the team may decide to interview the child and make a video recording of this interview. In this event they should adhere closely to the procedures recommended in the *Memorandum Of Good Practice* as this evidence may be used in later court proceedings: standards of practice will be open to detailed public scrutiny. If the video recorded interviews are not up to a standard acceptable to the courts the investigating teams, who have for so long been critical of the judiciary for its unacceptable treatment of child witnesses, will be judged similarly inept. The video recorded interview should replace the statement usually taken of the first detailed account given to the police of alleged abuse. It should be conducted as soon as is practicable after the inter-agency consultation and planning and after any possible medical examinations. 'If an interview takes place shortly after allegations or disclosure it will usually provide the freshest account least tainted by subsequent discussions and questioning' (Pigot 1989).

Early discussions prior to the substantive interview should be clearly recorded. Here other professionals or family members will be able to assist the interviewers. It will be important to know about any disabilities or special needs of the child or any communication or cultural issues that may be relevant.

At the beginning of the investigation the Memorandum recommends workers should 'Listen to the child, rather than directly question him/her. Never stop a child who is freely recalling significant events. Make a note of the discussions, taking care to record the timing, setting and personnel present as well as what is said. Record all subsequent events up to the time of the substantive interview' (Home Office 1992).

If it becomes clear that a criminal offence has been committed the child should be given an explanation of the interview to follow. The conditions for the video recorded interview should then be set up as soon as possible – this should reduce the child's stress and the risk of important details being forgotten. The Memorandum advises the use of appropriate settings for such an interview and also the type of equipment to use. The interview must be planned and pertinent questions carefully listed, and should take account of the child's age, understanding, vocabulary, language and emotional state.

Attention must be paid to the child's comfort and it should be the child who dictates the pace of the interview. The interviewer should be someone experienced in communicating with children and familiar with the basic rules of evidence and the elements of the criminal offences. As the Memorandum says: 'This is a formidable job specification' (p.6).

It may not always be the police or social services who are best able to communicate with the child: a teacher or school nurse may have the child's

---

2   Community Care (11.2.93.) reported the recent findings of Professor Graham
     Davies, Leicester University, who is monitoring the implementation of video
     recorded evidence in child abuse cases for the Home Office. His preliminary
     findings suggest that many social services departments are not yet ready to video
     children's evidence for the courts due to lack of training of joint police and social
     service investigation teams and also a lack of resources to set up and operate the
     expensive video facilities.

confidence and trust. If that person is willing to cooperate they should not be excluded from the interview process as their skills and knowledge may be invaluable to the success of the interview – they might even conduct part of the interview. In trials using the Memorandum in Oxfordshire joint teams found that 'Whoever has a rapport with the child would be the lead interviewer, with an earpiece so that the other person could act as a consultant outside the room' (Neate 1992).

The interviews should follow the 'stepwise process', a systematic interview technique pioneered by Professor John Yuille of the University of British Columbia. This begins with the 'rapport stage' – building a rapport between the child and the interviewer – which includes discussions of truth and the introduction of the purpose of the interview. The child needs to know that it is fine to say they don't know in answer to any questions.

The child should then be asked to give an account of events without being prompted or asked leading questions. Next, the child may be asked open-ended questions for more information, but again there should be no leading questions or pressure put on the child. Specific questions maybe asked for clarification, and non-suggestive interview aids such as drawing pads and crayons may also be useful. These questions will seek to extend and clarify only the information that the child has already given. Only experience and training will equip interviewers in this extremely difficult area of work.

The Memorandum recommends that there should be a closing phase to the interview, possibly returning to some of the more 'neutral' topics discussed in the rapport stage. An explanation of what happens next should be given to the child and it is important that the child is given a contact name and telephone number in case the child needs to discuss further matters (this number may be for the keyworker appointed at the child protection conference).

What the Memorandum does not do is suggest alternatives or acknowledge the difficulties in interviewing children. There are many factors to do with fear, damage, trauma and personal circumstances in long-term child abuse cases which prevent children from telling.

> Such children are unlikely to respond to the spontaneous recall and free narrative style the memorandum advocates. (Wattam 1992)

> Conducting interviews with child sexual abuse witnesses must rank as one of the most demanding interview situations due to the sensitivity of the topic, the reticence of the victim and the potential conflict between evidentiary and therapeutic goals. (Spencer and Flin 1990)

If the interview is skilfully conducted it will enable the video to speak to the court on any fact related by the child which the child could have given in person to the court. However, if the video is subsequently used at a trial the child must be available to attend court to be cross-examined by the defence.[3]

---

3   Recent reports in Community Care 11.2.93. suggest that in some areas where
     video evidence has been used the legal process may backfire on agencies taking
     the case to court. They quote a recent case in Dorset where a case using video
     evidence was thrown out by the judge before it came to court. The judge argued,
     after viewing the video, that it would 'not be in the child's best interest' to proceed.

THE NEED FOR PROFESSIONALS TO WORK TOGETHER FOLLOWING THE INVESTIGATION

Almost all the literature in this area focuses on the issues surrounding disclosure, the investigation and the interviewing of child witnesses. Although the success of these stages is crucial to the eventual outcome of any trial, there is also the period of time between the investigation and the final court hearing as well as the aftermath of the trial.

The interim period, waiting for the trial, can be one of considerable upheaval in cases of inter-familial abuse: the child and his/her family must try to pick up the pieces and return to some kind of normality and routine. For some children a return home is not possible and they may be looked after by the local authority or placed with other relatives; for those who can return home it may be that a family member is in custody or living away and the family must come to terms with this loss. Other children in the family may not fully understand the changes and the abused child may experience guilt and recriminations. In some cases the extended family may be angry and try to exert pressure on the child to withdraw the allegations. There also may be other legal proceedings, possibly civil proceedings, which again will place stress and anxiety on the family. The child may become withdrawn and isolated. Whatever the situation the child and family will need considerable ongoing help. The keyworker and the core group of involved professionals appointed to implement the child protection plan need to work closely together at this time to ensure that the child's welfare is paramount.

The police, via the Crown Prosecution Service, will be best placed to monitor the progress of the criminal case as it proceeds through the court system. The keyworker needs to be kept closely informed, particularly with information relating to possible bail conditions of the accused and any issues of child protection which may need to be addressed by the social services. The child may need special help and consideration at school, in which case teachers or nursery staff will play an important role in coping with any behavioural or emotional difficulties manifested by the child. Family or foster parents need to be kept informed and involved during these months of waiting so that they can answer the child's questions, and they too will require support and reassurance. As Plotnikoff (1990) points out 'Emotion can be communicated contagiously to the child by non-verbal as well as verbal means.' I have known cases were families have felt abandoned and isolated at this time and as a result have had to seek help from their doctor for sedatives and other medication as a way of coping with the stress and uncertainty as court proceedings seem to drag on for months.

The core group must liaise and plan their intervention so that maximum support is offered: families often initially seem to cope well and signs of trauma may go unnoticed. Conversely, however, if too many professionals are offering help the assistance can be counter-productive and inconsistent. Contact must be coordinated.

The case first goes through the Magistrates Court and is eventually committed to the Crown Court. The Crown Prosecution Service may apply to the Crown Court for an early 'Plea and Directions' hearing – witnesses are not called at this stage and this may be the first time that the prosecution are informed of the defendant's plea. The prosecution will give advance warning to the court of the specific directions and arrangements it will be seeking in the event of a not guilty plea. The court will be told that the case involves a child witness and informed of the reasons for requesting certain facilities. The police and 'keyworker' need to advise the prosecution well in advance of this hearing if screens or live television links are required. Judges have a wide discretion to vary procedures in court and preparation of the child for court will be made easier if as many procedural matters as possible can be decided in advance. If a video-taped interview is to be part of the evidence the judge can make a decision as to its admissibility either at an early stage or in the event of a disagreement between the prosecution and defence about admissibility of whole or part of a video-interview.

The keyworker will need to explain to the family the purpose of such a hearing. Families receive formal notification of court dates and these letters are frequently written in unfamiliar jargon that is incomprehensible to them. They may become very anxious if they do not understand what is happening.

Eventually, notification will be received of the trial date. The police and keyworker should be alerted to that date via the Crown Prosecution Service so that representations can be made to the court listing officer to arrange an appropriate courtroom. Sometimes a prior visit to the court can be arranged for a child, which may help to familiarise the child with the court arrangements and layout. A child maybe permitted to sit in the witness box and practice speaking out loud, they may be allowed to see the television link room and speak through the microphone. Plotnikoff (1990) describes how in some cases arrangements have been made for a child to meet a judge (not the judge in their case). Such visits are usually organised by the social worker, who should contact courthouse personnel prior to the visit. Lunchtimes can be a convenient time as the court room is then empty and visits do not interfere with the busy working of the court. Custom and practice does vary around the country – in some areas these arrangements are seen as an integral part of the process for child witnesses, whereas in other areas they are not encouraged.

There are some useful pamphlets available from the Children's Legal Centre: *The Child Witness* and *Being a Witness* explain the system in simple language which may be of help to the child and the family.

A few days prior to the trial the child can read through any statements or transcripts of recorded evidence that they made at the time of the investigation to 'refresh their recollection of events'. The Police retain copies of these documents but can delegate the job of assisting the child to read through them to whoever the child chooses.

DAY OF THE TRIAL

Careful planning is necessary to transport the child to court on the day of the trial. I have known instances when children have arrived at court and come face to face with the accused and his/her family waiting in the same area of the courthouse – this could be disastrous and can cause considerable distress to all concerned. Many courts do not have adequate waiting facilities or separate waiting areas, and I have known children to wait in barristers' robing rooms and probation offices. The child should be able to wait in a separate room within the courtbuilding where they can relax and feel safe. Crown Prosecution Service personnel usually make these arrangements but again care must be given to ensure that these details have been coordinated prior to the trial date.

There maybe considerable delays before the child is called to give evidence and activities and refreshments should be provided. Television and video games may be available in waiting areas, and books and magazines. I remember a small boy and his teacher quietly getting on with sums in the barristers' robing rooms, absorbed and busy.

Plotnikoff (1990) suggests that it should be possible for a child to be introduced to both prosecution and defence counsel together before the trial, as this may allay fears and anxieties. I have never come across this and am aware that many barristers strongly disapprove of such a practice. However, a portly and bewigged barrister can appear quite startling to a child. A preliminary meeting could be helpful but this would depend on the communication skills of the barrister.

When the child is finally called to give evidence he/she will be led by the usher to the courtroom or live-television link room. In some courts there are no special entrances for witnesses and the child may have to pass the dock – in these circumstances the accused will be removed until the child is positioned in the courtroom behind a screen. The judge may allow a parent or social worker to sit with the child. Where a child is giving evidence via the television link it was the case until recently that a decision would be made by the judge as to who would be allowed to sit with the child, and I have seen social workers, foster parents and ushers perform this role. The task is difficult: the Court of Appeal described the role as one 'to be undertaken with considerable care, the court has to be astute to see that nothing improper passes and no undue encouragement is given to the child witness to make him or her say something other than the truth' (Home Office 1992).

The Lord Chancellor's office has now directed that the usher is the most appropriate person to sit with the child. However, as the main purpose of the link is to enable children to give their evidence in the least stressful surroundings away from the austere and formal court setting, it makes little sense to place the child in a room with a complete stranger. A more helpful arrangement would be to allow the child, as is presently permitted in the court witness box, to have a parent or trusted adult to accompany them, with a court usher also present to ensure that there is no improper communication. It is the judge who decides this issue.

In a recent case in the Sheffield Crown Court a child was taken to the video link room with an usher but on being questioned she refused to answer. She cried out 'I'm not answering, why can't you leave me alone'. The trial was adjourned for twenty minutes and during this break a court official was sent out to buy a doll to help the child describe what had allegedly taken place. Both prosecuting and defence counsel then argued against the use of the doll. Such scenes can only lead to confusion and distress, and this is a good example of a case in which a video recording of the initial interview would have been more helpful.

In my experience judges are sensitive to the needs of young children and where possible they do try to put children at ease during their court appearance; for example, barristers and judges often remove their wigs in an attempt to reduce the formality of their appearance. Barristers do not have any formal training in communication with children and often experience difficulties in simplifying their questions and using childlike language. Children frequently use slang or colloquial words and barristers need to be familiar with these expressions.

Language can lead to misunderstandings – in a recent case a child was being asked about his clothing and when asked 'What else did you have on?' The child answered 'Only the television'. It should be made clear to the child that they can answer 'I don't know' or 'I don't understand' when being questioned. The quality of a child's evidence is dependent upon the skill of the barrister.

Probably the most distressing part of the proceedings will be when the child is cross-examined by the defence counsel. When challenged by seasoned barristers children may think they are not being believed or may become confused – it is at this point that I have often seen children become distressed and break down. The defence counsel plays a dangerous game of trying to discredit the child's evidence, but does not want to alienate the jury from his cause.

After the child has given evidence the judge will often say a few words to the child. Children remember these words vividly. A young girl recently told me that after she had given evidence the judge had said to her 'I hope you can now go and get on with your own life and put all this behind you'. She had found this particularly comforting. Following this the child can leave the court and, unlike adult witnesses they are not usually permitted back into court to observe the rest of the trial.

It is imperative that support continues – the family need to be kept informed as to how the case progresses and the final outcome. In the event of a not guilty verdict anger can be intense and the child can be left with a feeling that they were not believed. The verdict needs to be explained to the child: 'Whatever the verdict, the explanation should relieve the child of responsibility for the outcome' (Plotnikoff 1990).[4]

It is now that social workers will take on the significant role of helping the child and family to come to terms with the outcome and begin to help them rebuild their lives.

4	A. Wade (1993) describes how in Canada, where children are helped to understand their evidence and to view their role as only one part of the overall case, they more readily see that they do not therefore carry the full weight of responsibility for the success or failure of a prosecution. Children are encouraged to see themselves and their supporters as a team who will attend court together.

SUMMARY

No matter how much information is provided to all those working in this difficult area of child protection the success or failure of the child's court experience will depend on the care and support offered at all stages from the initial investigation to the final hearing and the time of offering therapy or treatment when the court case is over. Courts in different areas vary in their custom and practices, and it is vital that joint teams clarify and demystify the acceptable procedures in their courts. It may be that where problems arise they will need to be addressed at the level of the Area Child Protection Committee or Joint Working Meetings for all court users. Constant monitoring and coordination is essential to improve and tailor the court arrangements to meet the needs of child witnesses. Children should not be revictimised by the internal wranglings of agencies whose main aim is to ensure the care and protection of abused children.

EXERCISE 13.1

1. Brainstorming exercise. All students record words that are used for breasts, genitals, intercourse, touching in a sexual way and so on, thinking of words that children use, such as slang.

   Objective: To be aware of the many different words used that can cause confusion and difficulty when asking a child to relate events around an incident of sexual abuse.

2. Familiarising students in practical use of the technology, video cameras and video recording equipment. The trainer will need to be arrange for the appropriate equipment to be available for two 3–hour sessions. Each student should have the opportunity to be instructed in the use of the equipment and become familiar with how to use it.

   Objective: To be comfortable and skilled in the use of such equipment.

3. Making video-recorded interviews. In small groups students take it in turns to record interviews of each other relating their first sexual experience.

   Objective: To become sensitive to the difficulties of any child having to relate intimate and often embaressing details in an interview faced by intimidating equipment which is to be recorded.

4. The trainer needs to provide copies of *Memorandum of Good Practice* and *Working Together under the Children Act 1989*. Students are given time to read and become familiar with these codes.

Objective: To have the basic knowledge of the Codes.
Exercises: Essay questions are set asking students to examine the codes critically and think of practical problems that might hinder (a) inter-agency work and (b) the making of video-recorded interviews with children.

5. Visit to a Crown Court. The trainer needs to liaise with court to arrange visit – students should spend at least two days sitting through a trial, preferably where television link facilities are to be used and/or video recorded evidence.

Objective: To be aware of the process and difficulties that may arise and to see first hand the facilities and equipment in use.

Exercises: The students have 30 minutes to work in small groups and discuss their impressions of the court. They should identify the key figures, for example the Defending Barrister, Prosecuting Barrister, Probation Officer, Police, Representative of the Defence Solicitor, the Usher, the Family of the accused, and ask questions such as: Is anyone sitting at the side of the Judge? Who are they? What is their role? After 30 minutes they rejoin the class to discuss these roles and check factual information.

Objective: To be aware of how difficult it is to identify key figures. To clarify who does what and why.

REFERENCES

Butler Sloss, E. (1988) *Report of the Inquiry into Child Abuse in Cleveland 1987.* London: HMSO.

Conroy, Fielding and Tunstill (1992) Research quoted in *Criminal Justice and the Prevention of Child Sexual Abuse.* London: NACRO.

Davies, G. and Noon, E. (1992) *An Evaluation of the Live Link for Child Witnesses.* London: Home Office.

Department of Health HMSO (1988) *Protecting Children. A Guide for Social Workers Undertaking a Comprehensive Assessment.* London: Department of Health, HMSO.

Editorial 'Comment' (1990) *The Guardian,* 22 December.

Flin, R.H. (1990) *Child Witnesses in Scottish Criminal Prosecutions* Report to the Scottish Home and Health Departments.

Flin, R., Davies, G. and Tarrant, A. (1988) *Children as Witnesses.* Final Report to The Scottish Home and Health Department, Grant 85/9290.

Flin, R., Stevenson, Y. and Davies, G. (1989) 'Children's knowledge of court proceedings'. *British Journal of Psychology,* 80, 285–297.

Godfrey, M. and Hopkins, C. (1992) 'Taking Evidence' *Community Care* 13 August.

Home Office (1989) *Report of the Advisory Group on Video Evidence.* (The Pigot Report) London: Home Office.

Home Office, Department of Health, Department of Education and Science, Welsh Office (1991) *Working Together Under The Children Act 1989.* London: HMSO.

Home Office, Department of Health (1992) *Memorandum of Good Practice.* London: HMSO.

Ivory, M. (1993) Child Video Evidence a non-starter, say S.S.D.'s'. *Community Care* 11 February.

NACRO (1992) *Criminal Justice and the Prevention of Child Sexual Abuse.* London: NACRO.

Neate, P. (1992) 'A Question of Focus'. *Community Care* 19 March.

O'Hara, M. (1990) 'A Competent Witness'. *Community Care* 21 May.

Owen, H. and Todd, I. (1990) 'The Courtroom Ordeal of Child Victims'. *The Independent* 6 July.

Plotnikoff, J. (1990) *The Child Witness.* The Children's Legal Centre.

Plotnikoff, J. (1990a) *Going to Court.* The Children's Legal Centre.

Spencer and Flin, R.H. (1990) *The Evidence of Children, The Law and The Psychology.* London: Blackstone.

Wasik, M. and Taylor, R.D. (1991) *Blackstone's Guide to the Criminal Justice Act 1991.* Blackstone Press.

Wattam, J. (1992) 'For Justice or Therapy' *Community Care* 27 August.

Wade, A. (1993) 'The Canadian Experience' *Community Care* 4 February.

CHAPTER 14

CHILD PROTECTION
THE POLICE PERSPECTIVE

COLIN WALKE

The involvement of the police in cases of child abuse stems from the historical principle that they have a duty to protect life and limb and to prevent and investigate crime.

Initially, one may imagine that the role of police officers in investigating child abuse is relatively straightforward: has a crime – be it a sexual or violent crime or one of neglect – been committed? Is this child a victim or witness to this crime? What can they tell us? If there are other witnesses, what, if anything, can they tell us? What evidence have we got? Sadly, it is not as easy as that. There are any number of other significant factors which need to be considered and addressed in line with both criminal and/or civil proceedings.

Today, with the emphasis on multi-agency co-operation, the role of the police in child protection extends beyond that of only criminal investigation. It embraces other duties and responsibilities, especially as the welfare of the child and his/her needs are the overriding and paramount considerations.

Throughout the process of an investigation, much information is collected by a variety of agencies. It is essential that as much appropriate information as possible be shared between the agencies to ensure both the child's safety and an effective investigation.

In cases where a criminal prosecution is being pursued, the evidence obtained during the joint police/social worker investigation and held by the Crown Prosecution Service may be invaluable in securing the long-term safety of a child through the civil courts. It is, therefore, equally essential that good and co-operative communication exists between the Crown Prosecution Service and the Social Services legal departments. The police, along with all other professionals and agencies involved in an investigation, need to have a clear recognition and understanding of where they fit into the whole process.

The police are a constituent member of the local ACPC (Area Child Protection Committee), and policy, procedure and training will need to be in line with ACPC guidelines. It is important, therefore, that police training, both in-house and multi-agency, fits ACPC agreed strategies. It is assumed that the training outlined in the following paragraphs would need to be fully dis-

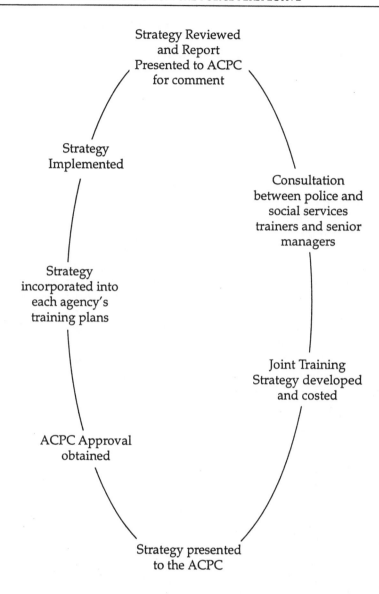

Figure 14.1: Yearly cycle for the implementation of a joint training strategy.

cussed and agreed by whichever ACPC structure exists locally (see Figure 14.1).

I have identified three key areas of training/awareness raising for police officers which, I believe, may go some way to achieving the recognition and understanding to which I previously alluded.

1. For probationers and other police officers.
2. For managers.
3. For practitioners.

PROBATIONERS AND OTHER POLICE OFFICERS

In-house training for police probationers, that is, those in their first two years of service, and other police officers would need to focus predominantly on general principles.

Prior to commencing in-house training for probationers there will be a need for trainers to establish what, if any, input has been made at the District Training Centres, and tailor their needs accordingly. During one of the Post-Foundation phases (the Foundation phase is spent at District Training Centres) adequate time – at least a day – should be allocated for relevant exercises and issues to be addressed. These should include The Children Act 1989, the implementation and use of police powers, and various aspects of child abuse. Unless the trainer feels suitably qualified and comfortable, this should be done by a member of a child protection team or a child protection trainer. The issues that need to be focused on include such matters as:

- What is child abuse?
- How do I recognise it?
- Who do I contact?
- What will happen?
- What will I be starting?

In reality, police officers often attend incidents which involve violence or severe disturbance and, upon arrival, discover children present. Officers need to be mindful of the child protection issues as much as the public order or other more obvious criminal aspects. Care must also be taken by officers not to appear to be socially judgemental and to treat each incident separately and uniquely.

Until such time as every police officer has received this basic training, the following aspects will be necessary for all officers.

Formal in-house training may be totally impractical due to workload and resource/abstraction problems. In general terms, the development and distribution of *aide mémoire* cards highlighting the key points above is a start. Explanatory articles appearing in police magazines and journals, both nationally and more locally, may also 'spread the word', as may videos produced to raise awareness and instill confidence in would-be referrers.

A keystone for all police officers, especially – but not exclusively – those interested in becoming child protection investigators, is the potential to be involved in, and attend, multi-agency child protection training, if it exists in their area. This training can be developed and tailored to accommodate officers' attendance for half a day, one day or two days, as individual forces may deem appropriate. Although many areas do not have such multi-agency training, I have found locally that officers attending these courses, along with a variety of people from other agencies and disciplines, have thought them to be extremely worthwhile. Areas considered and explored include: what is child abuse?; recognition of signs and indicators; principles and local procedures for all agencies; the legal framework; and professional dangerousness.

Such training and awareness raising within the police service may dispel some of the myths that surround child protection work and, it is hoped, prevent such inane and derisory comments such as, 'it's not real police work', 'it's a policewoman's job', 'leave it to the Social Services', 'we get few convictions at the end of it', and 'Monday to Friday, 9 to 5, nice'.

MANAGERS

Practitioners have known it for a long time, Home Office circulars have mentioned it, and so has the Orkney 1992 report: investigation into alleged child abuse is very stressful and 'requires a corresponding degree of support' (Orkney Report 1992).

If child abuse investigations are to be fully and skilfully completed, the role of a supportive and knowledgeable manager is essential. If workers feel isolated and abandoned, or if managers appear uninterested and aloof, investigations may not be satisfactorily concluded and unnecessary problems or barriers may impede future working practice.

In-house management training for police may include issues surrounding the interviewing of alleged child abuse offenders, legal and procedural requirements and liaison with the Crown Prosecution Service, child care legislation, such as the Children Act 1989 and its implications for the police.

Under the auspices of the ACPC, Joint Management courses (Police and Social Services) should be, and have been, run. Preferably, these should be residential, as (a) this makes it easier for people to concentrate and focus their minds on the training, and (b) the opportunity for both formal and informal exchanges of ideas and experiences is enhanced by participants not having to go home at the end of each day.

These courses should include:

- Understanding and appreciation of the investigative process and its effects on families and professionals
- Knowledge of legislative changes/government guidance/judicial review and stated cases
- Good practice in relation to child protection
- An understanding of each other's functions
- Joint decision making in line with procedures
- Staff support needs
- Skills in reviewing video interviews
- Gender and sexuality issues

- Race, culture, religion and language considerations.

The frequency and length of these courses will undoubtedly be determined by cost and resource implications, but if children are to receive the best service possible, we should strive to develop and run these courses. Subsequent, timely seminars to review work practices, update on current theory, practice and legislative changes should not be overlooked when devising future training plans.

PRACTITIONERS

From a variety of reports and inquiries – from Cleveland in 1987, the 'Working Together' documents and Home Office circulars through to Orkney 1992 – much reference has been made to the selection and training of child abuse investigators.

There are no national criteria laid down for this, and individual police forces will, therefore, have devised and developed their own selection and training methods. This may well be determined by whichever child abuse investigation system they operate, be it dedicated teams/units or otherwise. The length and content of training courses will also universally vary. Some forces may provide in-house training, or supply appropriate pre-read material, to workers prior to their attendance on a basic Joint Investigation course. This is in order to ensure that workers receive a basic grounding in important key areas such as race, culture, religion, sexuality, disability, gender and so on, and to make the most effective use of course time and material.

What I propose to do is to identify key practice related issues which may need to be addressed on Joint Investigation (Police and Social Services) training courses for practitioners.

The course needs to be structured to:

1. • enable Police and Social Workers to develop an understanding of each other's functions within child protection procedures

   • provide Police and Social Workers with the necessary knowledge and skills to enable them to undertake investigations into cases of sexual, physical and emotional abuse and neglect

   • consider together the evidential issues relating to statements from children i.e., previous statements and hearsay, leading questions and bad character of the accused

   • develop interview skills based on an understanding of child development and the effects of abuse

   • address the personal issues for investigators which may surface in work with abused children and their families

   • provide a model for carrying out investigations within the framework of the Children Act 1989, taking into account race, culture, gender and disability.

2. Equip the participants with the following knowledge:

   • relevant aspects of human development

- theoretical explanations of human development
- research findings relating to child sexual abuse and possible outcomes
- signs, indicators and assessment of risk in all forms of abuse
- interview techniques
- child protection policy and local procedures
- the effect of investigation into abuse on the child, the family and others involved
- relevant child care law and evidential issues.

3. Equip the participants with skills in:

- working with another agency
- communicating and consulting with children
- conducting a joint investigation interview into child abuse in line with the *Memorandum of Good Practice*
- working within the context of the law and local child protection policy and procedures
- working with families and other agencies
- using, and appearing on, video.

4. Enable participants to explore their own feelings in relation to all forms of abuse on children.

Appropriate participation of skilled and qualified guest speakers is essential. These may include consultant child psychiatrists, community or consultant paediatricians, forensic scientists, representatives from the Crown Prosecution Service (to explain the 'sufficiency of evidence' requirement) and a child care solicitor.

A time consuming, but particularly important, component is a post-course meeting between participant, line manager and trainer(s). This is to evaluate learning on the course, to identify future training/learning needs and to discuss any issues raised on the end-of-course evaluation forms.

It may very well be that not all of what I have identified for training practitioners can be properly achieved during one course. Consideration, therefore, needs to be given to on-going or 'top-up' training within an appropriate and reasonable time scale.

Some Police forces and Social Services Departments may already have installed video equipment in their interview suites in line with the *Memorandum of Good Practice* recommendations and guidelines. Practice in operating this equipment is vitally important.

Practitioners should also be aware of dual-agency Child Protection Protocols (if they exist in their area). Protocols may address such matters as:

- principles applying to all investigations
- the aims of a Joint Investigation
- procedures for referrals
- timing of investigations

- planning
- recording
- parental involvement
- the video interview
- post interview issues (progress meetings/decisions, etc.).

Although course participants may have differences of opinion, these may be resolved through sensitive confrontation and discussion. There should be an awareness, acknowledgement and sharing of individuals' skills, strengths and limitations. Developing genuine mutual trust and respect for each other's roles and functions, without blurring one's own responsibilities, leads to a more tolerant and open-minded approach.

An exercise which has received particularly favourable comment from all the participants in the Joint Investigation course I am involved in running is centred on video interviewing 'live' children from a local middle school.[1]

What needs to be established is a school that is willing to participate. The exercise should come towards the end of the course when all of the theoretical aspects of communicating with children and the legal constraints, the phased approach and 'use of questions' exercises have been completed.

About a month before the course, a letter is sent to all the parents of the children in the class involved explaining the object of the exercise. The letter is jointly signed by the Headteacher of the school and the trainer (on behalf of the Social Services Department and the Police) and sent out via the school. A return slip is attached in order for any parent not wishing their child to participate to indicate this. Care is taken not to involve this particular child and not to embarrass them should they indicate a desire to take part on the actual day of the exercise.

On the day before the exercise, subject to the class availability, 2 or 3 people (perhaps police trainers in ordinary clothes/jeans, etc.) enter the classroom and 'stage an incident', for example, measure up windows/curtains/carpets or do something fairly unusual and attempt to involve the class teacher and children. A minor altercation or disagreement between the 'workers' may also take place. This entire scenario is video recorded. The whole episode may take no more than, say, 10 minutes.

Also on the day before the exercise, the course participants are informed that they will be attending the school in order to 'interview' the children. The purpose of the exercise is explained, that being to allow them to practice the phased approach and their questioning skills with a child on video. They are told that 'an incident' took place in the classroom in front of the children. Their task, using the phased approach and their questioning skills, will be to determine what the child can remember, if anything. This will also be videoed. Subject to the size of the course and the constraints within the school, each pair of interviewers is usually allocated 15 minutes. As far as possible, they are paired off with a member of the other agency with whom they may actually work in the future.

---

1   Credit for the original idea for the exercise must go to Inspector Keith Lawrence of West Yorkshire Police.

Before the exercise starts, the trainer carefully explains why the Police and Social Workers are here – that is, to practice talking with children. None of the police officers throughout the course should be in uniform. In the introduction to the children, the trainer should make no reference to the videoed incident of the previous day. Volunteers are asked for to speak with the 'interviewers'. Following deliberate discussion with the class teacher, in order not to upset anyone and to obtain a cross-section of children, it is the class teacher who selects the children to be interviewed.

The children are taken to the interviewers and introduced. At the end of their interviews the children are returned to their class. Care should be taken to ask them not to tell other children in the class about their interviews until all the interviews have been completed. Once this is done, the trainer should return to the classroom and explain the exercise in full detail to all the children and thank them for their co-operation. A thank-you letter and donation to the class may also be sent later.

On returning to the course venue, the videos are watched and participants de-briefed, usually in two groups with a trainer to each group. Feedback and observations are offered sensitively to all interviewers.

CONCLUSION

If the training strategies mentioned here are to be implemented, police forces will need to be willing to commit sufficient funds for child protection training. In addition, if multi-agency co-operation in developing training is to be effective, a designated child protection trainer will need to be identified and the specialist skills and knowledge required to implement training strategies be recognised.

ACKNOWEDGEMENT

I am indebted to Jane Wonnacott, Surrey Social Services Staff Development and Training Manager (Child Protection) for her help and permission to refer to multi-agency training in Surrey and to use material referred to for Management and Joint Investigation training jointly developed. Also, to Detective Chief Inspector Derek Short and Sgt. Bob Maidment, both of Surrey Police, for their time and valuable comments.

REFERENCES

Home Office Circular 84 (1991).

Home Office and Deparment of Health (1992) *Memorandum of Good Practice*. London: HMSO

Home Office, Department of Health, Department of Education and Science, Welsh Office (1989) *Working Together Under the Children Act*. London: HMSO.

The Report of the Inquiry into the Removal of Children from Orkney in February 1991. Edinburgh: HMSO.

Surrey Child Protection Committee, Manual of Procedures.

Surrey Social Services/Surrey Police Child Protection Protocol.

CHAPTER 15

SUPERVISION AND SUPPORT OF WORKERS INVOLVED IN CHILD PROTECTION CASES

DOROTA IWANIEC

INTRODUCTION

Numerous public inquiry reports have indicated a lack of national policies and clear procedures in child protection work, as well as a lack of constructive supervision for the staff dealing with highly stressful cases (see Brent Borough Council 1985, Butler-Sloss 1988, Greenwich Borough Council 1987, Lambeth Borough Council 1987). While issues of policies and procedures have been addressed and dealt with, those of staff supervision (especially on a professional and supportive level) still have received little attention. Very few agencies have clearly defined and developed departmental policies on staff supervision that embrace all the supervisory functions, and not many training courses are available to help those who supervise child protection workers to do the job effectively. There seems to be a consistent under-estimation of the time required and the skills needed for the tasks.

Adequately organised and facilitated supervision should be seen as essential in any agency that deals with child protection work and should be available to all ranks in the organisational structure. Tragic events in recent years (both in parental homes and in various institutions) clearly point to serious shortcomings at grass-root and management levels in social work. Constant hammering of social workers and their managers by the media has shaken the public's confidence in social work practice.

Extensive literature on child abuse points out dilemmas with which child protection workers are faced: 'care and control'; disputes and confusion about workers' accountability and how they work in the supervisory relationship; uncertainties in decision-making; and judgement of risk situations. Other issues are the question of collusion between families and other professionals, and the prevailing sense of optimism that things will somehow work themselves out. Social workers may even be severely demoralised because of the emotional impact of the work they do and atmosphere in which they do it, which may lead to the development of passive 'policing' and a denial of the very real problems involved (see Hallett and Stevenson 1980, Clare 1988).

PURPOSE OF SUPERVISION

Supervision implies overseeing appropriate functioning of the worker within specified tasks given by the employing agency. It also implies guidance, advice, correction, encouragement, teaching, and support. Child protection work, with its tasks and responsibilities, will be dictated by legislation, policies, procedures, and available resources. The content and the quality of work will be determined by the workers' level of knowledge, their skills, judgement, confidence, stamina, and the support and help given to them to do the job effectively and efficiently. The supervision of workers should be the major legitimate function that can safeguard the quality of work and guard against things going wrong, and should be seen as mediating between the requirements of management and professional practice. Supervision, therefore, has to bridge the worlds of management and of practice, and this is by no means an easy task.

All too often supervisors find themselves being stretched to the limit, often managing large teams where supervision of staff is only one of many responsibilities and demands. Consequently they only attend to the managerial function of supervision to make sure that the policies and procedures are adhered to and that the job is done. Frequent crises and set- backs take precedence, so there is little time left to attend to the developmental/professional and supportive functions: the result leaves a lot to be desired, and seriously affects quality control. This state of affairs makes *quantity* rather than *quality* the main concern of controllers. I will come to discuss this issue later on.

THE NEEDS OF SUPERVISORS

Needs of supervisors are not that different from those of their staff, for supervisors need full supervision themselves, including advice, guidance, clarification, reassurance, assistance, help and support. Being accountable to their own managers they will have to show that the policies and procedures are in place, resources are used properly, and that work is managed effectively. Essential needs are:

- time for the supervisory task
- training in the supervision of staff
- resources to manage workloads efficiently
- quality supervision for themselves
- management training
- support

Assumptions that the supervisor does not need preparation in terms of training in supervision skills, and that everyone who has reached the first line-manager level can do the job effectively, are costly fallacies. Supervisors in child protection work should have sound professional knowledge, managerial and organisational skills, teaching supportive and enabling skills – management skills alone are not enough when one has to deal daily with the complexity and unpredictability of human behaviour and when professional judgement in decision making is vital.

EXPECTATIONS OF THE SUPERVISOR

Supervisors have expectations, but there are also expectations of supervisors. Among them are:

- good knowledge of agency policies, procedures and resources
- up-to-date knowledge of child protection work
- sound knowledge about child development, child care and family work
- sound knowledge of child care legislation
- understanding of human behaviour
- ability to recognise risks and make appropriate judgements
- skills to manage workers' workloads
- ability to manage and allocate appropriate resources
- ability to use given authority and power when appropriate
- ability to pick up workers' stresses and anxieties and attend to them
- willingness and capacity to support staff
- ability to keep good morale in the team
- willingness to address workers' professional and personal needs
- ability to represent workers' needs outside the team (e.g. training, resources)
- ability to promote antidiscriminatory practices
- ability to establish and promote a multidisciplinary approach to problem-solving.

FUNCTIONS OF SUPERVISION

Literature on staff supervision puts forward three basic functions: managerial, developmental/professional and supportive (Kadushin 1976, Pettes 1979, Payne and Scott 1982, Richards, Payne and Shepperd 1990). Richards, Payne and Shepperd add mediation as a fourth function of supervisors which in Table 15.1 is described as representative. This table outlines the essences of each function.

Table 15.1: Functions of Supervision

Managerial	Developmental	Supportive	Representative
Checking, monitoring, ensuring that the agency policies and procedures are observed; managing workload and resources; prioritising short- and long-term objectives; evaluating work.	Encouraging staff to become familiar with new knowledge and methods of working; encouraging professional growth and job satisfaction; creating opportunities for learning; acknowledging achievements and performance; using constructive crticism to improve practice.	Helping and enabling workers to cope with stress and anxiety; perceiving stress and anxiety as a legitimate reaction and not as a weakness.	Representing workers' needs with senior management when negotiating resources; facilities and training of staff; representing workers on multi-disciplinary forums.

All these functions are inter-related and need to be considered as integral parts of the supervision process. Full quality supervision will determine quality work, morale of staff and professional development of staff. In recent years there has been a preoccupation, or obsession, with the management function at the expense of the professional and supportive functions – this will not determine the quality of work alone and indeed may not even ensure that the work is done to any adequate standard; ticking boxes according to laid down procedures will not improve judgement, understanding or awareness of the problem. These aspects of child protection work can be enhanced by challenging and pro-active supervision style. Questioning, exploring, directing, informing are as important as management procedures, policies and resources. Below are some suggestions of the 'what', 'how' and 'why', variety of questions that might be asked when discussing a case:

Why might this be a reason?

What is the reason for this conclusion?

What evidence is there for this statement?

How was the evidence collected?

How many people were interviewed?

What do other professionals, connected with the case, think about it?

Could there be another explanation?

What does the observation of the child care in this family suggest?

How do they relate to each other?

How does the child behave when in this person's company?

What is the child's reaction to that person, place or circumstances?

How is the child perceived?

What level of attachment and commitment is there?

Why has an opinion been formed that abuse will take place?

This sort of exploration is useful for the following reasons:
- It clarifies and points out what is going on
- It gives the worker a sense of direction
- It enhances confidence in decision-making
- It suggests different ways of approaching and working the case
- It decreases anxiety level
- It gives the supervisor some idea of the knowledge, understanding, and skills possessed by the worker
- It provides information about what is needed for future training.

It may be useful at this point to illustrate the use of the different functions of supervision by means of an exercise. Exercise 1 can be used by training supervisors or by individual supervisors in private study when they are preparing for the supervision session.

EXERCISE 15.1

This exercise can be done in three or four groups, each working on one function of supervision. It will take 25–30 minutes to complete, after which each group should present its outcome. There might be differences of opinion between the groups, so discussion is needed to clarify the issues which arise.

Case Study

You have carried out a joint visit with a social worker who is fairly new to your team and to the area. You have found a child (18-month-old boy) to be badly neglected and possibly ill. The child is extremely thin, small, withdrawn and lethargic, and sits in one place looking blankly at you. There is little response to your attempts to play and talk to him. When his mother approaches him he bursts into tears. The mother complains that he is stubborn, will not do what he is told and is too lazy to talk or do anything. He appears to be hungry all the time and she says he feels happiest when he is left alone. There are hardly any toys for him to play with. The mother does not seem to be very concerned about the child's appearance and development but rather preoccupied with her financial difficulties.

Once the child has been admitted to hospital, you gather from a brief discussion with the social worker on the way back to the office that you will have to spend substantial time during the next supervision session with her discussing and analysing this case. The worker appears to be quite anxious and not confident about how to deal with it.

Exercise Task

Work out how you would deal with the case and how you would help your social worker through the use of supervision covering all aspects of supervisory functions.

Function	Tasks
Managerial	
Professional/Developmental	
Supportive	
Representative	

THE SUPPORT OF CHILD PROTECTION WORKERS

Workers who deal with child abuse (whether in the field, residential, or day care settings), experience anxiety and stress on a daily basis. Crises, set-backs, hostility of the care-givers (and at times of other agencies), uncertainties as how to manage difficult situations, facing the misery of children and the breaking-up of the families, all create stress and pressure. There are also at times overwhelming senses of helplessness and of impotence to be able to offer help. This emotionally charged work can be draining both physically and psychologically, and emotional fatigue can affect judgement and alertness most catastrophically and can lead to reactive responses or passive neglect. Continuous support and monitoring of the workload are needed for both the workers' and clients' sakes and for it to be acknowledged by senior management. Direct support, however, will be expected from the supervisor/line-manager, as she/he is closest to stress experienced by the workers, although this may, at times, create a barrier, as workers fear that they might be perceived as weak, unprofessional, and that they cannot function under pressure.

Workers are quite often reluctant to ask for help, to admit that they find it difficult to cope, to accept that stress affects them as people and as professionals, and to face up to the fact that they find it hard to function confidently and effectively. Whether the fear of exposure is rational or not, it is there, and it needs to be dealt with. Reassurance and permission to share these feelings without being judged should be given when negotiating supervision agreements. Support of workers can be provided directly and indirectly; it should be given directly on an everyday basis, during formal and informal supervision, group supervision and team meetings; and it should be provided indirectly by allocating resources outside the teams or units. It can include a stress-management training course, relaxation training, consultancy to help with particularly difficult issues or problems (e.g. anti-racist casework), pairing workers to do some joint work in difficult cases or, occasionally, joint visits with the supervisor. It is also useful to add an item to the team-meeting agenda labelled 'sharing difficulties' where workers can talk about their experiences which provoke anxieties. Supervisors should bring their own worries to encourage others to talk freely. Having lunch together once a week as a group provides another informal forum for support and the building of trust. Supervisors should be able to pick up stress factors amongst the staff, acknowledge them and facilitate support (e.g. giving a worker a day off when exhaustion is recognised), spend time talking about it, and examine current pressures of work and the workload. In residential work, particularly, stress is often present and yet is seldom recognised. Residential workers have to deal daily with the victims of all kinds of maltreatment and abuse, and the disturbed and unpredictable behaviour of damaged children requires a lot of energy and skills from the workers if help is to be given. Support on individual and group levels is essential to enhance the quality of work and the morale of staff.

STARTING AS A SUPERVISOR

The best way to find out what workers expect from the supervisor and to establish what personal and professional qualities they are looking for is to ask supervisees. The following exercise can be used in training, team-building, or between supervisor and worker alone:

EXERCISE 15.2: WHAT WORKERS EXPECT FROM THEIR SUPERVISORS

There are some people from whom we can learn a lot. In everyone's life there has been at least one person who influenced our personal and professional development. What has made them successful in shaping up our personality, attitudes, and skills?

There are some people who cannot influence or teach us even when they try very hard. What is it that prevents them and us from benefiting from each other's experiences?

Task 1:   Discuss both questions openly for a few minutes. Recall some pleasant and unpleasant experiences and share them with each other.

Task 2:   Write down on a big piece of paper what personal and professional qualities are essential to being a good and effective supervisor.

(10–15 minutes)

Workers' Group

'What do workers expect to get out of the supervision session?'
Write the answers on a big piece of paper.
(10–15 minutes)

Managers' Group

Write down what the supervisor aims to achieve during the supervision session.
(10–15 minutes)

Once the answers are written both groups join together to complete the second part of this exercise.

Task 1:   How many expectations were the same?
(Compare answers from Group 1 and Group 2)

Task 2:   Write down those answers.

Task 3:   How many expectations were different?

Task 4:   Write down those answers.

Discuss discrepancies between the worker and the supervisor expectations.

SUPERVISION AGREEMENT

Once it is established what supervisor and supervisee expect from each other on a general level then precise negotiations regarding the supervision process should take place. As a matter of good practice a formal agreement should be negotiated between the supervisor and each individual worker, as there are going to be different needs amongst the team members. The supervisor will need to take into consideration the level of experience in child protection work; the confidence and stamina of the worker in dealing with conflicts and painful situations; and the knowledge and skills of the worker. All workers will have some common general needs which could be dealt with in group-supervision and training courses. Individual professional needs will have to be addressed during the supervision session, and built into a supervision contract.

There are several reasons why there should be formal agreements on supervision:

- It clarifies what is expected from the supervisor and supervisee
- It clearly states frequency, time, place, and duration of the supervision session
- It obliges both parties to plan the supervision session
- It provides structure for the work between supervisor and supervisee to be done together
- It motivates both parties
- It is a good reminder of what is intended and hoped for
- It is an obligation to provide an agreed content
- It provides data for later evaluation
- It takes care of individual needs for workers
- It protects both parties in the event of dispute.

The agreement should be:

- written
- should clearly specify frequency, place, duration and time
- should clearly specify goals
- should clearly state what is expected behaviour of the supervisor and the worker (e.g. confidentiality)
- should state expected content of the sessions
- should state the duration of present agreement and expected time for the revision and evaluation
- should be signed by the supervisor and the worker.

Figure 15.1: Specimen Supervision Agreement

Between: Ms Jones – Team manager/supervisor and Ms White – Social worker, Child Care Team, South Division.

1. Both parties agree to have a formal supervision session every three weeks on Thursday from 11.00am to 12.30pm.
2. If for an unavoidable reason the session has to be cancelled an alternative day will be arranged.
3. Supervision sessions will take place in Ms Jones' office and instructions will be given for no unnecessary interruption.
4. Both parties will prepare an agenda and agree to prioritise items to meet their needs and obligations.
5. Both parties agree that supervision style will be pro- active and challenging.
6. Both parties agree to observe confidentiality regarding matters discussed in supervision unless superseded by the departmental policies and procedures.
7. Both parties agree for the supervision session to be briefly recorded by the supervisor and signed by both of them, stating: *issues brought for discussion, decisions taken, action plan.*
8. Both agree to evaluate supervision openly and honestly every three months and use the outcome constructively.
9. Both parties agree to give regular feedback to each other regarding their performance.
10. Both parties agree that the terms of the agreement will not be changed except by mutual decision to do so.

Ms Jones would want Ms White:

1. To give her three case-recordings on the day before the supervision session (different cases each time).
2. To keep recording up to date.
3. To report uncertainties and major difficulties without delay.
4. To share with her anxieties and worries about work.
5. To bring one fully worked out 'action plan' for the family or an individual child (for discussion).
6. To observe child protection procedure.

Ms White would like Ms Jones:

1. To address her professional development during the sessions (focus on skills development).
2. To attend to her personal needs as a worker.

3. To direct her to appropriate training regarding working with abused children.
4. To review her workload systematically.
5. To provide support and guidance when under pressure.

Signed: Ms Jones

Ms White

Date: 30.10.1992

Figure 15.2 Sample of Agenda for the Supervision Session

Date: 12.,10.1992

Place: Ms Jones' office

Supervisor: Ms Jones

Worker: Ms White

1. Organising the agenda for the session.
2. Review of the current work (checking whether statutory obligations were met, procedures observed, necessary paper work was done).
3. Comments on a sample recording provided a day before.
4. Issues arising from current work (management of workload, stress and difficulties experienced, progress made, availability of resources, etc.).
5. Cases or issues brought by the worker. Exploring, analysing and planning 'action'.
6. Any other business, for example providing information, discussing professional needs, such as training, courses, promotion, sharing anxieties.
7. Recording and signing outcomes of the supervision session.
8. Feedback on supervision session and work performance.

Figure 15.3: Supervision record

Issues brought for discussion	Outcome	Action Plan
1. Social worker concerned about John, aged 3, who appears to have lost weight, looks ill, and is detached and lethargic. Parents do not seem to be bothered about the child's poor appearance and lack of responsiveness, and have little physical or emotional contact with the child. No stimulation or meaningful contact was observed.	1. Child seems to be physically and emotionally neglected.	1. GP to see the child re health and failure to thrive.
	2. Possible failure-to-thrive.	2. Possible referral to the paediatrician.
	3. Almost no existent parent–child interaction and stimulation.	3. Consider whether medical and social findings indicate need to convene child protection conference.
	4. Parent–child relationship lacks warmth and concern. There is little evidence of commitment and affection.	4. Alert the health-visitor to monitor weight
		5. Arrangements to be made for the child to attend day-nursery.
		6. To discuss concern with both parents and involve them in proposed action.

Signed: Supervisor _____
             Worker _____
             Date _____

RECORDING SUPERVISION

There are several reasons why supervision sessions should be recorded:

- It provides evidence of what has been discussed and dealt with
- It avoids misunderstanding and confusion
- It provides instruction regarding what needs to be done
- It disciplines both parties to prepare for the next session
- It motivates the use of supervisor constructively, according to the agreed agenda
- It helps to evaluate supervision.

Each supervisor might like to develop an individual system of recording or might devise it in consultation with the team members. Some supervisors write it in a form of minutes, but that is quite time-consuming. Recording should be brief and to the point. When discussing a case or an issue, three points should be recorded:

1. Description of a situation or issue.
2. Outcome – identifying problems.
3. Action plan – what are we going to do about it?

This process tends to encourage disciplined thinking and clear analyses of the situation. A sample of this type of recording is given in figure 15.3.

A written outcome of the supervision session is helpful to the supervisor and supervisee. It gives the worker clear 'go ahead' with the action plan and the supervisor assurance that action was prepared to the best of their ability and available information.

Conclusion

This Chapter aims to detail the importance of well-balanced supervision and support in child protection work, and it provides some ideas on how to prepare for the supervision task and how to provide achievable support rather than work for the workers. The exercises included in this chapter can be used on staff-supervision courses, group supervision or in team-seminars. Examples are given relating to: supervisor/worker agreements on supervision; agendas for the supervision session and supervision records in terms of presenting problem-outcomes and action-plans. These can be adapted according to individual needs and circumstances.

References

Butler-Sloss, L. (Chair) (1988) *Report of the Inquiry into Child Abuse in Cleveland.* London: HMSO.

Brent Borough Council (1985) *A Child in Trust.* (The Report of the panel of inquiry into the circumstances surrounding the death of Jasmine Beckford, Chair Louis Blom-Cooper). London: Brent Borough Council.

Clare, M. (1988) *Supervision, Role Strain and Social Services Department.* Birmingham: British Association of Social Workers.

Greenwich Borough Council (1977) *A Child in Mind: Protection of Children in A Responsible Society.* (Report of the Commission of Inquiry into the circumstances surrounding the death of Kimberley Carlile). London: Greenwich Borough Council.

Hallett, C. and Stevenson, O. (1980) *Child Abuse: Aspect of Inter-Professional Cooperation.* London: George Allen and Unwin.

Kadushin, A. (1976) *Supervision in Social Work.* New York: Columbia University Press.

Lambeth Borough Council (1987) *Whose Child?* (The report of the panel appointed to inquire into the death of Tyra Henry. Chair: Stephen Sedley). London: Lambeth Borough Council.

Payne, C. and Scott, T. (1982) *Developing Supervision of Teams in Field and Residential Social Work (Part 1).* London: National Institute for Social Work.

Payne, C. and Scott, T. (1985) *Developing Supervision of Teams in Field and Residential Social Work (Part 2).* London: National Institute for Social Work.

Pettes, D. (1979) *Staff and Student Supervision: A Task-Centred Approach.* London: Allen and Unwin.

Richards, M., Payne, C. and Shepperd, A. (1990) *Staff Supervision in Child Protection Work.* London: National Institute for Social Work.

CHAPTER 16

Support and Supervision of Social Workers Working in the Child Protection Field

Jacki Pritchard

We all think we know what we mean by supervision, and most workers know whether they get it or they do not. What we do get, however, might not be what we want. From my experience over the years I have learnt that there are numerous different ideas about what constitutes *good* supervision. I am also aware that supervision has been low on the agenda of many team leaders.

As child protection work has gained a higher profile in recent years, people are gradually realising how crucial it is for workers to get proper and appropriate supervision on a regular basis. If workers are not supported in the correct manner then we shall lose them in a number of ways, for example sickness, burn out syndrome, finding employment in another authority which does offer support and understanding, or finding an alternative career to social work.

My aim in this chapter is to consider how *social workers* in the child protection field can be supported and supervised in a constructive and helpful way, which will benefit the service to clients. Supervision and support in regard to other professionals is discussed elsewhere (Chapter 15). I will be addressing some very general topics, but relating them to social work. I wish to identify some of the needs, both practical and emotional, of social workers working in the child protection field.

Throughout the chapter there will be a number of exercises, some of which can be adapted for use in other work settings. The exercises can be used in normal one-to-one supervision sessions (worker and line manager), group supervision or team development meetings, or training sessions for child protection work. Some of the exercises can be adapted to help managers when they are receiving supervision from their line managers. Anyone who is leading the exercises, be they line manager, team leader, team worker or trainer, will be referred to as the trainer in this chapter. In most of the exercises, some examples of material will be given. However, it is anticipated that most trainers will want to use their own case material and examples.

Because of the sensitive nature of child protection work, many workers may feel uncomfortable in participating in certain exercises and may not want to share their feelings with certain people. It is important that the trainer checks out whether workers wish to participate in a group or whether they would prefer to do the exercise in a one-to-one situation.

WHAT IS SUPERVISION?

This question would probably be answered in a variety of ways if put to individuals of a social work team or to workers across one department. Some typical answers may be:

> Getting help when I need it.

> A way of letting off steam.

> Her [team leader] way of checking up on me.

> I don't know – I never get any.

Few departments actually set out formally what should constitute supervision and this needs to be addressed. One Department which has implemented a policy statement on supervision and practice guidelines is Sheffield Family and Community Services. The policy statement on staff supervision states:

1. All staff have a right to receive regular and formal supervision. It is the duty of a supervisor to ensure that this happens.
2. The object of supervision is the promotion of sound and consistent practice and decisions of high quality.
3. Supervision establishes clear accountability and enables the sharing of responsibility in situations of risk.
4. Supervision ensures that policy procedures and good practice are being followed.
5. Supervision is a valuable tool in the support of staff working with highly complex and stressful workloads.
6. Supervision should be an enabling process and involves the professional development of the worker concerned.
7. Sound and consistent supervision will provide benefits to both the organisation and to staff working in all areas of service delivery.
8. Supervision should ensure consistency in the delivery of services throughout the department.
9. Throughout the supervision process managers should be able to identify the training needs of staff across the department allowing effective training strategies to be developed.
10. Supervision should enable the development and maintenance of an appropriate value system and a positive climate for quality services.
11. Supervision should enhance and re-enforce anti-discriminatory practice throughout the department.

(Sheffield Family and Community Services Department 1992)

WHY HAVE SUPERVISION?

In my view supervision is a forum where a worker can talk about cases, look and ask for guidance, express his/her feelings, learn about procedures, policies and methods, and evaluate practical and emotional needs. The line manager has a duty to listen, facilitate, teach and organise ways of fillings the gaps in knowledge and experience.

Supervision needs to be at regular intervals, but the word 'regular' will mean different things to different workers – 'weekly', 'every two weeks', 'once a month', 'when I feel the need'. I have heard both experienced workers and team leaders express the view that someone who is experienced does not need so much supervision. I totally disagree with this on two counts: First, it is very important that a line manager knows what a worker is doing. An experienced worker can develop bad practices or become very isolated if they think that they know it all already. A lazy or inefficient worker can keep bad practices or their lack of knowledge well hidden if she or he does not receive regular supervision. Second, a worker, no matter how experienced, needs to express his/her feelings. Social workers are supposed to learn how to cut off from situations and act in a professional manner, much in the same way as doctors do with their patients. The reality is that the work is sometimes so stressful it is very difficult to 'cut off' and not to 'take it home with you'. I have heard it said that 'it is not professional to break down and cry'. Some workers in training sessions have expressed their reluctance to tell their line managers how they feel, because they are frightened that they will be seen as 'not coping'. Therefore, it is crucial that workers have the opportunity to express their feelings and are supported through these difficult situations. Exercise 16.1 can be used to help achieve this.

EXERCISE 16.1: FEELINGS

Objective

To enable the worker to express his/her feelings about situations.

Participants

This exercise is carried out in a large group which is sitting in a circle.

Equipment

The trainer needs to prepare the cards in advance.

Time

10 minutes to carry out exercise, followed by discussion to identify common feelings.

Task

Each card is the beginning of a sentence, which the worker has to complete verbally. Each worker is given a card to read. S/he has one minute to think of how they will complete the sentence. The trainer goes round the circle, asking each worker to say his/her completed sentence.

Preparation

Each card needs to start off with 'In child protection work...'and the following added (1 to each card):

what I like most is...

what I hate most is...

what I find most difficult is...

I laugh when...

I cry when...

I become upset when...

I get angry when...

I lose my temper when...

I feel uncomfortable when...

I feel happy when...

I feel sad when...

I feel sick when...

I feel nervous when...

I worry when...

It is also crucial that workers should be allowed to express their innermost fears. The term 'experienced worker' is used frequently and with that go certain expectations. However, even the most experienced worker still has fears. There are moments you dread and things that you hate doing. There is nothing wrong in having these fears and it is good for workers to share these fears so that people know it is normal to feel like this.

EXERCISE 16.2: FEARS

Objective

To enable a worker to talk about what they fear in the child protection work they do.

Participants

This exercise can be carried out in pairs or small groups; perhaps in preparation for a supervision session or in a team development meeting.

Equipment

Flipchart paper and pens.

Time

20 minutes for task, 30 minutes for feedback and discussion.

Task

The worker has to list what they fear in child protection work. Each sentence must start with either 'I fear' or 'I dread' or 'I worry', for example

- 'I fear that I won't know what to say or what to do next'
- 'I dread having to confront the perpetrator'
- 'I worry that I am going to get it wrong'

How Can Good Supervision Be Achieved?

Because supervision can often be organised in a haphazard way, it is useful to agree a formal/written contract, which states how often supervision will take place and the structure for supervision sessions. Through my experience as a team leader, I have learnt that every individual likes to use supervision in different ways. Sessions should *not* be conducted to suit the needs of the manager. Therefore, supervision should not be seen as a set time where a worker comes in, talks about cases, the manager responds and that is it. It needs to have more depth to it, so that both the worker and manager will look forward to the sessions, which should be challenging, stimulating and interesting.

Before agreeing a written contract, consideration should be given to the following:

- frequency of supervision
- length of supervision sessions
  (it is important for the individuals involved that the correct amount of time is allotted so that sessions do not have to be cut short because they run over. It is better to overestimate the time rather than underestimate it)
- preparation for sessions
  (writing up files, time limits for presenting files to manager before sessions)

- agenda to be set by worker and manager
  (how far in advance of supervision session?)
- Use of written material, exercises, role play
- Written record of supervision sessions
  (what is included in the written record, who writes up the session,
  who keeps the written record, who sees it?)

Before agreeing a contract it may be useful to use Exercise 16.3. in order to
identify what a worker and his/her manager expect of each other.

EXERCISE 16.3: EXPECTATIONS

Objective

> To identify what a worker and manager expect of each other in a
> supervision session and of supervision in general.

Participants

> Worker and line manager.

Equipment

> Pen and paper.

Time

> 15 minutes to complete task and 30 minutes for feedback and
> discussion.

Task

> Each participant will be expected to answer a question by making
> a list of one word or one sentence responses.
> Question for worker: 'What do you expect from your line manager
> in supervision?'
> Question for line manager: 'What do you expect from your worker
> in supervision?'

STAFF APPRAISALS

Whenever I have taken up a new post as team leader and introduced the idea
of staff appraisals, most of the workers have cringed and grimaced! After
some gentle persuasion, all of them have participated in six-monthly appraisals. What needs to be stressed to workers is that appraisals are for their own
benefit.

What I find fascinating about appraisals is that you never see yourself as
others see you. When I was practising as a generic social worker and my line

manager carried out an appraisal of me, she saw strengths in me which I had never recognised before. This has also happened when I have told my workers what I think their strengths are. The effect is that workers come out feeling good about something, but also hopefully they will learn and feel positive about what they need to improve on.

The purpose of the appraisal needs to be explained clearly before the worker and manager agree the agenda. Once workers realise that they can set part of the agenda for the appraisal, they feel less threatened. It gives them the opportunity to say how they are feeling about their work, how they are functioning, the support/supervision they are getting and a chance to consider the way forward. Appraisals have to be a two way process and both the worker and manager have to agree to be honest with each other. Again, having a format and agenda is useful, but they do not have to be restrictive. Some general questions/headings which may be useful are:

What is my role in regard to... clients, team, department?

What have I achieved in the past 6 months/year?

What have I messed up/failed at in the past 6 months/year?

What are my strengths?

What are my weaknesses?

What do I want to improve on/get better at?

How can I do this?

Who will help me?

Where am I going?

My objectives for the next 6 months?

Some workers prefer to address certain issues/topics/concerns in appraisals rather than have general headings for discussion. They do this by making a statement and then contemplating what to do about it. Some topics which have been addressed are:

'I am bored and stale with the work, how can I get out?'.

'I don't think I'm any good at child protection work'.

'My casefiles are a mess. I can't keep up with the written work'.

TIME OUT

I have always been a great advocate of workers taking time out for their career development, and I think this is crucial for workers in the child protection field. By 'time out' I mean allocating time to do the things that you are always 'going to do when time allows' and in fact never do because there is never enough time.

Managers should actively encourage workers to strike out days in their diaries at regular intervals, so that they can pursue certain activities and interests related to their work. Other managers have often laughed at me when I have suggested this and said that it is impossible to do because of all the pressures we have. My answer to that is that there are pressures, but we can prioritise and give workers some space for their own development, because the end result will be a better quality service. If workers have time out they will feel valued by the department and be able to develop in a way which keeps them skilled and enthusiastic about the job they are doing.

I have operated a 'time out programme' with my workers on a regular basis. Time out can be the odd day at regular intervals or a block of days. Days out are agreed in supervision sessions and it is important that once the worker has struck out the day in his/her diary, s/he does not let work intrude on that day (unless it is unavoidable, such as having to go to court). Line managers have to agree to take responsibility for the worker's caseload on that day, which would be normal practice if the worker was off sick or on annual leave!

The work or activity to be undertaken is discussed in supervision both before and after the time out. Some workers use the day to catch up on file recording when they are under a great deal of pressure. In these situations, the worker works at home or somewhere else quiet where they will not be disturbed. The effect is that the worker feels so much better for having caught up and feels on top of things again.

Other workers have used the time to visit particular units, therapeutic centres, work settings (within and outside of their own department) or spent the day with a particular specialist/professional (e.g. a paediatrician dealing with child abuse, policewoman working in an abuse unit, health visitor). Other workers like to catch up on reading about current issues (e.g. female genital mutilation), social work methods (e.g. step-wise interviews). One worker I know spent a day in the library to do a literature search on a particular topic.

GROUP SUPERVISION

One-to-one supervision is important, but supervision can also be done in a group setting. This certainly would not suit everyone as many individuals do not like talking in groups – individuals often feel intimidated and threatened in a group – however, if a group of individuals get on together reasonably well and would not mind conducting supervision in this way, then a great deal can be learnt and achieved. This way of conducting supervision can facilitate team development and ways of working together. The manager will be able to identify the particular skills and knowledge of team members, but also their gaps in knowledge and weaknesses. Specialisms can be created within the team and team members build up support mechanisms within the team itself.

Again, format and agendas have to be agreed. For group supervision to take place, it is necessary for people to feel that they can speak their minds, be honest, helpful, supportive, be able accept criticism and abide by confidentiality.

TRAINING

It is the responsibility of team leaders to identify the training needs of their workers and pass this information on to the appropriate people within the department. Unfortunately, the standard of training offered in social work departments varies terrifically – some is excellent, some is appalling. Workers in the child protection field need regular training of a high standard. Where there are gaps in training offered, then managers should attempt to fill the gaps by undertaking training themselves or trying to obtain help from other colleagues or professionals (see Chapter 5).

A team leader does not have to have training experience in order to facilitate team training sessions. A team can decide what training they require and how they would like to learn. A particular team member may have certain skills which could be shared with the team, by that member taking the lead role in the training session.

SOME IDEAS FOR SUPERVISION

In this final section, I would like to put forward some exercises which could be used in supervision to address some key issues in child protection work. Very often it is useful to use brainstorming exercises to discuss practices and procedures, hence identifying what workers know or do not know.

EXERCISE 16.4: BRAINSTORMING

Objective

To get as many ideas as possible on how to proceed.

Participants

Group exercise.

Equipment

Flipchart and pen.

Time

5 minutes for brainstorming, followed by full discussion.

Task

The trainer gives the group an issue/problem and asks the group to brainstorm ideas.

Preparation

The trainer needs to identify issues/problems which are of relevance to the group. The topics can be extremely broad or very specific. It may be helpful to present a direct question to the group. Some examples:

What is abuse?

What checks do you carry out before going out on an investigation?

Who do you go to in order to get information?

Who do you go to for advice?

Who are the key people in child protection work in this agency?

On which parts of the body are you most likely to find non-accidental injuries?

What emotional traits/signs might a sexually abused child present?

Who is invited to a case conference?

What are the boundaries regarding confidentiality?

Brainstorming is useful to get workers thinking and learning from each other, but also for producing ideas for further discussion. However, it is necessary to move on to work on specific methods in working with child protection. Some workers and supervisors may find it useful to analyse and evaluate practice over a period of time, while undertaking ongoing training. Exercise 16.5. is designed to encourage workers to keep a diary of their actions and feelings on a daily basis.

EXERCISE 16.5: KEEPING A DIARY

Objective

Sometimes it is easier to write something down rather than talk about it at the time. Also, sometimes there is no time for talking or the person you need to talk is not around. This exercise has been developed for such occasions, but it also has the purpose of evaluating situations over a period of time.

Participants

Worker and supervisor.

Equipment

A proper diary can be used (preferably with a day to a page) or a loose leaf file, so that a worker can write as much or as little as necessary.

Time

The worker and supervisor should agree on how long this exercise should be carried out. The shortest time span should be one week. Some participants may agree to conduct the exercise over a long period of time (e.g. 6 months), but evaluation should occur on a regular basis.

Task

The worker will be asked to keep a diary in between supervision sessions. The idea is that the worker will write about his/her actions, thoughts, feelings either as they occur (e.g. in the heat of the moment when s/he is angry) or at the end of the day (no matter how tired s/he is). The purpose is to briefly state what happened, the feeling and what caused it. The diary will act as a stimulus for discussion in supervision sessions.

Workers must be given the opportunity to analyse their own practice, that is, what they actually say and do in certain situations. It has to be recognised that at times even the most experienced worker flounders or is lost for words. I think it is always useful to go back to basics at regular intervals. For example, what you say after knocking on the door when you are out on a child protection investigation. Exercise 16.6 can be used to consider the most simple interaction or a very complex situation.

EXERCISE 16.6: SAY AND DO

Objective

To make participants think how they would react/respond in certain situations.

Participants

Small groups.

Equipment

Flipchart paper and pens.

Time

20 minutes in small groups; followed by feedback and discussion in large group.

Task

Each group will be given a situation. Participants are asked to discuss what they would do and list their activities on paper.

Preparation

The trainer will need to prepare the situations beforehand and present them to the groups either on small cards or sheets of A4 paper, so that each participant has the situation in front of him/her. Participants are asked 'What would you say and do?' Some examples:

- You are the duty social worker. A headteacher reports bruising on a 6-year-old girl and asks you to interview her before contacting the parents. What do you say and do?

- You are on a home visit. While mum is making a cup of tea, 9-year-old Sarah says 'Daddy put his willy up me last night?'

- A father confides in you 'I have sexual urges towards my 12-year-old daughter'.

- You walk into a playroom at a local nursery and see the child care assistant slap a child across the face.

- A mother breaks down and tells you her husband deliberately burnt their son with a cigarette last night. She begs you not to tell anyone.

- You find out that one of your clients, who has three children, is now co-habiting with a Schedule 1 offender.

- It is 4.30pm on a Friday afternoon. A teacher rings to say that she forgot to ring you at lunchtime, but s/he has been worried about the bruise she saw on 7-year-old Jenny's back during a gym lesson.

There is the old cliche that 'you learn by your mistakes'. It may be very painful to talk about how you 'messed up', but we all do it. If workers can share their mistakes, their colleagues will be able to reflect on and learn from the errors that have been made. Exercise 16.7. will make workers think about what procedures should have been followed or what should have been said in a certain situation.

EXERCISE 16.7: SHARING YOUR MISTAKES

Objective

To reassure workers that no-one is perfect and that everyone makes mistakes.

Participants

Large group sitting in a circle.

Equipment

None.

Time

Each worker is allowed to talk for 5 minutes; the group can ask questions for a further 5–10 minutes.

Task

Each participant in the group is asked to talk about a situation in their child protection work where they made a mistake (either in what action that they took or in what they said/told someone) or where they felt they had not done or said the right thing.

It is absolutely crucial that case files are up to date and give factual information. Neither pre- nor post-qualification training courses give enough attention to file recording. Therefore, it is the responsibility of line managers to ensure that workers can record information in an appropriate and useful way. Workers need continuous practice in and regular assessment of their recording skills. Supervisors will find Exercise 16.8 helpful in promoting recording of a high standard.

EXERCISE 16.8: FILE RECORDING

Objective

To help workers improve their recording of interviews.

Participants

This exercise can be carried out in individual supervision sessions or in a small group (6 maximum).

Equipment

Video showing interviews in child protection work.
Pen and paper.

Time

After the scenario has been shown on the video, participants have 30 minutes to record the interview. Time for feedback will depend on whether the exercise is done by a supervisor and worker (feedback will take 30–45 minutes) or in a group (where there is a group of 6, feedback can take between 1 and 2 hours by the time participants have read each other's records).

Task

A scenario of an interview will be shown. Participants will then be given time to do a write up of the interview as if they had been the worker involved in the scenario. They will then present what they have written and discussion will focus on key points which have been missed/included.

Preparation

The trainer will need to identify a video which shows a situation in which a worker is involved and would subsequently have to write up on a case file. It could be a home visit, an interview with a client (this may be a child, parent) or a meeting or telephone conversation with another professional. If a video is not available, the participants could be asked to view and write about a role play situation which is performed before them.

One of the first lessons to be learnt in child protection work is that workers must 'think before they act'. It is not good practice to rush out to see a child as soon as an allegation of abuse has been referred. It is very important to gather information and plan the investigation by formulating a strategy:

> It is essential that there is an early strategy discussion, which may not require a meeting, between the statutory agencies, i.e. Police and social services, to plan the investigation and in particular the role of each agency and the extent of the joint investigation. It is the responsibility of the agency receiving the referral to initiate this. Other team members should be involved as soon as possible. (Section 5.13.1. Home Office *et al.* 1991).

Workers must get in the habit of arranging strategy meetings and learning how to present information in a helpful and clear way. This can achieved by using Exercise 16.9.

EXERCISE 16.9: STRATEGY PLANS

Objective

To help workers develop a strategy before going out on a child protection investigation.

Participants

Small groups.

Equipment

Flipchart paper and pens.

Time

30 minutes for work in groups, then 15 minutes to feedback and discuss the strategy that had been formulated.

Task

Each group is given a case example, which requires a strategy plan. Each member of the group is asked to take on the role of a particular professional (from different agencies) and participate in a strategy meeting. By the end of the meeting the group will have formulated a strategy, which is written down on flipchart paper.

Preparation

The trainer needs to check his/her Department's Child Protection Procedure Manual about guidance for strategy meetings. Any specific requirements should be set out clearly on a flipchart for the participants to refer to and it will clarify what is expected of them. For example, the Sheffield ACPC Procedure Manual says that a strategy discussion should seek to establish:

- a detailed timetable for the investigation
- the roles and responsibilities of the various professionals involved (Who is to do what, when, and how)
- responsibility for co-ordination of the investigation on a day-to-day basis
- how operational difficulties/disputes between professionals will be resolved
- arrangements for keeping senior managers informed.

(Section 3.172 Sheffield ACPC 1992).

CONCLUSION

This chapter has not been able to cover every aspect of supervision and support a worker may require. My intention has been to highlight some of the key elements in the supervision of child protection work. Supervision has often been lacking in the past, but now as child protection work becomes more specialised, managers have to recognise that workers must receive supervision and support of a high standard, and supervision must occur on a regular basis.

REFERENCES

Sheffield Area Child Protection Committee (1992) *Child Protection Procedures.* Sheffield: ACPC.

Sheffield Family and Community Services Department (1992) *Supervision – Departmental Policy Statement and Practice Guidelines.* Sheffield: Family and Community Services.

Home Office, Department of Health, Department of Education and Science, Welsh Office (1991) *Working Together Under the Children Act 1989.* London: HMSO.

Contributors

Eve Brock, is a Freelance Trainer and Team Leader of teachers in H.M. Prison Lindholme.

Lola Brown, is a Senior Race Relations Trainer (Child Protection) for Lambeth Social Services.

Marian Charles, is a Senior Lecturer, School of Social Studies at The University of Nottingham.

Jo Crow, is a Sister in Accident and Emergency at The Children's Hospital, Birmingham.

Anne Hollows, is Senior Development Officer, for the Child Abuse Training Unit of the National Children's Bureau.

Professor Dorota Iwaniec is a Professor in the Department of Social Work at The Queens University of Belfast.

Tony McFarlane is a Multidisciplinary Training Officer for the Northern Health and Social Services Board.

Pat Monro is a Solicitor with Wilford McBain Solicitors.

Hilary Owen is an Assistant Child Protection Co-ordinator, with the Child Protection Section of Sheffield Family and Community Services Department.

Jacki Pritchard is a Freelance Trainer and Team Leader with Sheffield Family and Community Services Department.

Philippa Russell is Director of the Voluntary Council for Handicapped Children.

Lindsey Savage is a Child Protection Administrator, Sheffield Family and Community Services Department.

Dr Alice Swann is a Senior Clinical Medical Officer with Eastern Health and Social Services Board.

Isobel Todd is a Court Welfare Officer, South Yorkshire Probation Service.

Sergeant Colin Walke is a Police Trainer for the Surrey Constabulary's Training School.

Subject Index

References in italic indicate figures or training exercises

Name Index

Group Work with Children and Adolescents
A Handbook
Edited by Kedar Nath Dwivedi
Foreword by Dr Robin Skynner
ISBN 1 85302 157 1 pb

'It is a particular and very personal pleasure to contribute a
foreword to this important book... I congratulate the authors
and editor on their achievement, and warmly recommend
Group Work with Children and Adolescents as vital reading for
all those involved in the treatment of children's emotional
problems.'

– from the Foreword

Bringing together the skills, practical experience and expertise
of a wide range of contributors, this comprehensive handbook
provides analysis and practical guidance on all aspects of the
subject under five broad headings: theoretical and practical
issues, including organisational aspects, conceptual
frameworks, evaluation; developmental perspectives, including
emotional development, empathy and prosocial development;
tools and techniques, including the use of play and games, art
psychotherapy, relaxation, drama and interpretation; themes,
including bereavement, encopresis, victims and perpetrators of
sexual abuse, young offenders and racial identity; and contexts
and settings, including schools, residential institutions, mental
health services, youth services and therapeutic communities.
Group Work with Children and Adolescents will be an invaluable
resource for all those involved in the field.
Dr Kedar Nath Dwivedi, MBBS, MD, DPM, FRCPsych, is
Consultant Psychiatrist for the Northampton Child and Family
Consultation Service.

Jessica Kingsley Publishers
116 Pentonville Road, London. N1 9JB Tel: 071 833 2307

Child Abuse and Child Abusers

Protection and Prevention

Edited by Lorraine Waterhouse
Foreword by Olive Stephenson
ISBN 1 85302 133 4 hb
Research Highlights in Social Work 24

> 'By its scholarly quality, [this book] raises a host of questions
> remaining to be explored... The range and depth of the
> matters here considered set child abuse in a wide context;
> social, legal and professional... There is much in this book
> which affords us a valuable opportunity to stand back and
> reflect critically at where we stand.'
>
> *— from the Foreword*

Lorraine Waterhouse is senior lecturer in the Department of
Social Policy and Social Work at Edinburgh University.

Jessica Kingsley Publishers
116 Pentonville Road, London. N1 9JB Tel: 071 833 2307

Play Therapy with Abused Children

Ann Cattanach

ISBN 1 85302 193 8 pb
ISBN 1 85302 120 2 hb

'Ways of starting play therapy with abused children are described, as well as various forms of therapy such as story telling, roleplay, or playing with dolls. Case histories are given of children who have experienced physical, emotional, or sexual abuse... They show how play therapy helped them come to terms with the past and prepare for the future... This is a book which is shocking at times but extremely valuable.'

– Nursery World

'Her accounts of the ways in which play is used to make sense of traumatic experiences are full of insight and often moving. All aspects of the work are covered, including preparation for play, starting play, boundary testing and the play therapy process. There is a good book list. The effects on the therapist of working with these problems and the type of support and supervision needed are described. This exceptional volume... goes far beyond a mere text book.'

– Therapy Weekly

'Ann Cattanach has written an excellent succinct and eminently readable book which reveals her considerable personal experience in helping abused children. ... about actual practice as opposed to dogmatic speculative theories. The descriptions of sessions are particularly effective...'

– Rostrum

Ann Cattanach MSc, CTSD, DTh lectures at the Institute of Dramatherapy and the Roehampton Institute. She is a therapist at the Harrow Health Authority Child and Family Service.

Jessica Kingsley Publishers
116 Pentonville Road, London. N1 9JB Tel: 071 833 2307

Grief in Children
A Handbook for Adults
Atle Dyregrov
ISBN 1 85302 113 X pb

'Dyregrov's writing is clear in its description, and explicit in
its advice, and demonstrates that the daunting task of
helping a child through grief is both manageable and
rewarding… The book will, I am sure, become
required reading for all those touched by the care of
bereaved children.'

– Bereavement Care

'An invaluable resource for parents, pastoral workers and
those in caring professions.'

– Methodist Recorder

'…a handy, small book ideal for teachers, social workers,
counsellors, parents and others faced with the task of
understanding children in grief and trying to help them.'

– Assn for Child Psychology & Psychiatry Newsletter

'an excellent guide'

– School Psychology International

Atle Dyregrov is a clinical psychologist and is Director of the
Centre for Crisis Psychology in Bergen, Norway. For more than
12 years he has worked with families who are the victims of
crisis surrounding sudden death.

Jessica Kingsley Publishers
116 Pentonville Road, London. N1 9JB Tel: 071 833 2307

Chain Reaction
Children and Divorce
Ofra Ayalon and Adina Flasher
ISBN 1 85302 136 9 pb

As we approach the end of the twentieth century, increasing numbers of children are going through the often shattering experience of the separation, divorce and remarriage of their parents: an experience which creates a perpetual 'chain reaction', affecting children at every stage and in every aspect of their lives. Using a range of methods including literatherapy and storytelling, play and art therapy, cognitive reframing, problem solving and values clarification, all illustrated and supported by case studies, *Chain Reaction* identifies and suggests ways of dealing with divorce-related stress. The individual and group oriented processes of intervention will be invaluable to therapists in the clinic, teachers in the classroom and parents who are eager to support their children.

Dr Ofra Ayalon is a psychologist and family therapist, internationally known for her creative contributions in the psychology of stress and coping. A senior faculty member at the University of Haifa, she teaches in many different countries. **Dr Adina Flasher** works in education as a counsellor, child therapist and bibliotherapist. She teaches at Haifa University and at Oranim and Gordon teacher training colleges in Israel.

Jessica Kingsley Publishers
116 Pentonville Road, London. N1 9JB Tel: 071 833 2307

Good Grief
Exploring Feelings, Loss and Death with Over Elevens and Adults
Barbara Ward and Associates
ISBN 1 85302 162 8 pb

'a unique curriculum pack, in that it gives children the opportunity to explore a range of both positive and negative feelings within a safe environment.'

– *LEA Advisor/Inspector*

Good Grief
Exploring Feelings, Loss and Death with Under Elevens
Barbara Ward and Associates
ISBN 1 85302 161 X pb

'*Good Grief* has been put together with love and deep understanding of children's needs in facing loss and death.'
– *Barbara Kahan, National Children's Bureau*

'The 22 cooperating contributors provide a superbly constructed resource of information, activities and ideas... Incredibly sensitive in everyway... Thanatology is an embryo discipline – these two books represent a major contribution to the caring aspect of that discipline. Barbara Ward... is to be congratulated and commended.'
– *Journal of the Institute of Health Education*

Jessica Kingsley Publishers
116 Pentonville Road, London. N1 9JB Tel: 071 833 2307

The Abuse of Elderly People
A Handbook for Professionals
Jacki Pritchard
Foreword by Professor Eric Sainsbury
ISBN 1 85302 122 9 pb

'This book provides a ready-made training package
containing an abundance of carefully thought-out scenarios,
simulation and role-play exercises which are ideal for
multidisciplinary workshops. Of particular interest is the
exercise designed to help staff learn how to prioritise their
workload... this is a good, practical guide to the subject and
will be of use to all staff involved in care of the elderly.'

— Nursing Times

Jacki Pritchard is Principal Social Worker in the Sheffield
Family and Community Services Department, Nether Edge
Hospital.

Handbook of Theory for Practice Teachers
in Social Work
Edited by Joyce Lishman
ISBN 1 85302 098 2 pb

'There is no need for practice teachers to feel at sea when the
student's personal tutor comes calling... one can recommend
the volume as effectively covering the traditional knowledge
base for social workers.'

— Community Care

Professor Joyce Lishman is Head of the School of Health and
Social Work at the Robert Gordon's Institute of Technology in
Aberdeen.

Jessica Kingsley Publishers
116 Pentonville Road, London. N1 9JB Tel: 071 833 2307

WITHDRAWN
FROM STOCK
QMUL LIBRARY